Labour under the Marshall Plan

Also by ANTHONY CAREW

Democracy and government in European trade unions

The lower deck of the Royal Navy

Labour under the Marshall Plan

The politics of productivity and the marketing
of management science

ANTHONY CAREW

Wayne State University Press

Detroit, Michigan   1987

Published in the United States by
Wayne State University Press,
Detroit, Michigan 48202

Printed in Great Britain

Library of Congress cataloging-in-publication data applied for

ISBN 0-8143-1825-8

CONTENTS

ACKNOWLEDGEMENTS

In researching material for the book I have been generously assisted by the staff of various archives and libraries, notably at the Walter P. Reuther Archives of Labour and Urban Affairs, the Public Record Office, the Trades Union Congress, the Labour Party, Independent Labour Publications, the American Federation of Labour–Congress of Industrial Organisations, the International Ladies' Garment Workers' Union, the University of Pennsylvania, the State Historical Society of Wisconsin, the Harry S. Truman Presidential Library, the United States National Archives, the London School of Economics, the Modern Record Centre at Warwick University, the Tamiment Institute, and the library staff at the University of Manchester Institute of Science and Technology. A number of individuals helped by making personal papers or reminiscenes available, including George Doughty, Jack Jones, Ian Mikardo, Ted Fletcher, Albert Carthy, Frank Ward, George Foggon, Jim Mortimer, Austen Albu, Robert Garland, Bernard Dix, Richard Clements, Filmer Paradise, Victor Reuther, William Kemsley, Newman Jeffrey, George Wheeler, Morris Weisz, Nelson Cruikshank, Paul Porter, Joseph Keenan, Ted Silvey, James Toughill, Dan Benedict and Louis Wiesner.

Several friends and colleagues have given material help and encouragement in a variety of ways, especially Bill Schaap, Ellen Rae, Louis Wolf, Ike Krasner, Heather Nicholas, Colin Garvey, Ian Bullock, Jon Williams, Alan Milward, Barry Winter and Paul Martin.

My biggest debts are to the British Academy and the Nuffield Foundation for the generous grants which helped me to undertake much of the initial research on which this book is based, to the Walter Reuther Archives at Wayne State University, Detroit, for awarding me a Rockefeller Foundation Residency which enabled me to spend a year completing the research and to Richard Fletcher, who first interested me in this area and made his own large collection of research material freely available.

A.C.
Rockefeller Fellow
Walter P. Reuther *Library of Labour and Urban Affairs*
Detroit, April 1987

ABBREVIATIONS

AACP	Anglo-American Council on Productivity
AFL	American Federation of Labour
ALCIA	American Labour Conference on International Affairs
BPC	British Productivity Council
CEEC	Committee on European Economic Co-operation
CED	Committee for Economic Development
CFTC	Confédération Française des Travailleurs Chrétiens
CGIL	Confederazione Generale Italiana del Lavoro
CGT	Confédération Générale du Travail
CIO	Congress of Industrial Organisations
CISL	Confederazione Italiana dei Sindacati Lavoratori
DGB	Deutsche Gewerkschaftsbund
ECA	Economic Co-operation Agency
EPA	European Productivity Agency
ERP	European Recovery Programme
ERP-TUAC	European Recovery Programme Trade Union Advisory Committee
FO	Force Ouvrière
FOA	Foreign Operations Agency
FTUC	Free Trade Union Committee
ICA	International Co-operation Agency
ICFTU	International Confederation of Free Trade Unions
ILP	Independent Labour Party
ITF	International Transport Workers' Federation
MSA	Mutual Security Agency
NAM	National Association of Manufacturers
OEEC	Organisation for European Economic Co-operation
OSR	Office of the Special Representative
PCF	Parti Communist Français
PCI	Partito Communista Italiano
PSI	Partito Socialista Italiano
PSIUP	Partito Socialista Italiano del Unita Proletaria
SFIO	Parti Socialist, Section Française de l'Internationale Socialiste
TUC	Trades Union Congress
UIL	Unione Italiana del Lavoro
WFTU	World Federation of Trade Unions

For MARILYN, ROSIE and JOE

When they desire to place their economic life on a better foundation, they repeat, like parrots, the word 'productivity', because that is the word that rises first in their minds, regardless of the fact that productivity is the foundation on which it is based already, that increased productivity is the one characteristic of the age [...] and that it is precisely in the century which has seen the greatest increase in productivity since the fall of the Roman Empire that economic discontent has been so acute. [R. H. Tawney *The Acquisitive Society*, 1920]

It is true that efficiency and mass production are not the highest of human goals. But they have become an indispensable condition for sheer national survival in this dangerous and dynamic world. Only when it has emerged from the sea of stagnation can [...] democracy permit itself the luxury of muddling through [...]. [Herbert Luthy, *Socialist Commentary*, December 1951]

Political issues are illusions created by evil men. Society's true problems are engineering problems. [Elton Mayo]

INTRODUCTION

The Marshall Plan for economic aid to Europe is now but a dimly remembered phase of the first Cold War. Yet during its currency it was not simply another international programme affecting Europe and America, it was *the* central ingredient in the relations between the two continents. For at least the years 1947–55 and perhaps for longer it defined the mood of the time. In a real sense this was the Age of the Marshall Plan.

Today there are different perceptions of what it was about. Some take it at face value and look back at a humanitarian programme aimed at getting post-war Europe back on its feet. Among others it is vaguely seen as part of a post-war American economic offensive in Europe which helped generate the long boom of the 1950s and 1960s and in the process undermined the radicalism of the trade union and socialist movement. In this respect it often tends to be lumped together *holus bolus* with CIA intrigue abroad and McCarthyite reaction at home in America – the economic manifestation of a massive project aimed at ensuring world dominance by American capitalism through the export of its economic and social values.

Neither of these perceptions is adequate. It is naive to regard the Marshall programme purely in terms of philanthropy. But it is also mistaken to view it entirely in terms of dark, anti-labour conspiracy. Too often, it seems, trade unionists and people on the political left seek to explain away their failures in terms of the manipulative skills of their opponents: many times over the years 'Catholic Action' or 'CIA money' have been invoked as convenient alibis. The Marshall Plan too fits into this category. None of which is to deny that covert funding or anti-labour programmes hatched by government intelligence agencies have not had an important influence from time to time. The point is merely that programmes like Marshall Aid – which had organised labour as a central focus – should be examined closely to see exactly what were their strengths and weaknesses, their achievements and their failures. And in reviewing the impact of Marshall Aid it has to be constantly borne in mind that organised labour was not simply on the receiving end of the programme but was, through American union officials and their counterparts in Europe, deeply involved in administering it. No doubt some would dismiss such activity as a cover for CIA work – and indeed there were labour officials within the Marshall Plan who operated thus. But the uncomfortable fact is that some of the most vigorous critics of Marshall Aid were to be found among labour personnel working in the programme. That is a complicating factor for consideration by those whose inclination is to sum it up in simplistic, unidimensional terms. Moreover, it should be noted that, in general, contemporary scholars of the Marshall Plan are increasingly inclined to play down claims about its impact beyond the immediate sphere of post-war economic recovery.

Given that there is no history, adequate or otherwise, of the Marshall Plan as it affected labour, the present work is an attempt to outline its major phases and programmes and to do so in a way that enables some judgement to be made as to its impact on the development of labour politics. Was the socialist 'revisionism' of the 1950s something to which Marshall Aid made a significant contribution directly or indirectly, or did its roots lie elsewhere? Were the organisational weaknesses and divisions in the European labour movement of the 1950s attributable to the influence of the American economic aid programme, or were they already in the making before the full impact of American foreign economic policy was felt? Was the attempt to export American labour practices a 'good thing' or a 'bad thing'? More important, did it succeed? If Marshall Aid had an impact on the world of labour, was it through the specific programmes of support for anti-communist labour organisations or more generally through the cultural norms it helped to implant in a society gradually accustoming itself to economic growth and consumer affluence? In other words, was it in the field of organisation – through the superior material resources at their disposal – that the Marshall Plan authorities were most able to influence European labour, or was it in the realm of ideas? And if in the latter, may this not have been due at least in part to the inadequacy of labour's own ideological perspective and theoretical prescriptions?

One of the major themes in what follows is the Marshall Plan's role in developing among European workers a consciousness – indeed, an acceptance – of the need for an ever increasing level of productivity, with all that that implies for the role of labour in the workplace and its relationship with capital. Indeed, it is arguable that this was the Marshall Plan's greatest achievement and the factor that has had the most lasting effect on labour in its struggle for greater material rewards and more control over the process through which wealth is created. Given that, it is astonishing that the Marshall Plan is so neglected in studies of the development of so-called management 'sciences' – especially since so many of the techniques of management and their underlying value system were honed, refined and elaborated under the auspices of Marshall Aid. Of course it is a feature of management disciplines that they tend to be taught as a series of universal truths, timeless and neutral, without reference to history or the current political and economic power structure that they sustain. Such an approach simply will not do. Many techniques of management science were imported into post-war Europe as part of an ideological offensive by liberal capitalism. Our research indicates how, in academia as well as industry, a particular set of managerialist values and beliefs came to constitute a powerful conventional wisdom largely as a result of the financial clout of their influential promoters within the Marshall Plan and related institutions.

As labour history and an account of the development of post-war industrial relations, this study is unconventional in that much of the source material it draws on is in the form of government diplomatic records. Few perhaps would consider the Foreign Office, the US State Department or the embassy staff in various national capitals as a valuable source of information on labour matters, still less as influential in shaping labour–management relations. But in the Marshall Age that certainly was the case. The future of industrial society and the shape of its key institutions were closely bound up with the outcome of power plays in the world of international politics. Indeed, it is a refreshing change to go beyond the dreary bounds of conventional academic industrial relations literature with its often pedestrian explanations of events and structures to record how post-war industrial society really was moulded. (In this connection one wonders how many people who debate in scholarly terms the merits of Allan Flanders's academic writing on industrial relations and his influence on the 'Oxford school' know the first thing about his far more important practical political work as a British evangelist of Atlanticism in the age of the Marshall Plan.) By and large the people who figure prominently in this account are not the well known national leaders in their field, be it management, unions or government, but second-tier officials and back-room boys, civil servants and trade union technicians – the people who so often really do shape history. Frequently it is from their own records rather than the official pronouncements of the organisations for which they worked that the most accurate account of events is to be obtained. It is, then, a study that necessarily operates on different levels – a mixture of diplomatic and labour history, all the time seeking to understand labour's grass-roots response to workplace changes foisted upon it as an indirect result of geo-political trials of strength.

This does not pretend to be a general history of the Marshall Plan: only the four main industrial powers in Europe – Germany, France, Italy and Britain – are looked at in any detail. Far less is it a history of the labour movement in those countries. Its main focus is the Marshall Plan's Labour Division and what they set out to achieve in a broad sense. Western Europe was their oyster, and tempting as it is to restrict the focus to one country, to do so would be to distort the nature of their enter-prise. Marshall Plan staff tended to think in terms of continents, not countries. However, the hope is that this study of an ongoing international programme will help to illuminate some of the conditions peculiar to different countries. Dealing with a number of national labour movements dictates the need to engage in some prior scene-setting in order to establish the context in which the Marshall Plan operated in the donor and recipient countries. But this also helps to establish what changes were afoot *before* the aid programme started. Such background is provided in chapters 2, 3 and 4. Chapter 5 examines the circum-stances surrounding the organisational split in the World Feder-ation of Trade Unions caused by disagreements over the correct response to the offer of Marshall Aid. This was, perhaps, the aid programme's first major accomplishment. Chapters 6, 7 and 8 describe the Marshall Plan's labour operations and consider developments in the Labour Division in the first two years of the programme. Chapter 9 focuses on the American-inspired pro-ductivity programme in Britain, which provided a testing ground for ideas and practices that were later to be exported to the Continent. Chapter 10 looks at the Americans' frustrating experience of trying to launch productivity drives and change the industrial culture in various European countries. The European Productivity Agency, largely created and financed by the Americans for the purpose of continuing the productivity crusade on a continent-wide basis up to the end of the 1950s, is the subject of chapter 11, and chapter 12 considers the experience of European labour in the 1950s under this continual pressure to achieve higher levels of productivity. In the concluding chapter an assessment is made of the claims that the Marshall Plan and the American labour presence in Europe were a force for the deradicalisation of European labour movements.

CHAPTER 1

The Marshall Plan

It was a humanitarian programme to aid Europe's postwar recovery and to extend a helping hand to those in need. It was a political programme to preserve civilisation out of which the American way of life had developed. [...] It was an economic programme to promote Europe's financial, fiscal, and political stability; to stimulate world trade; to expand American markets; to forestall an American depression; to maintain the open-door policy; to create a multilateral trade world which could be dominated by American capitalists; and to maintain a capitalist hegemony over the regions later to be called the Third World. [...] a programme to stop communism, to frustrate socialists and leftists, to attract the Soviet Union's satellites, and to contain or roll back the Russians. It was a programme that promised reduction in military expenditures, but it also provided Americans with opportunities to stockpile strategic materials and maintain friendly access to military bases abroad. [John Gimbel, *The Origins of the Marshall Plan*, 1976]

Originating with a very general offer of economic aid to Europe made by Secretary of State George C. Marshall in a Harvard graduation day speech on 5 June 1947,[1] there emerged ten months later – after much high-level diplomacy, the intensive deliberations of an international committee of officials of European governments, exhaustive Congressional hearings and three Presidential committees of inquiry – the Foreign Assistance Act of 1948. This umbrella legislation established the Economic Co-operation Agency (ECA) to administer the European Recovery Programme (ERP) – Marshall Aid. Over the next four years $13 billion in aid was made available to sixteen western European countries who were prepared to sign bilateral agreements with the USA committing themselves to four broad aims – a strong production effort, expansion of foreign trade, the maintenance of financial stability, and the development of European economic co-operation. Before the four years were up the ECA was superseded in 1951 by the Mutual Security Agency (MSA) as the programme now assumed an essentially militaristic purpose. Further changes in structure and nomenclature followed as the MSA was transformed into the Foreign Operations Agency (FOA) in 1954, thence to become the International Co-operation Agency (ICA) in 1955 and finally the Agency for International Development (AID) in 1961. By that time economic aid to Europe had ceased and other parts of the world were the focus of attention. But as long as Europe was receiving aid during the 1950s under these successor programmes it makes sense to view the operation as a continuation of Marshall Aid.

The immediate background to Marshall's offer of aid, and the factor that lent urgency to the project in the summer of 1947, was the chronic dollar shortage in Europe, in particular Britain's increasingly desperate trading position.[2] Her invisible earning capacity was much reduced as a consequence of the war; foreign investments had been wiped out. The harsh winter and fuel crisis of 1946–47 had cost her two months' worth of exports and put her export drive back by nine months, and she was crippled both by huge military expenditures[3] and by the cost of feeding the German population in the British zone of occupation. In fact Germany was the key to the problem. No progress had been made in reaching a political settlement of the intractable German question, and the most recent failure to break the stalemate at the Moscow session of the Conference of Foreign Ministers in April 1947 – a failure that could only prolong Britain's economic agony – impelled the United States to take some dramatic initiative to reconstruct the economic base of Europe, with Germany reintegrated into the Continental economy. But, Germany apart, it was possible to exaggerate the need for physical reconstruction. Europe had already made much progress since 1945 in rebuilding its industrial base and, on average, production was once again up to 1938 levels by 1947.[4] The real problem lay in the unbalanced trading relationships between America and Europe, and within Europe itself. That imbalance was not a temporary feature, but a permanent result of the way the war had devastated many economies while benefiting the Americans'.

Marshall Aid was represented as an act of great humanitarianism, as a result of which much needed supplies of raw materials, bread grains and other cereal crops would alleviate hunger in Europe. But this dimension of the plan has to be seen alongside the earlier decision of the United States in August 1946 to terminate its crucial contributions to the United Nations Relief and Rehabilitation Administration (UNRRA) on the grounds that further aid was not needed. The truth was that, beyond some legitimate criticisms about maladministration in UNRRA, the United States had grown impatient of general relief programmes which offered no political pay-off. UNRRA finally closed down in June 1947, just as America's massive aid programme was to be announced. Significantly, the United States deliberately chose not to have the aid administered by the United Nations' recently created Economic Committee for Europe (ECE). Nor did the humanitarian element in the Marshall Plan extend so far as to envisage higher general living standards for Europeans by the termination of the four-year programme. Improved levels of consumption were deliberately deferred until after 1952. Dean Acheson was to defend the Marshall Plan in terms of 'our duty [...] as human beings', but he was even more emphatic in saying that the United States was involved in the programme 'chiefly as a matter of national self-interest'.[5]

For many people, of different political persuasions, the Marshall Plan was in essence an anti-communist, anti-Soviet programme designed to undermine and isolate the Soviet Bloc and to defeat indigenous communism in the nations of western Europe. This purpose is hard to deny, since such intentions were frequently proclaimed in the Congressional debates that preceded the passing of the Foreign Assistance Act. Economic power was to be used to attack what one writer referred to as 'submerged problems like the psychological and diplomatic hold of the USSR on Europe'.[6] For the Administrator of the Marshall Plan, Paul Hoffman, the recovery programme was the economic manifestation of what was at bottom an ideological battle needing to be fought concurrently on military, political and psychological fronts. In his pithy phrase, it was a contest between the American assembly line and the communist party line.[7] In western Europe the possibility of communism triumphing on the back of extensive economic and social deprivation in countries such as France, Italy and Germany was a real one for American foreign policymakers to reckon with.

However, anti-communism was only part of the story. Indeed, Marshall Aid was offered to all the eastern European countries, including the USSR, though with what sincerity cannot be known, since the USSR rejected the terms as unacceptable and was therefore in no position to test the *bona fides* of the American offer. It is also relevant to note that the Soviet Bloc was not so monolithic in June 1947 as it subsequently became. The various national economies were not yet integrated as closely as they were under the Molotov Plan; tighter Soviet discipline over communist parties had yet to be established through the Cominform; no *coup* had yet taken place in Czechoslovakia; and the rigid division of Germany into east and west had not been finalised. Indeed, all these developments might be viewed as consequences of the Marshall Plan rather than its justification. That the notion of containment was a prominent strand in American thinking was reflected in the selection in spring 1947 of the Russian specialist George Kennan to head the important Policy Planning Staff of the State Department which was given the task of drafting the outline of the aid programme. But Kennan clearly perceived the European problem primarily in economic terms rather than as a political threat from communism.[8] That was a contingent problem, and his notion of containment held that a successful attack on Europe's economic ills would undermine the scope for the growth of communism. In short, anti-communism was to some extent a convenient, emotive rallying call that the State Department was happy to ride in order to get its foreign economic policy through an economy-minded Congress.

Opponents of Marshall Aid made much play of the argument that it was essentially a measure to ward off the recession that was widely expected to hit the United States in the late 1940s, and did arrive in 1949. Long before the political division of the State Department had turned serious attention to the challenge of communism, economic experts within the department had foreseen the danger that Europe's economy might seize up, with dire consequences for the United States' export trade and the domestic economy generally.[9] At the end of the war, over-capacity in industry dictated that she find markets for $14 billion annually in extra exports. That such domestic concerns lay behind the programme was clearly the assumption of the British Foreign Secretary, Ernest Bevin, and his Russian and French counterparts, Molotov and Bidault, when they met in June 1947. American commentators were claiming that the recession had definitely begun.[10] Before the end of the year, three presidential committees had advised that generous foreign aid was necessary if American prosperity and full employment were to continue. The Council of Economic Advisers warned that, without dollar aid to finance trade, American exports would fall by over one-third within a year, necessitating a 'drastic adjustment in the domestic economy'.[11] Indeed, a fall in exports to Europe of that magnitude occurred during the ten months the aid programme was under consideration.

A more far-reaching explanation of Marshall Aid is that the programme was not so much about restoring western Europe to economic health as to do with a fundamental restructuring of the international economy such as would permit the United States to draw the full advantage from its vast economic strength. Seen in this light, it has been suggested that the question was not whether capitalism would survive, but whether it would survive in the form most beneficial to United States business interests.[12] A failure to solve the dollar problem would, if nothing else, reinforce autarkic tendencies in world economics, with trade reduced to a series of bilateral/barter arrangements and the United States excluded from large potential markets for its exports and deprived of access to essential raw materials.[13] As the *Department of State Bulletin* put it, 'It is idle to think that Europe left to its own efforts [...] would remain open to American business in the same way that we have known in the past.'[14] The basic problem, then, was to reconstruct international capitalism in a way acceptable to America. To do this, political diplomatic and economic measures would have to be used to influence the political economy of other governments. This is precisely what was attempted under the Marshall Plan. Implemented as an economic programme, it was in fact conceived as a major element of United States foreign policy. As the Senate Foreign Relations Committee Chairman, Senator Vandenberg, saw it, the Marshall Plan was destined to be 'the turning point in history for 100 years to come'.[15]

The Americans drove a hard bargain over the ground rules for aid. Initially they invited the Europeans to draw up their own programme, but within a matter of three or four months the State Department was effectively dictating the terms. Following Marshall's offer to Europe and its acceptance in principle by Bevin and Bidault, Britain and France convened a Committee on European Economic Co-operation (CEEC) comprising officials from the sixteen participating countries to draft their overall aid requirements. However, their tendency to behave as a collection of autonomous national representatives and to put forward what seemed to the Americans to be inflated requests caused concern in the State Department. In August 1947 State Department economist, Paul Nitze, briefed US ambassadors Caffery (France), Douglas (Britain) and Murphy (Germany) on the American design for Marshall Aid, including details of commitments required of the Europeans on high production, liberalised trade, monetary stabilisation and European integration. State Department officials George Kennan and Charles Bonesteel were sent to Paris to monitor the CEEC deliberations, and from mid-August the Americans took an increasingly firm line in telling the CEEC delegates what their requirements and expectations of aid ought to be. In particular, every opportunity was taken to impress upon European governments that the chances of getting the aid programme through Congress would be greatly improved if they would only pursue policies of financial orthodoxy and balance their national budgets.[16] By the end of the CEEC report-drafting exercise the State Department had asserted its authority, and the report produced by the Europeans followed very closely the department's original concept of the Marshall Plan.

In the subsequent process of negotiating bilateral agreements with participating countries the United States attempted to go further and include clauses that infringed the sovereignty of the countries. For example, the draft treaty with Britain required her to balance her budget annually, restrict her tariffs and extend most-favoured-nation status to Germany and Japan. The treaties would also have allowed America to apply pressure to recipient countries to require them to alter interest rates, and one provision that was universally rejected by the participating states would have made it mandatory to consult the International Monetary Fund regarding proposed devaluation of the currency should the United States think it desirable. This and certain other restrictive clauses were dropped, but the theme of monetary stability was still the *sine qua non* of the aid programme and the *Department of State Bulletin* could claim an historic breakthrough: 'Never before in history [...] has any nation undertaken by solemn international agreement [...] to stabilise its currency, establish or maintain internal financial stability.'[17] The Europeans were compelled to agree to close monitoring of their economic policies by the Americans. They were to supply quarterly progress reports and provide any information relating to the recovery programme that the United States might want. If the recipients reneged on their commitments, the Administrator of the programme would have the power to cut off their aid.

The Americans were always torn between the intention of extracting significant concessions and the desire to appear as friendly benefactors without any plans for dictating policy to the Europeans. But as Senator Cabot Lodge argued in the Foreign Relations Committee:

> I think this whole question of interfering in Europe's internal affairs is going to come up all the time, and God knows this Marshall Plan is going to be the biggest damned interference in international affairs that there has ever been in history. It doesn't do any good to say we are not going to interfere. [...] I don't think we have to be so sensitive about interfering in the internal affairs of these countries [...].[18]

The United States had to be cautious if it were not to invite charges of American imperialism through the export of ideological values. The official position of the ECA reflected the line successfully advocated by Administrator Paul Hoffman as a member of the President's Committee on Foreign Aid (the Harriman Committee), which had considered in detail the mechanism by which economic aid would be rendered.

> Aid from this country should not be conditioned on the methods used to reach these goals, so long as they are consistent with basic democratic principles. [...] While this committee firmly believes that the American system of free enterprise is the best method of obtaining high productivity, it does not believe that any foreign-aid program should be used as a means of requiring other countries to adopt it.[19]

Hoffman always denied that there were strings to Marshall Aid, that the expenditure decisions of the ECA were taken on ideological grounds: pragmatic business considerations were what weighed most. Under questioning from Congressmen on the possibility of aid being used to further nationalisation of industry, he paraded his pragmatism: 'We would have to decide whether socialisation would make for recovery.' But his mind was far from open on this question, and he was quick to qualify

his answer: 'My guess is that it would not.'[20] Hoffman's hostility
to the nationalisation of the British steel industry was hardly in
doubt, as was evident from statements made before various
audiences. He told the Congressional Appropriation Committee
in May 1948 that the scheme did not have his sympathy, and he
later asked the British government to postpone the measure.[21]
American business hostility extended to the whole range of social
welfare measures being pursued in various European countries,
notably by the Labour government in Britain. Expenditure on
welfare and government subsidies was said to threaten monetary
stability, while policies of social egalitarianism were reckoned
to stifle initiative and entrepreneurship. As such they had to be
discouraged. Thus as the Labour government developed its
public-sector house-building programme the Americans would
consider reducing their exports of vital timber supplies to the
United Kingdom.

If intervention was, as has been suggested, a 'sometime
thing',[22] a course to be followed pragmatically as and when the
climate permitted, it was still not difficult to discern a consistent
sticking point beyond which the ECA would invoke a right of
veto. Hoffman might claim that nationalisation was exclusively
a matter for national governments to decide, but he summed up
the ECA's general position on British government policy in this
way:

> [...] what they do with their economy is their business, and what we
> do with our dollars is our business and if they start playing ducks and
> drakes with their economy to such a point that they cannot recover
> and our investment is not worthwhile, we are going to hold up the
> investment [...]. They should not use our dollars to engage in social
> experimentation [...].[23]

One of the major potential sources of American influence over
the domestic policies of participating countries was through
control over what were termed 'counterpart funds'. These were
sums of money in local currency, equivalent to the dollar value
of exports provided by the ECA. A European importer who bought
American goods under the programme had to deposit with his
government an amount in local currency equivalent to the dollar
price. The ECA shared authority with the national government
in question in determining the use to which the bulk of the
counterpart fund was put. It might be used to finance public

projects or loaned for investment purposes. In an inflationary situation other options were to immobilise the fund or use it to retire government debt. Ninety-five per cent of counterpart was jointly controlled in this way. The remaining 5 per cent was paid over direct to the ECA for its exclusive use in covering administrative costs, stockpiling strategic materials and other miscellaneous expenditures. And part of the 5 per cent was available for use by the Administrator himself on a secret basis, without need for public disclosure.

The Americans were reluctant to spell out the various purposes to which counterpart would be put, since that involved delicate policy decisions.[24] But two basic objectives were listed in the Marshall Plan legislation – the stimulation of production and the promotion of monetary stability. The value of counterpart to the United States as a means of exerting pressure on participating countries was contested within the ECA. In France, where the ECA applied strong pressure to force deflationary policies on the government, the Americans were forced to soft-pedal their approach from time to time or risk the collapse of the French government and its replacement by one hostile to the United States.[25] In Britain, where the ECA would have preferred to spend the money on specific investment programmes, it was forced to settle for using 99 per cent of it – some $1·4 billion – for debt retirement, a means of reducing liquidity and, in American eyes, forcing a measure of anti-inflationary discipline on the Labour government.[26] Counterpart was not released to assist any British welfare or social programmes, and this helped to reduce the resources available for consumption by the Labour government. In 1945–46 over a quarter of the budgetary resources available for domestic use had been consumed by the government. The figure was down to 18·2 per cent in 1948, and the ECA expected it to be down to 16·8 per cent by 1951 following cuts in housing, health and educational programmes.[27] Officials still complained that the British government deliberately created a type of official debt which they then retired with counterpart.[28] The policy of using the fund for this purpose was strongly criticised by the Deputy ECA Administrator, Richard Bissell, who argued that the United States had thereby passed up an opportunity to exert maximum pressure on European countries.[29] However, he later modified his view and agreed that counterpart had sometimes been very successful in influencing monetary and fiscal policy.[30]

Hoffman's own view was much more positive. He claimed that counterpart was a decisive feature of the Marshall Plan:

> I can say flatly that it made the difference between success and failure for the Marshall Plan in every nation that had a shaky government, and it helped mightily with those that had strong ones. It was, I believe, the indispensable idea – the essential catalyst.[31]

Even where the pressure was subtle rather than direct, it was nonetheless capable of being effective. As Thomas Finletter, who headed the ECA's London mission during the first year of the plan, testified:

> As to actually influencing policy – there is no doubt about it. I would not want this quoted, but there were cases where they actually went over documents with me before they presented them officially to us. True, there was nothing like the direct intervention in the United Kingdom that you had elsewhere [...].[32]

As the aid programme developed, the Americans lost many of their early inhibitions about interfering in the domestic affairs of participating countries and were increasingly inclined to dictate to the Europeans. In 1950 the ECA concluded that the tendency for European countries to feel that they were entitled to their share of aid was undermining the American purpose in the programme. Consequently, up to a quarter of the following year's aid appropriation was to be withheld and only allotted on a drip-feed basis if the Europeans performed according to ECA requirements.[33] In this more hard-nosed approach, aid was to be based on performance, not on need. Later in the year, following the outbreak of war in Korea, the participating countries were told abruptly that a substantial diversion of their resources from economic to military purposes would now be required. This significant change of emphasis was announced as a *fait accompli* rather than a matter for discussion.[34]

These various aspects of the Marshall Plan all had important implications for organised labour. Trade unionists in Europe and America naturally warmed to the humanitarian aspects of the programme, though for communists in Europe, who stood to benefit from prolonged economic and social dislocation, the aid was clearly a poisoned chalice. The agonising by the Italian trade unions, strongly influenced by communism, before declaring against the aid programme, was the sharpest manifestation of this dilemma. The American labour movement was clearly enthusiastic about the economic pump-priming in Europe, which would generate exports for the United States and ward off the depression that had been threatening there ever since the end of the war. Likewise, American unions were beneficiaries of those provisions in the programme that protected American jobs in industries such as shipping and agriculture. The protectionist element in the plan was not to the liking of European labour; nonetheless their short-term interests were served by any programme that enabled their industry to acquire raw materials for manufacturing and to increase the exports of such output.

In general the European trade unions took the view that they were in no position to balk at the basic terms under which aid was offered. Certainly the British, the Germans and the Scandinavians approached it philosophically: as with collective bargaining, it was an unavoidable exercise in which labour would have to make some concessions, but through which there were also gains to be made if they played their cards carefully. Though not without some misgivings, they chose, for the most part, to regard the Marshall Plan in the best possible light, essentially a virtuous measure. In this they were encouraged by American labour, which insisted that its own involvement in the scheme was proof that aid was being given without 'strings'. As the AFL President, William Green, said, '[...] the AFL has an indispensable service to perform. The wage earners of this country can convince the wage earners of Europe that our government does not seek power over their lives or wants to possess their land. Neither our government nor our employers can carry this important message convincingly.'[35] The CIO's position was that Marshall Aid was 'a people's programme' whose administration needed to consist of people representing all walks of American life. Philip Murray and Walter Reuther both argued at the Senate Foreign Relations Committee hearings on Marshall Aid that there should be no strings. But of course there were conditions attached and they had important implications for labour. That was understood by the CIO Secretary Treasurer, James Carey, although he tried to play it down: 'While we frankly realise that there are ideological questions residual in the implementation and administration of the ERP, these cannot be considered as separate or even primary.'[36]

The hidden agenda was the long-term restructuring of Western capitalism. The American design was to generate an international economy of abundance based on high growth and productivity which would, in turn, provide high levels of employment and income. Secure jobs and high wages would, if they materialised, naturally be welcomed by trade unions. The long-term effects of Marshall Aid on organised labour could not be precisely foretold, but the price to be paid in the long run might be the consolidation of power among business elites, the abandoning of measures to extend social equality, and the capacity to plan national economies in the interests of wider social welfare.

The plan's challenge to communist influence affected the internal politics of the labour movement in all the recipient countries. Not only communists but socialists and groups simply favouring a reform of capitalist society were to some extent caught up as objects of that challenge, the result being that the aid programme also had a serious influence on domestic labour movement politics in countries other than those where communism was strong, including the United States itself, where divisions between communist and anti-communist trade unionists were becoming sharper. While liberals, influenced by the experience of wartime co-operation with the USSR and amenable to the rhetoric of the grand alliance, often shied away from policies designed to challenge communism head-on, socialists, who had frequently been the first victims of communist attacks, had fewer reservations about identifying with such steps. Projected on to the international labour screen, the aid programme became a catalyst hastening the polarisation of the world labour movement, which was already subject to increasing tension between communist and non-communist tendencies. Before the first shipment of Marshall Aid supplies arrived in Europe in May 1948, the World Federation of Trade Unions (WFTU) was well on the way to a permanent split over this issue. It was, arguably, the first achievement of the Marshall Plan.

The sequence of events through which the WFTU was divided over Marshall Aid will be looked at in greater detail in chapter 5. As a preliminary, and to indicate what sort of world the

Marshall Plan was meant to influence, it is necessary to outline some of the important elements of labour politics in western Europe in the early post-war years, and also to establish the context in which industrialists and organised labour in America were operating on the eve of the announcement of Marshall Aid. These are the concerns of chapters 2, 3 and 4.

CHAPTER 2

The politics of European labour, 1945–48

In the Europe of 1945 [...] the communists replaced the social democrats as the essential anchor of social stability. Only by means of their aid did the established order accomplish the difficult transition to a new normality and re-establish the old organs of state power, military and judiciary, substantially unchanged from an earlier age. [Walter Kendall, *The Labour Movement in Europe*, 1975]

Who had ever dreamed that Utopia would begin in bankruptcy court? That the Socialist Zion would have to be subsidised by American capitalism? In short, that the advent of Socialism would make so little difference to the character of life? [John P. Roche, *New Leader*, 31 August 1959]

Popular Front politics were much to the fore in Europe at the end of the war. The spirit of the grand alliance continued after the end of hostilities, helping to bind the anti-fascist parties together. And in countries such as France and Italy communists played a particularly important role in the Popular Front as a result of the considerable prestige they had earned in the Resistance. For the first two post-war years the balance of forces within this coalition framework, and especially the relationship between communists and socialists, was a central factor in labour movement politics.

Although labour was in the ascendant at the war's end, and the prospects for a far-reaching transformation of European society looked good, the political programme of the left was generally restrained. Modest measures of socialisation, the development of social welfare policies and the pursuit of full employment were the hallmark of Popular Front politics as the left concentrated on reconstruction rather than revolution. Communist parties were largely responsible for this orientation. Whether it stemmed from a genuine belief that the European working class would not accept anything more radical, or a calculation that the interests of the Soviet Union required a period of consolidation rather than radical change, the weight of their influence was thrown behind policies of economic reconstruction and moderate social reform.

Whereas the French Communist Party (PCF) regarded nationalisation of industry essentially as part of a policy of national reconstruction that would ensure French economic independence, their socialist partners (SFIO) in the post-war coalition government spoke in terms of the gradual transformation of society and insisted that it was *socialisation* that they wanted, a programme leading ultimately to a socialist society. But communists regarded this as irresponsible talk, and the result of their considerable influence was that the nationalisation measures adopted in 1945–46 in half a dozen industries represented 'more an advance to state economic management and technocratic overhaul than a breakthrough to socialism'.[1] The PCF and their allies in the main trade union centre, the Confédération Générale du Travail (CGT), participated enthusiastically in the early postwar 'battle for production', the centrepiece of their strategy for reconstruction. The CGT's 1946 congress manifesto announced, 'The first duty is to raise production [...].' Communist Party Secretary Thorez told miners that to dig coal 'was the highest form of their duty as Frenchmen'. Ambroise Croizat, the communist Minister of Labour, who was also leader of the metalworkers' union, publicly condemned workers who undermined the battle for production by striking.[2] The unions agreed to lengthen the basic working week to forty-eight hours. Works councils had been introduced by law in 1946, partly as a gesture towards the syndicalist idea of workers' control but also as a vehicle for expediting economic recovery. In fact, with the CGT under communist domination, they became exclusively instruments for waging the battle of production.

Italian experience closely approximated that of France. The failure of the left to capitalise on the radical opportunities presented by Italian labour's significant contribution to the defeat of the fascist state dated back to the 1944 decision of Palmiro Togliatti, Secretary of the Italian Communist Party (PCI) and recently returned from Moscow, to reverse the policy agreed with the other Resistance parties not to participate in government without the abdication of the king, who had been closely identified with Mussolini. In joining the government headed by the ex-fascist military leader General Badoglio, the communists were giving notice of their intention to play down radical policies while quietly entrenching themselves in positions of influence in government. Under Togliatti communist strategy aimed not at achieving socialist revolution but at establishing a working-class hegemony in society. Fearing that they might be excluded from power, the other political groups of the Resistance, and especially the socialists, put aside their objections, followed the lead of the PCI and joined them in the government.

The PCI's cautious line was determined by Togliatii, who considered that the United States and Britain would block any attempt to build socialism in Italy, and that the Catholic Church was such a powerful influence that the communists would have to come to terms with the Christian Democrats. Almost certainly, too, the Soviet Union would have viewed precipitate action to implement socialist policies as destablising from its standpoint. Given this analysis, the PCI settled for presenting itself as a non-revolutionary party of reconstruction, content to collaborate with bourgeois parties in coalition government.[3] The communist goal was thus to achieve a working relationship with the Church while advancing modest economic and social proposals for a welfare state. There was never any intention of challenging the capitalist basis of society. Togliatti said in 1945 that even if the PCI were governing alone it would rely on private initiative for reconstruction. Even with their own members in economic Ministries the communists made no radical impact on government policy. Standing for improved social services, income redistribution through taxation, increased public consumption and the nationalisation of some basic industries, they were, if anything, less radical than the Labour government of Britain. There was no call for thoroughgoing planning, and arguments in favour of a voice for workers in managerial decision-making soon died out.

The Italian socialists (PSIUP) were far more optimistic about the prospects of radical change in society after the war and they expected to play a leading part in effecting it. Their general assumption was that Italian capitalism was too weak to be revived. They were unwilling to accept the validity of the emerging spheres of capitalist and communist influence or Italy's inevitable membership of the Western Bloc.[4] They were critical of the PCI's opportunism in accepting office in Badoglio's government, whose links with fascism had not been broken. Equally they were critical of PCI subservience to Moscow.[5] Yet about all they placed the need for left-wing unity so as to avoid the damaging split that had first given Mussolini his chance in 1922.

In Britain the circumstances were rather different. The Communist Party (CPGB) was influential in the trade union movement, though politically it was of no significance. It had favoured the continuation of the wartime coalition, but Labour chose to fight the 1945 general election on partisan lines and duly formed the first post-war government. Still, there was an important element of continuity with wartime policies. Labour's leaders had formed close ties with their Conservative counterparts and with senior civil servants during the coalition years, and their unquestioned respect for the institutions of the state and Parliament restricted their scope for radical change. Party leaders were hesitant in their approach to the socialisation of industry, the programme of nationalisation being agreed only belatedly and under pressure from the rank and file. Likewise the Labour Party failed to advance any radical policies for the democratisation of industry, thereby missing the opportunity to shift the balance of power in society. The quest for increased output was the foremost concern of the government. As Herbert Morrison said in 1947, echoing dozens of such statements by his Cabinet colleagues, 'the battle for socialism is the battle for production'. And, while many in the trade unions and the Labour Party argued that this could best be achieved by democratising industry, the government and employers put their trust in the traditional hierarchical structures of industrial leadership, albeit in some instances newly coated with a gloss of scientific management. Much of Labour's thinking and practice was indeed rooted not in a class analysis of society but in a corporatist, 'one nation' value system. As Party Secretary Morgan Phillips declared in 1945 during the general election campaign, 'Let me remove at the outset any lingering impression of the outworn idea that the Labour Party is a class party.'[6] And, in the administration of industrial controls within this corporatist structure, businessmen on secondment from their companies played a dominant role. The result was that, despite its protestations that the socialist state was killing enterprise, private industry emerged from the years of Labour government remarkably unscathed.

A major goal of the British Communist Party after the war was to affiliate with the Labour Party. Through its influence in the trade union movement it sought agreement on this before the 1946 Labour Party conference decisively rejected the proposal. On the Continent the issue of organic links between communists and socialists was also a matter of contention. Unity of the left was clearly the communist strategy, as was evidenced by the enforced merger of the communists and socialists in the Soviet zone of Germany in 1946.

Although the French Socialist Party performed well in the first post-liberation municipal elections, when they won control of most major cities outside Paris, in organisational terms they were far less powerful than the communists and not nearly as united in strategic thinking. While the PCF's internal discipline was strict, the socialists indulged in the luxury of open doctrinal debate, with all their divisions on view.[7] In particular they engaged in an extended debate on the organisational and ideo-logical basis of future political activity. Following Leon Blum's leadership, many wanted the party to assert humanitarian values as against the totalitarianism of the communists − not so much as an antidote to class struggle but in opposition to the way, in PCF thinking, production had become the measure of all things. Indeed, a substantial section of the SFIO membership were attracted to the idea of creating a broad-based Labour Party committed to parliamentarianism, with the industrial and political wings of the labour movement in close alignment, as in Britain. However, Blum's position was narrowly rejected by the party congress in 1946. The SFIO stuck to its traditional Marxist line, making few concessions to the changing circum-stances of the post-war world. And though the idea of closer links with the trade unions was attractive, the problem for socialists was that they lacked a base in the mass labour movement, where the communists monopolised support. Attempts to strengthen the SFIO's ties with the trade union movement amounted to little, though the socialists may have provided encouragement to some of the dissident workers who broke with the CGT in 1946 as a result of its domination by the communists and its obsession with the battle for production.[8]

The PCF offered to unite with the SFIO in a mass labour party in June 1945, but the socialists declined, fearing, as they continued to fear throughout the Fourth Republic, that their loosely disciplined organisation would effectivley be swallowed by the communists if they ventured too close. The SFIO even rejected a united campaign with the PCF in the general election in October 1945. Reflecting the bitter experience of previous attempts at co-operation with the PCF, Jules Moch told the SFIO congress that there could be no united action without mutual loyalty and confidence in one another, meaning that both parties had to be open and frank in their policies and avoid opportunistic action. Moreover the PCF would have to demonstrate that it was democratic in practice and not tied to any foreign government.[9] Thus unity of the left was not a realistic prospect, but in declining the PCF overture the socialists ensured that they would remain essentially a parliamentary group with no direct line to the organised working class. Their vacillation over the question of unity cost them popular support, and in the October 1945 election they came in third, behind the Catholic MRP and the communists. The tide had now turned against the socialists.

The Italian Communist Party, which before the war had never amounted to more than a sect, also emerged in 1944 organisationally strong, having maintained cadre discipline during the years of exile under Mussolini and in the Resistance. As in France, the organisational discipline of the communists put them at a distinct advantage in relation to the much more loosely organised Socialist Party with its tolerance of different currents and perspectives. Yet in the first post-war elections in June 1946 the socialists polled more heavily than the communists and were the second largest party in the National Assembly behind the Christian Democrats. Socialist leader Pietro Nenni's hope was for the fusion of the two parties in order to create a wholly new type of political organisation with the emphasis on tolerance and democracy and devoid of dogmatism and sectarianism.[10] But in subordinating all else to the goal of unity with the less scrupulous and more disciplined communists the PSIUP leaders soon allowed themselves to be cast in the role of the junior partner, in the process causing a split in their party.

A proposal for total fusion with the PCI was defeated at the Socialist congress in April 1946, the party opting narrowly to retain its independent existence. But in October 1946 the leaders signed a new unity of action pact with the communists, tying the two more closely together than had been the case before and committing them to joint decisions on all problems at all levels.[11] It was this that provoked a secessionist move by the social democratic followers of Giuseppe Saragat, whose conception of socialism placed more emphasis on parliamentary reform than on class conflict. Hitherto the socialists had managed to accommodate revolutionary and revisionist currents in Marxism, but the tension created by the alliance with the communists had prised the two apart. Saragat's break-away party, the PSLI, failed to attract a large following. Cut off from the mass base of socialist support, it was largely a rump of parlimentarians, distinguished by Tammany-style politics. However, the split was to be permanent and deeply harmful to the cause of democratic socialism in Italy.

Everywhere in Europe the key to left-wing strength lay with the trade union movement. In Germany, amidst the complexities of quadripartite military rule, a particularly vigorous struggle for political dominance in the re-emerging trade union movement was taking place. With the activities of political parties restricted, trade union organisation provided the focus of left-wing politics. Much depended on the political leanings of the military authorities, who were in a position to confer favours and allocate resources to their preferred group. Within the British and American occupations a mixture of anti-German sentiment, fear of a Nazi resurgence and anti-trade unionism, especially among members of the military, delayed the serious work of rebuilding trade unions for many months after the war. The approach reflected the lack of any clear policy towards Germany on the part of the two governments. On the other hand the Red Army was quick to promote the development of the trade union movement in the Soviet zone from the top down under strong communist leadership. The anticipated prize for acting so swiftly was the likelihood of being able to set the agenda for the wider German labour movement following the reunification of the zones. The Russians also took the lead in reconstructing the trade union movement under strong communist influence in Berlin, which was jointly administered by the occupying powers. It was, in part, their achievement in this area and what it presaged for the spread of communism throughout the German labour movement that prompted a rethink of the official approach to trade unionism in the Western zones, especially among the Americans.

Within the United States military government the situation was complicated by a fierce struggle that raged in the second half of 1945 between those in the Manpower Division who favoured the reconstruction of trade unions on the basis of shop stewards and plant-level organisation and those who wanted the German trade union leaders of the pre-Nazi period to play a leading role in organising the movement at a higher level. The two sides accused each other of delaying the re-emergence of German trade unionism. Each invoked 'democracy' in arguing its case, and the issue of whether the trade union movement should be oriented to social democracy or should be 'apolitical' was a prominent theme in the dispute. But what added real passion to the conflict was the fact that the alternative approaches were seen as stratagems designed to favour in the one case the communists and in the other the social democrats. The issue was viewed by the protagonists in terms of a struggle between communist-sympathising military government officials and pro-capitalist labour supporters of American business unionism. Both sides rejected this characterisation by the other, but it was almost certain that continued emphasis on the plant-based approach (which was officially favoured until the end of 1945) would have given the communists an advantage over the social democrats in a 'non-political' trade union movement, whereas the policy subsequently adopted in early 1946, allowing former union leaders to take the organising initiative, handed the advantage to social democrats in the labour movement.[12]

In the British zone, which contained the biggest concentration of the industrial labour force, the military government also gave general support to social democratic trade union leaders and, after taking advice from a TUC delegation to Germany in November 1945, insisted on a federal structure of autonomous industrial unions for Germany as opposed to the more centralised format favoured by German trade unionists of all political persuasions. British opposition to union centralisation was that it would facilitate authoritarian control – especially in the hands of communists. The model preferred by the British was accepted by the Americans and was gradually put into effect in the two zones over the next two years. But before the trade union move-ment in the Western zones took final shape a protracted effort was made to amalgamate it with the unions in the Soviet zone.

The project was vigorously supported by the World Federation of Trade Unions (WFTU), which saw the unification of the German labour movement as perhaps its most urgent task. The increasingly communist-leaning leadership of the Federation recognised this as a major opportunity to extend communist influence from the East to the Western zones, and for exactly the same reason it was equally strongly resisted by the American military government and the American Federation of Labour. In the context of polarising politics the failure of the German zonal trade union organisations to agree a basis for unification between 1946 and 1948 paralleled the more general failure of WFTU affiliates to reach agreement on the Marshall Plan.

In France communist trade unionists traded on their acknowledged record of leadership in the Resistance. And, resorting where necessary to unscrupulous methods to defeat their political rivals, they used the opportunity presented by the purge of union officials who had collaborated with the Germans to remove opponents who had no taint of collaboration. By spring 1945 communists were sufficiently strong to insist on parity with non-communists on the CGT executive, and their nominee, Benoit Frachon, became joint general secretary of the Confederation and effectively the leading official.[13] In individual unions members of the PCF consolidated their hold, abandoning the system of factional truce which had previously allowed members of different political persuasions to work together without domination by one or another group.[14] In spring 1946 the voting system in the CGT was amended to allow greater influence by the larger communist-dominated unions. Rule changes also allowed, for the first time ever, CGT executive members to remain members of the executive of a political party, a move clearly intended to bring the CGT and the PCF into lock step.[15]

In Italy a unified trade union centre, the Confederazione Generale Italiana del Lavoro (CGIL), embracing communists, socialists and Christian Democrats, had been created in 1944. But although there was nominal parity between the three party factions in the Confederation, the disciplined strength of the communists soon began to be felt, and the CGIL's policies mirrored the moderation of the Communist Party. The major challenge to capitalist industry in this period was posed by the spontaneous growth of councils of administration, plant-level institutions which had their roots in Mussolini's regime but which became the focus of popular rank-and-file pressure for the socialisation of enterprise under workers' control at the end of the war. The CGIL supported the development of the councils of administration, attempted to co-ordinate their activities and over a period of two years pressed unsuccessfully for them to be given legal status.[16] The aim was to incorporate the network of councils into a system of government economic planning. However, CGIL support for them was in the context of efforts to preserve the stability of the post-war coalition, a strategy that aimed at best to create a progressive democracy in Italy, not socialist revolution. The CGIL's major economic concern was to maintain the level of employment by resisting proposed lay-offs in industry. As secondary objectives, it sought to prevent profiteering and to protect the purchasing power of wages in an inflationary situation. But primary concern for the protection of jobs and fear of the effects of inflation on employment ruled out any aggressive wage strategy. Against a background of rank-and-file unrest over inflation, the lack of job-creating public works projects and failure to punish ex-fascists, the CGIL discouraged strikes in a bid to manage the discontents of the labour force. Indeed, there were hardly any national strikes in the first two years after the war, and in January 1947 Togliatti boasted that Italy had fewer strikes than many other European countries.[17]

Through all this the Italian Communist Party bent its efforts to secure factional dominance in the Confederation. Communist trade unionists were diligent in making sure that newly recruited members were also introduced to the party.[18] The communists' 40 per cent share of CGIL support in early 1945 had been translated into majority support among delegates at the 1946 congress, and early in 1947 the PCI moved to end formal equality between the three political groups, promoting the communist faction leader Di Vittorio to the position of effective head of the CGIL in June 1947.[19] Meanwhile the Christian Democrats organised a strong factional grouping through membership of the Association of Catholic Trade Unionists (ACLI), which attacked the CGIL for abandoning its supposed political neutrality and allowing itself to be used as a weapon against de Gasperi and his government. The communists, on the other hand, accused ACLI of interfering in CGIL affairs.[20] Lacking the same discipline and sense of purpose, the socialist faction in the CGIL was no match for the communists. Discord between leading socialist trade unionists and their counterparts in the party organisation – the former being more inclined to adopt moderate positions – compounded the socialists' relative weakness. And on a personal level the leader of the CGIL's socialist faction, Fernando Santi, was quite overshadowed by Di Vittorio.[21]

The moderation of French and Italian trade union leaders and their single-minded support for policies of reconstruction came under fire from their own rank and file in the course of 1946 and early 1947. In Italy the CGIL was palpably failing to protect the economic interests of its members. An agreement with the employers in early 1946 ceded to them the right to declare lay-offs, and this paved the way for an increase of 750,000 in the number unemployed in the twelve months following March 1946. Likewise they were party to a cost of living agreement whose terms failed to compensate workers for a loss of real earnings. Spiraling inflation in 1946 precipitated a wave of strikes in October, and this finally prompted the socialists and communists to insist on the resignation of de Gasperi's Treasury Minister.

As the political climate grew more turbulent the communists proved more resilient than the socialists. They appropriated the language and symbols of the left and were ever ready to deride the socialists as weak and reformist if they failed to toe the communist line. Yet this populist demagogy went hand in hand with their membership of a conservative coalition. As Horowitz points out, the party supported balanced budgets while making populist demands for more government spending. They denounced inflation while advocating wage increases. They were for a secular state and yet supported the government's concordat wtih the Vatican, which resulted in a firm Catholic hold over the educational system.[22] However, the scope for such political gymnastics was rapidly diminishing in both Italy and France.

In the course of 1946 French workers became disillusioned as reforms promised by the Resistance failed to materialise. Living standards were depressed and prices escalated as wealth was redistributed away from labour. In these circumstances exhortations from the communists and the CGT to join the battle for production began to pall. Some anarcho-syndicalists had broken away from the CGT following its capture by the communists in April 1946. Non-communist members now protested about the politicisation of the CGT as communist leaders pressed the Confederation to follow the party line. Strikes on the railways and in the postal service in the summer of 1946 led by socialists discomfited the CGT and increased tension between communist and anti-communist trade unionists, with break-away unions being formed in consequence.[23] The result was that the CGT was forced to press more vigorously for wage increases and for an end to the controls on wage bargaining, while still striving to give pride of place to the production campaign.

Throughout 1945 and 1946 the left-wing French and Italian parties remained in the conservative-led coalition governments, making no move to strike out in a more radical direction despite the fact that in France the socialists and communists together attracted some 50 per cent of the vote whereas in Italy their combined electoral support made them the biggest political bloc, ahead of the Christian Democrats. Meanwhile European governments found themselves increasingly forced into the arms of the United States for financial assistance, with the result that their room for political manoeuvre was further constrained. This factor, combined with the growing industrial unrest among workers, would finally lead to a break-up of the Popular Fronts in 1947.

Britain's Labour government was the first to find itself in the position of seeking American financial aid in 1945 following the abrupt termination of Lend-lease. The American and Canadian governments offered a $4 · 4 billion loan at 2 per cent interest on condition that Britain ratified the terms of the Bretton Woods agreement. It meant eliminating protectionism in trade, ending restrictions on United States imports by the end of 1946 and agreeing to make sterling freely convertible as of July 1947. The terms were designed to force Britain into the American-dominated multilateral trading world. In practice the stiff conditions proved unworkable and led direct to the sterling crisis of summer 1947. The US Congress had grave reservations about making a loan to facilitate the programme of a socialist government in Britain. But eventually the Americans came to see the importance of the measure as a means of stabilising the Western economy and progressing towards a system of multilateral free trade. Failure to approve the loan ran the risk for the Americans that Britain would be driven into the arms of the Soviet Union. In that sense it was a means of combating communism.[24] There was vocal opposition to the terms of the loan from the Labour Cabinet Ministers Aneurin Bevan and Emanuel Shinwell, who preferred the gamble of an independent policy. But interestingly, in view of what was to happen later during the negotiation of Marshall Aid, the two communist members of Parliament supported the loan.

Was there really any alternative to accepting the loan on those conditions? Lord Keynes, who negotiated the transaction, saw it as an essential stepping stone to the kind of multilateral trading world he favoured and conjured up an apocalyptic picture of the consequences of rejecting it. That involved social violence and the loss of civilisation, with Britain becoming 'a secondary power, a slum of squalid living and loutish ways'. But as Pimlott has observed, Keynes' perspective was that of a 'Bloomsbury patriot', not a socialist.[25] The more sober judgement of Treasury Under-Secretary Otto Clarke was that 'we could pull through without having to embark upon such austerity as would reduce the British economy to a standstill'. When pressed, Keynes himself was ready to agree on a similar view: the loan was primarily to meet Britain's political and military role overseas, otherwise the country was capable of managing without excessive interruption to her domestic programme.[26] In other words, without the loan the government would have experienced constraints on its high-spending social programme and would have had to take firmer control of economic management. At the same time its failure to agree terms with the Americans might have led it to cultivate other alliances and would undoubtedly have imperilled at the outset the American objective of a multilateral free-trading world. Thus the loan helped steer Labour away from those radical alternatives, with the result that British economic and foreign policy remained broadly compatible with American interests in 1946–47 until the influence of the United States really began to be felt in Europe with the introduction of Marshall Aid.

The dollar gap in France likewise caused its government to send Léon Blum to Washington in May 1946 in search of a loan. Jean Monnet accompanied Blum and took with him an early draft of his plan for economic recovery, a scheme which involved the lowering of consumption levels and a boost for heavy capital investment. The Americans welcomed the plan but demanded certain concesions in return for a loan, including the relaxation of import duties, the abolition of government purchasing organisations and the consequent privatisation of trade. The Americans also expressed concern about the French government policy of nationalisation, but Blum protested that it did not impede a return to free trade and insisted that the US administration drop the subject.[27] The result of the mission was that France was granted a loan of $650 million for 1946–49 with a further $250 million to come later. Reports that the American Secretary of the Treasury had urged Blum and the socialists to join an anti-communist coalition government were denied by the French and American authorities. Blum stated that no political, diplomatic or military conditions attached to the loan. However, in granting the credit the Americans were acutely conscious that a general election would be held before the end of 1946 and that friendly politicians like Blum needed to be supported. Indeed, the loan and the Blum visit were an important landmark in the process of drawing France into the United States orbit.[28] Characteristically the PCF voted for the loan while denouncing it as an instance of American intervention in French affairs. When the second instalment was paid in May 1947 the communists again voted to accept it and at the same time claimed that it was an attack on France.[29] In fact the PCF managed to ride the growing popular disenchantment with the government, successfully projecting itself as a party of protest while simultaneously sharing government office. On the other hand the socialists lost heavily in terms of public support as a consequence of their identification with unpopular policies.

However, the pressure of popular resentment over the French government's lack of success in economic and social policy was mounting in the early months of 1947. With real wages depressed, Frachon at the CGT was already warning of the danger of strikes. Communist support for wages based on incentive systems had not been well received on the shop floor. In a dilemma, the CGT leadership began to mobilise unions to press for general wage increases, all the time hoping that it would not lead to strikes. In the National Assembly divisions began to appear between PCF deputies and PCF Cabinet Ministers.[30] By March prospects for continued communist participation in government seemed doubtful as a result of international developments: the worsening situation in Vietnam; the failure of the Moscow Conference of Foreign Ministers to resolve the German problem, and the announcement of the Truman Doctrine. What brought matters to a head was a strike for better wages at Renault at the end of April 1947, led by socialists. The communists in the CGT tried at first to break the strike but, fearful of being outflanked on the left by the socialists, reversed gear and assumed leadership of the action. Unable to support the government's wage policy any more, the communist Ministers were dismissed on 4 May.[31] The crisis had arisen over a domestic issue but international considerations also pointed to the government's need to be rid of the communists. There was much press speculation of a massive new American aid programme, and the chances of its materialising were likely to be greater with the communists out of office.[32]

Food rioting occurred in June and was accompanied by major strikes among dockers, gas, electricity and railway workers. It was at this point that all hope of future co-operation between the SFIO and PCF effectively disappeared. At the SFIO congress in May, Socialist Party secretary Mollet led a move in favour of immediate withdrawal from the government in order to prevent the isolation of the socialists from the wave of popular militancy now unleashed. Though it attracted a large minority vote the move was defeated.[33] Developments now guaranteed that the socialists would remain in office. Firstly, the announcement of the Marshall Plan was welcomed by socialists. With their brethren elsewhere they rationalised that the aid programme would make sense only under democratic socialist planning. The second key development guaranteeing that the socialists would cling to office was the formation of De Gaulle's RPF in summer 1947 and the sudden prospect of a political take-over by the extremist right when his party polled 40 per cent of the popular vote in the October municipal elections. If for no other reason than to stave off this challenge and the accompanying threat of destruction of the free labour movement, the SFIO felt they had little option but to remain in office.

However, it was not just a challenge from the extremist right that the French government had to contend with but also a challenge from the communists, who now adopted insurrection-ary tactics in a bid to defeat the government and block the Marshall Plan. It was a desperate piece of adventurism that ran the grave risk of opening the door to a take-over by the Gaullists.

On being dismissed from government the communists had not gone into total opposition, anticipating a return to office in the near future. When Marshall Aid was announced a month later the PCF response was uncertain: their opposition only became hard and fast once the Cominform had laid down a firm line. When Molotov brought a large Soviet delegation to Paris to explore with Bidault and Bevin the nature of the proposed aid, the PCF Secretary, Thorez, retracted his earlier view that the plan was a Western trap.[34] As late as September 1947 the *Cahiers du Communisme* reasoned: 'Of course, France like England must not refuse American aid but, as our comrade Thorez made clear, its independence must be jealously maintained.'[35] But after the USSR had rejected the terms for aid and proceeded to organise the Cominform to stiffen discipline among communist parties, the PCF were forced to admit that they had been remiss in not denouncing American imperialism with sufficient vigour. They were now committed to rectifying this mistake, even while recognising that France desperately needed aid and that a policy of opposition to the Marshall Plan would court unpopularity at home.[36]

Action to block the Marshall Plan was the overriding imperative in international communism, and the French com-munists seized the opportunity provided by growing unrest over living standards to lead a frontal attack against the government. Real wages had now fallen by a third from the level of January 1946, new price rises in gas, electricity and public transport fares were announced, and the general sense of grievance was fanned by the inadequacy of food supplies. Local strikes began spon-taneously in November 1947 but the CGT quickly assumed leadership, spreading the protest and linking grievances to the Marshall Plan. In effect it became a general strike, with 2½ million workers involved at the peak at the beginning of December. The communist strategy was evidently to force the SFIO out of the coalition: in the demagogy of the PCF, the socialists were required to choose between 'the workers' and 'the right'. Irregularities in the leadership of the strike – by-passing both the accepted procedures for consulting the membership and the responsible executive body within the CGT – was clear evidence of the communists' intention of utilising the action for sectarian purposes.

In the course of the strike wave the French government fell; the Socialist leader, Léon Blum, who was anxious to distinguish between the legitimate and illegitimate elements in the strike, failed to form a replacement government, and the reins of office fell to Robert Schuman of the Catholic MRP, who proceeded to introduce draconian anti-strike legislation, while Moch, the socialist Minister of the Interior, called in troops to deal with the strikers. The violence that accompanied the strike, and in particular the tactics of CGT commando units, eventually caused the movement to lose popular support, and it collapsed on 9 December with only marginal improvements gained.[37]

This strike action had catastrophic long-term consequences for the French trade union movement. First and foremost it precipitated a split in the CGT, with anti-communists, including many socialists and people with no political affiliation, breaking away to form Force Ouvrière. It also had lasting consequences for the Socialist and Communist Parties. If the communists were guilty of allowing foreign-policy considerations to determine their line of domestic policy, the socialists stood accused of placing too much faith in reformism. From now until after the next general election in 1951 the SFIO would move further in this direction, being represented in a succession of so-called Third Force governments – thus labelled to indicate their centrist resistance to both De Gaulle's anti-parliamentarianism and communist insurgency – comprising socialists, MRP and a motley group of radicals. But, unlike the embryonic international movement of the same name, the Third Force had no radical socialist pretensions and, in fact, moved progressively to the right in the next few years. It defined itself in negative terms – against De Gaulle, against communism – and came to be characterised by 'immobilism', merely surviving and unable to effect any significant change in French political life.[38] The SFIO became a prisoner of this shifting coalition, lacking the capacity to lead the government in a socialist direction, losing credibility among the labour movement for its ineffectiveness in this regard, and yet fearful of leaving the coalition lest it open the door to a communist or (more probably) right-wing extremist government.[39] Communist predictions of SFIO 'sell-outs' became self-fulfilling. It was a classic case of Stalinist tactics breeding a reformist opposition, while the failings of reformism provided further justification for Stalinism.

In Italy domestic and international political pressures were working in a similar direction, leading to a split in the labour movement some months after the division of the French trade unions. In January 1947, like other European leaders forced into the position of supplicants, the Christian Democrat Prime Minister, de Gasperi, visited Washington in search of a $250 million loan. He managed to secure $100 million, but there were apparently assurances of more generous patronage if he would drop his communist partners.[40] This same message was conveyed to the Italian ambassador to Washington, who reported on his talks with Truman and Acheson in April 1947, when the outline of Marshall Aid was already in preparation:

> I had to say that, in order to obtain sufficient support for our adequate recovery [...] the Italian government needed to be homogeneous, efficient and explicitly dedicated to a policy which combined dignity and independence with loyalty to the common aims so often proclaimed with our friends abroad.[41]

In May 1947 de Gasperi resigned, ostensibly as a result of the conflict between the PSI[42] and the Saragat group, which was preventing him from forming a government of national unity. When he formed a new administration the communists and their socialist allies were excluded from office, just as they had been only weeks before in France. As in France, the PCI was slow to respond to this development, believing at first that their exclusion from government would be only temporary. But from summer 1947 political polarisation grew as the economic climate deteriorated and the government took advantage of its new-found freedom to press ahead with its liberal economic policies.

The hardship inflicted on the working class by these policies led to an increase in industrial militancy to which CGIL attached its own political slogans. This intensified the strains between the various political factions within the Confederation, especially between the communists and Christian Democrats. In May 1947 the latter refused to support a general strike called over the killing of a union organiser in Sicily, claiming it was designed to embarrass de Gasperi.[43] At the Confederation's congress in Florence the following month the Christian Democrats failed to secure a constitutional revision precluding any political activity by the unions.[44] They claimed that whereas between August 1944 and May 1947 the CGIL had been identified with forty-seven political strikes, in the last six months of 1947 alone there were eighty-four such actions. Industrial militancy reached a peak in the closing weeks of 1947, and, with the Cominform now insisting on vigorous action to oppose the American offer of Marshall Aid, the CGIL seized the opportunity to give an explicit lead. The strikes were not on a comparable scale to the November upheaval in France, but general strikes at a local level were launched in Milan, Rome and other centres in November and December. Immediately before the strikes began, the CGIL had convened a national congress of the councils of administration. Partisans of the Garibaldi Brigade attended the event in a show of force, and it was evident from the manner in which the subsequent strikes were conducted that they were intended to threaten the government should the communists and socialists continue to be excluded from office. Christian Democrats among the CGIL membership protested that the strikes were political and had been called without a vote of the members. They in turn were branded as strike-breakers.[45] Their faction leader, Giulio Pastore, called for referendum ballots before strikes and, ominously, for greater freedom of action for minority currents.[46] With the debate over Marshall Aid yet to reach its peak it was only a matter of time before CGIL's increasingly fragile unity was shattered.

Between 1945 and 1948 the European left ceased to exude its early post-war optimism. Under military occupation the German industrial class was rapidly restoring its influence in society, while organised labour and the socialists were struggling to establish a presence. In Britain, France and Italy, where socialists formed, or participated in, government, there appeared to be no likelihood of a rapid move towards socialism. The most they were heading for was economic and industrial reconstruction with a greater degree of state control and planning, an admixture of nationalisation and a welfare state. In Italy and France the communists were, as much as anybody, responsible for this orientation. The emphasis was to be on consolidation rather than revolution. Even where industry was nationalised there was no real move towards industrial democracy and no attempt to challenge the capitalist organisation of work. The premise that the modern industrial order must, in the interests of technical rationality, operate under hierarchical chains of command remained uncontested.[47] By late 1947 the communist parties and their industrial allies were suddenly in revolt against the established order, but their change in direction was not motivated by a reconsideration of their ideological position so much as by the changing strategic interests of the USSR in the international arena. If European communists were only as radical as Soviet interests allowed them to be, the democratic socialist movement failed in large measure to compensate for this deficiency. A fundamental weakness among post-war socialist parties was their lack of cohesion across national boundaries, their failure to operate as part of an *international* movement in the way that communists did. Without a strong international orientation they were hard put to inspire their members in the same way that communist internationalism inspired its followers.

This failure was a product of British and Scandinavian socialist reasoning that it was not feasible for the different European parties, given their varied circumstances, to adhere to a common programme based on majority decisions. Against the French and Benelux desire to re-establish a strong International, these more powerful labour and social democratic parties successfully argued the case for piecemeal reconstruction of the movement based on 'concrete realities'. In particular they argued that in order to keep contact with the precariously placed eastern European parties it was necessary to opt for a loose federation.[48] It is not difficult to grasp the logic of the British and Scandinavian opposition to reconstituting the Socialist International as a cohesive body, but it is clear that the absence of a well organised international socialist movement in these years did irreparable harm to the cause of socialism.

It was really only in November 1947 at Antwerp that socialist parties regrouped under the loose umbrella of COMISCO, the International Socialist Conference, and then as little more than a debating society, for there could be only a tenuous unity.

At Antwerp a British resolution on the Marshall proposal acknowledged the potentially positive nature of American help in European reconstruction but rejected any attempt to attach strings. Under Soviet pressure the Eastern Bloc socialist parties were unable to support this and abstained in the vote.[49] For the sake of unity no further attempt was made to discuss the Marshall Plan within COMISCO. The socialists did not even have a regular forum within which they could debate such an important issue. When in March 1948 western European socialist parties got together on an *ad hoc* basis at Selsdon Park to decide a line on Marshall Aid it was at the joint invitation of the Labour Party and the SFIO. Other parties had looked at the British Labour Party for socialist leadership, but despite its plentiful statements regarding the need for socialist economic planning the lead Labour now gave was in no way based on the notion of a socialist foreign policy. With Marshall Aid on the horizon European socialism was hobbled by uncertainty and indecision.

CHAPTER 3

Post-war American business and foreign economic policy

As the largest producer, the largest source of capital, we must set the pace and assume the responsibility of the major stockholder in this corporation known as the world [...]. Nor is this for a given term of office. This is a permanent obligation. [Leo D. Welch, Treasurer, Standard Oil of New Jersey, 1946]

The American economy emerged from the war vastly more powerful and prosperous than that of any other country. As the 'arsenal of democracy' her industry had fuelled not only her own war effort but also that of her main allies. US production capacity was enormous. In terms of technology she had acquired a twenty-year lead over her rivals. But now the problem was one of finding peacetime markets for her output, and the general belief in the early post-war years was that domestic demand alone would be insufficient to absorb production capacity. To ensure the continuation of American economic prosperity, businessmen and government fixed their sights on an expansion of international trade as an outlet for their produce. In 1948 the United States was responsible for over 40 per cent of the world's goods and services and accounted for almost half its industrial output. In those early post-war years her export surplus almost doubled, but it was only through American aid extended to other countries that many of these international sales were effected.[1] As much as one-third of all American exports were actually financed by American aid. Thus aid was the indispensable link between production and trade.

The desirability of ongoing economic expansion had been clearly recognised during the war, and strategic policy-making focused on the notion of 'new frontiers', both international and domestic.[2] The 'open door' policy of expanding trade was accepted and with it the notion that the home frontier would also have to be opened up, with increasing domestic consumption providing the basis of full employment. The 'frontier' approach was important not only from the economic point of view but also socially and politically. In 1934 Walter Lippmann had written that the 'social disease of proletarianism is not serious where the frontier is still open'.[3] Assistant Secretary of State Dean Acheson told the Congressional hearings on post-war economic policy that full employment was the key, and failure to achieve it could have grave consequences for the American social system.[4] Thus commercial expansion abroad was equated with political democracy at home. The notion that economic industrial expansion through increased trade and international consumption could be a force for political stability and an antidote to radical political tendencies took deep root in American thinking. The 'open door' policy, which had originally been conceived as a way of serving American self-interest, was put forward in the post-war period as a policy to benefit the international community in general.[5]

From the early years of the war, business leaders had been steering the American economy. The Roosevelt administration, which had been at loggerheads with big business during the New Deal, recognised the need to build bridges to its leaders in the late 1930s. This was reflected in the key appointment of the investment banker Averell Harriman to advise the Secretary of Commerce, Harry Hopkins, and the subsequent recruitment of 'tame millionaires' such as Edward Stettinius and Donald Nelson to key positions in the war effort. Roosevelt's wartime administration was dominated by corporate figures such as Acheson, John Foster Dulles and James Forrestal. By the end of hostilities, with their success as administrators of the 'industrial war effort' behind them, business leaders were held in high esteem by the administration. Their influence in government circles was on the increase and, as Paterson points out, because of the economic nature of many foreign relations crises in the late 1940s and early 1950s, it was natural for the Truman administration to turn for help to those Americans who appeared to have the requisite knowledge and managerial skills. By 1948, when the Marshall Plan became operational, over 40 per cent of the people serving in the higher echelons of the executive branch of government had backgrounds in business, finance, or law.[6]

A highly influential group of businessmen in this context were the members of the Committee for Economic Development (CED), which had been founded in 1942. This body served as a private Brains Trust for foreign economic policy, just as the private citizens belonging to the Council for Foreign Relations (CFR) (some of whom also belonged to CED) helped mould American foreign policy.[7] During the first fifteen years of its existence almost one in three of the 150 people who served as CED trustees held elective or appointive office in the federal government at one time or another.[8] The founders of CED were Paul Hoffman, President of Studebaker and subsequently Administrator of the Marshall Plan, and William Benton, chairman of Encyclopaedia Britannica, later to become Assistant Secretary of State and subsequently, as a US senator, the architect of a key provision in the Mutual Security Act of 1951 which governed the second phase of Marshall Aid. Other influential members of CED were Philip Reed of General Electric, who became Chairman of the Anglo-American Council on Productivity; William Batt of SKF, who later headed the Marshall Plan mission to London; David Zellerbach of Crown Zellerbach, who held a similar post in Rome and was later ambassador to Italy; William C. Foster of Pressed & Welded Steel Products, who served as executive secretary of CED before becoming Assistant Deputy Administrator of the Marshall Plan.[9] Benton and Hoffman had been concerned to establish 'an ongoing national seminar' that would bring together businessmen and academics and conduct scientific research on a broad scale in the interests of American business. Their focus was long-term, the goal being to force corporations to plan purposefully for the future growth and prosperity of business. Several CED members, including Batt and Zellerbach, were also prominent members of the National Planning Association, an organisation embracing progressive businessmen, labour leaders and academics. At the outset CED launched a huge long-range planning exercise, its purpose being to promote high levels of employment (and thus consumption) through planning for new products and better services with new methods. By 1944 the exercise involved over 50,000 businessmen operating through over 2,000 community-level planning groups.[10]

The members of the CED were people who had come to terms with the New Deal and had then been enormously influenced by the scope for industrial growth and development that the war revealed. These two factors enabled them to slough off much of the free enterprise orthodoxy of the conservative business-men associated with the powerful National Association of Manufacturers while conducting their pragmatic search for ways of promoting American industrial interests. Their wartime experience had convinced them of the need for planning; they were sanguine about the need for a certain amount of state intervention and were attracted by the concept of a managed economy, which constituted a challenge to the engineering talents of American businessmen. As William Batt argued, 'American engineers can do more than any one group to modern-ise and restore productive capacity.'[11]

CED members were, therefore, concerned with the techniques of industrial and economic management rather than with the promotion of free enterprise ideologies *per se*. Yet when in the early years of McCarthyism their integrity was called into question they were quick to issue a statement confirming their belief in capitalism: 'We in CED believe in a free competitive, capitalistic economy. We are opposed to any measures which are a threat to its continuance and development.'[12] The hallmark of many of these progressive business leaders was their technicism, their belief in the power of economic rationality and in the need for planning. But their economic rationality was advanced in apolitical terms. As Maier puts it, 'American opinion generally viewed the transition to a society of abundance as a problem of engineering, not politics.'[13] Reflecting this viewpoint, Paul Porter, later to become a senior official of the Marshall Plan, was to argue that the differences between the United States and Europe were not really over public ownership and economic planning: that was a false polarisation. As he pointed out, there was already more planning in the United States than in Europe, since their planning was carried out on a continental scale and was based upon far more dependable assumptions.[14]

The non-ideological, technical approach to industrial problems went hand in hand with a measure of social reformism and was well illustrated in the values espoused by William Batt. He had been elected President of the International Management Congress in 1938 and his elevation marked a turning point for the profession of scientific management. Whereas previously it had emphasised efficiency as a way of making profits, now it

stressed an interest in management's general responsibility to
society. This required a bigger effort in the area of public relations
and greater attention to modern psychology. There was an
emphasis on work simplification aimed, so the line went, at
making jobs easier. All this was accompanied by a new, more
liberal attitude towards trade unionism which facilitated the
growth of collective bargaining.[15] Here was the new 'socially
conscious capitalism', as Paul Hoffman termed it.[16] The technical managerialism advocated by the American liberal business
elite was part of the compromise settlement of economic conflict
that was in the process of formation in the United States in the
1940s. Under the New Deal labour had made significant ad-
vances, but the resurgence of business influence over economic
policy had arrested this progress, and at the end of the war stalemate had been reached. As Maier has argued, the unresolved class
tensions were now channelled into a general quest for productivity and economic growth – with considerable success as the
wartime industrial record shows. What were really political
issues were transformed into problems of output. Instead of class
conflict, an attempt had been made to create a national consensus
on the need for growth. After the war this approach, which had
served well domestically, was deployed by the United States in
the international arena. Thus, Maier suggests, it is not enough
to explain American foreign economic policy in terms of growing
anti-communism:

> American concepts of a desirable international economic order need to
> be understood further in terms of domestic social divisions and
> political stalemate. US spokesmen came to emphasise economic
> productivity as a principle of political settlement in its own right.[17]

Solutions to economic problems were now sought through
technical means rather than ideological prescription. Reformers
would concentrate on measures to limit monopoly rather than
confronting the deep inequalities of power and wealth. But the
pragmatic application of this approach to foreign economic policy
did allow the United States to work with and through social
democrats and socialists in Europe so long as they went along
with the essence of the apolitical 'politics of productivity'. The
United States had no systematic strategy for suppressing socialism, but in practice her support for moderate social democrats
was an effective constraint on more radical politics.[18] In Britain

the Labour Party's International Secretary, Denis Healey, maintained that economic reconstruction in Europe could take place
only on democratic socialist or communist lines. That being
the case (and many Americans agreed it was so), the United
States had little alternative but to cultivate middle-of-the-road
social democrats.[19] As John Hickerson of the State Department
European Division wrote when the Marshall Plan was being
discussed, 'The trend in Europe is clearly toward the left. I feel
that we should try to keep it a non-Communist left and should
support Social-Democratic governments.'

Occasionally the socialist or labour groups contained elements
whose politics were unacceptable, and American help would have
to be given in promoting splits. Under-Secretary of State Lovett
advised the American ambassador to France, 'politically speaking
the break must come to the left of or at the very least in the
middle of the Socialist Party.'[20] Elsewhere such heavy-handed
tactics were not required and a more subtle approach sufficed as
American representatives cultivated, rewarded and guided the
more reliable middle-of-the roaders and Atlanticists among
Europe's labour leaders.[21] Growth-minded labour groups were
viewed with friendly eyes, while those that refused to accept this
basic thrust of Washington's foreign economic policy were
regarded with hostility. The American hope was that over a
period of time the centrist politics that they supported would
generate sufficient economic prosperity to pre-empt any moves
towards radical socialism. The more successful the United
States was in getting Europeans to concentrate on growth as
the overriding goal, the more the scope for political differences
narrowed.[22] Consequently, while much American rhetoric was
directed against socialism after 1945, crude ideology had been
tempered among the more sophisticated leaders of the business
community and government advisers, and they were prepared to
do business with European governments of the left whose programme posed no serious challenge to American capitalism. Thus
Henry Ford II could announce in 1948 that his company was
able to operate without difficulty under Britain's Labour government.[23]

It would be quite wrong to suggest that the CED reflected
the typical values of American business in the 1940s. The
National Association of Manufacturers provided a conservative

counterweight more in keeping with traditional free enterprise values, rejecting Keynesian support for government stimulation of growth and active control of fiscal and monetary policy. But the CED did have an influence beyond its numbers. As already indicated, it provided the Marshall Plan with several of its key figures. And the progressive, liberal gloss that CED policy prescriptions contained was something that beguiled many labour leaders and helped create in foreign affairs an effective alliance of liberal industrialists and labour spokesmen.

However, in the area of domestic labour relations policy, a more influential group was a coalition of NAM pragmatists who were concerned to safeguard as much as possible of traditional *laissez-faire* by freeing the spirit of enterprise and loosening the bonds of wartime government controls. The model for the new 'realistic conservatism' in industrial relations was provided by General Motors. There was still considerable anti-unionism in the business community, but the crude belligerence of the 1930s was yielding to more sophisticated approaches in which employers sought an armed truce with labour. The aim was to build an industrial relations system in which collective bargaining and responsible unions played an important but limited role and through which conflict would be institutionalised. Attention was focused on restoring managerial controls: most employers were opposed to any notion of democracy in industry, viewing business efficiency strictly in terms of hierarchical control. This was the broad philosophical framework that was to guide the employers' successful campaign for a revision of the Wagner Act and a redefining of the 'rules of the game'. American business had gained in confidence during the early 1940s and went on to an ideological offensive in the late 1940s. Having worked miracles in mass production and mass distribution, it was now time to foster mass understanding.[24]

CHAPTER 4

Labour in early post-war America

We still have a long way to go in the United States in making genuine working partners in each factory, of managers and workers, but we are on our way. [Clinton Golden, Chief Labour Adviser to the Marshall Plan, 1950]

I am more and more convinced, as I study the European labour scene, that they, the Europeans, have neither the ideas, power, courage, energy or leaders to lead this fight in the trade union world. Unless we furnish the drive, I don't know how it will all end. I think Irving Brown holds the same view. [Sam Berger, US Labour Attaché (London), to George Meany, 23 December 1948]

The post-war American labour movement was very much a product of a moulding process that took place in the turbulent years of the 1940s. During this period important changes in practice and outlook affected the trade unions, particularly the CIO wing of the movement. The 1940s saw youthful radicalism give way to mature respectability as labour became subject to a variety of conservative 'civilising' pressures. Founder members of the CIO had believed that their movement would amount to something more than mere business unionism in the AFL mould, but by the end of the 1940s they were embarked on a journey that was to narrow the gap between the two philosophies of trade unionism, with many of the differences ultimately disappearing.[1] It was from the milieu of a newly stabilising labour movement and industrial relations system that American union officials ventured forth into the world of the late 1940s as Marshall Plan officials – often with a socialist or social democratic past but an increasing disposition to accept liberal capitalism.

Industrial democracy and collective bargaining

The CIO had manifested considerable radicalism in the formative years of the late 1930s, especially in rank-and-file struggles at the point of production. But this militancy was never guided by any clear ideological perspective. On the other hand, there soon developed among the CIO leadership a labour philosophy that envisaged social reforms taking place in the context of democratic industrial planning supported by a rational, sophisticated system of labour–management relations. The CIO leadership aspired to erect such a structure during World War II.

It was an approach that had its origin in the experience of the clothing industry during the 1920s. There Sidney Hillman's Amalgamated Clothing Workers' Union (ACW) had succeeded in developing a co-operative relationship with employers through sophisticated bargaining and grievance machinery that yielded for the union social welfare gains that went beyond mere wage improvements. Clothing workers were encouraged by their union to exercise self-discipline in the interests of orderly industrial planning and to grasp the opportunity of industrial citizenship offered by this civilised system.[2] The practice of trade unionism was closely related to the ethic of efficiency, with the ACW welcoming the introduction of 'scientifically' determined piece rates and the installation of new technology. Regarded by the union as a form of 'industrial democracy', others have described it as a system of 'corporatist syndicalism' imposed from above which proved to be an effective bulwark against bolshevism.[3] What was particularly important about this was the possibilities it suggested for extending the successful corporate planning mechanisms of the clothing industry to the economy generally.

The practice of trade unionism in the clothing industry provided the model for influential theoretical writings by intellectuals within, or close to, the labour movement. Basically they argued that the peaceful road to industrial democracy and greater industrial efficiency lay in the development of civilised collective bargaining machinery. It was necessary to build up a system of 'industrial jurisprudence', in the phrase of Sumner Slichter, doyen of labour economists. Union leaders should become administrators of collective agreements rather than tribunes of the rank and file or leaders of popular mobilisation. In a 1941 report for the Brookings Institute, Slichter argued the case for what amounted to bureaucratic industrial unionism. If union leaders were recognised and drawn into elaborate bargaining relationships, they would be more disposed to take a longer view of industry's problems while becoming distanced from immediate rank-and-file pressures.[4] Four years later Slichter noted with satisfaction that America was gradually shifting from a capitalist community to a labouristic one. But it was a shift that was also full of potential for progressive managements. There was little in this development that would limit their ability to introduce change and run industry effectively. On the contrary, they would benefit from having greater legitimacy among the work force. Indeed, the unions themselves would become a disciplinary force. As Clark Kerr later observed, 'unionism often means that two bosses grow where only one grew before.'[5]

Within the labour movement Philip Murray, John L. Lewis's deputy and, from 1940, successor as President of the CIO, argued in a publication written jointly with Morris Cooke, the advocate of scientific management, that the efficient operation of industry required the full partnership of unions in management.[6] The theme was echoed in the writings of two labour intellectuals, Clinton S. Golden and Harold Ruttenberg, both members of the staff of Murray's Steelworkers' Union, who elaborated the case for industrial efficiency through this form of 'industrial democracy'.[7] Golden went on to play a central role in the events described in this book, and it is important to have some idea of his career development.

Over a period of forty years Clinton Golden graduated from radical socialism to become one of the earliest and most influential American proponents of class collaborationist industrial politics within a corporatist framework. A railroad fireman, a machinist and sometime Homesteader, he became a labour educationalist, a full-time union organiser, a national union official, and later a senior government appointee on the Marshall Aid programme, before retiring to teach at Harvard and become an international eminence among labour and business geo-politicians of the Atlantic community.[8]

As a clothing union organiser in the early 1920s Golden was first drawn to notions of industrial peace. It was on the staff of Brookwood Labour College later in the 1920s that he was able to propagate those views to a wider trade union audience. Mistrusted by some as a sympathiser of Taylorism, he was heavily influenced by, and worked closely with, Elton Mayo in a study of human relations among textile workers. By 1929 Golden was openly at odds with his former socialist friends. Attached to the CIO's embryonic Steelworkers' Union in the 1930s, he rose to be vice-president. He was responsible for recruiting Joseph Scanlon, the industrial engineer, to the staff of the union and in the late 1930s the two of them developed a co-operative productivity plan – forerunner of the Scanlon Plan – which up to fifty often struggling steel firms were persuaded to adopt.[9] In the early 1940s, in conjunction with Ruttenberg, he wrote *The Dynamics of Industrial Democracy*, which was to become an influential text in management circles, if not among trade unionists. Originally intended to be entitled *Paths of Industrial Peace*, the book argued the case for making the pursuit of productivity a central feature of industrial relations, with the discipline of the union shop contributing to stable relationships and industrial peace. Comprehensive union organisation and joint union–management co-operation for efficiency became the twin pillars of Golden's industrial faith. 'Industrial democracy', by which he understood management's willingness to consult with labour on production matters, would free the worker from the dead hand of scientific management.

Attempts were made during the war to give effect to these values. In 1940 CIO President Murray, who as a Catholic was particularly influenced by Church teaching on the need for harmony in industry, put forward his 'Industrial Council' plan for American industry under which key sectors would be subject to the joint control of unions and management.[10] The same year Walter Reuther, then a rising force in the Auto Workers' Union (UAW), advocated an imaginative variant of this in his highly publicised '500 planes a day' proposal, which envisaged the motor industry being rapidly converted to essential aircraft production and the union sharing with management in control of the overall planning process.[11] Reuther followed this up towards the end of the war with a proposal that the tripartate War Production Board, of which Clinton Golden was now vice-president, be replaced by a Peace Production Board to supervise the conversion of industry and to ensure full employment.[12] These schemes, which were all rejected by government and employers, suggested a form of industrial democracy operating within the context of state-sponsored private enterprise.[13] To their proponents they seemed to offer the prospect of reforming capitalism and subjecting it to social democratic imperatives.

Finally, in March 1945, Philip Murray unveiled a new corporatist proposal for a Labour–Management Charter in which leaders of industry would agree to a programme of high wages, full employment and the maintenance of the *status quo* in federal labour legislation in return for labour's acceptance of free enterprise capitalism and an implicit no-strike clause.[14] The CIO was, *par excellence*, the wing of the labour movement that depended on, and had benefited most from, the state's legislative support for collective bargaining under the Wagner Act. Representing production workers without scarce skills to monopolise, it was most vulnerable to economic recession and unemployment. By contrast, the craft unions of the AFL, rejuvenated by the full employment of the war years and the competitive challenge posed by the CIO, felt confident of their ability to survive in the free market conditions of the post-war period.[15] The CIO leadership, however, feared a post-war recession, especially in industries such as steel and aircraft. They concluded that trade unionism in these mass industries was still not sufficiently strong to thrive without continued government protection, and it was in this essentially defensive frame of mind – not the belligerence that the employers and legislators detected – that the CIO sought a comprehensive agreement with industry and the administration on wages, prices and labour legislation.[16]

The AFL's support for the charter was minimal but the proposal won the backing of the leadership of the chambers of commerce and the progressive liberal industrialists in the CED. They were not perturbed by the wartime increase in trade union power and wanted a more constructive relationship with labour, with collective bargaining furnishing the basis for a form of industrial democracy within capitalism. They were willing to boost the status of responsible union leaders, so long as management retained the initiative in industry. However, conservative businessmen could feel the tide of public opinion turning their way and were in no mood to strike a generous bargain with labour.

This became evident in November 1945 in the course of the Labour–Management Conference convened by President Truman for the purpose of establishing ground rules for post-war industrial relations. There, while the CIO leaders restated their desire to reach a corporatist settlement for industry in the context of a civilised, socially progressive capitalism, the employers, with the NAM voice dominant, called for an unequivocal recognition by labour of management's right to manage,[17] a demand that assumed greater urgency as a result of the aggressive bargaining tactics then being pursued by Walter Reuther and the UAW at General Motors. Contemptuous of the CIO's corporatist leanings and confident of its own capacity to survive, the AFL offered no solidarity and the conference broke up without any overall agreement.[18] Substantial agreement had in fact been reached on the principles of a new regime of institutionalised bargaining, but over the central issue of the extent of management's right to control industry there was no meeting of minds. In effect it was a defeat for the CIO leadership, who had staked most on a settlement. They now had the choice of retreating or going on the offensive, not only against industry but also against the Truman administration, and for that sort of battle they had no stomach.[19] No further attempt was made to seek an equal voice in macro-level industrial planning. In future the unions' attention would be confined to the company level and the pursuit of 'industrial democracy' through the agency of collective bargaining.

Post-war American industrial relations came to be characterised by the practice of highly elaborate institutionalised collective bargaining which left managerial prerogative intact in central matters relating to the production function and focused attention instead on rewards and compensation for worker compliance. That institutionalised framework had first begun to appear as a result of decisions by the National War Labour Board and was later elaborated in the course of the early post-war rounds of collective bargaining between 1945 and 1950 and as a consequence of the 1947 Taft-Hartley Act. By 1945 the War Labour Board had successfully established the principle that disputes and grievances arising during the currency of a collective agreement should be arbitrated rather than resolved by trial of strength. By the late 1940s this was standard practice in unionised industry, and, in combination with the legalistic approach to arbitration that came to be used, it had the effect of denying shop-floor workers the opportunity to challenge at the point of production the exercise of managerial prerogative over the all-important production decisions that lay at the heart of industrial politics. In the 1950s the National Labour Relations Board was to go on and build up a body of case law which held that managerial decisions in such matters as sub-contracting, technological change and location policy were also non-bargainable matters. All that could legitimately be negotiated by unions was their effect on employees.[20] With some justification it has been argued that this legislation and bureaucratisation of bargaining blocked any significant future redistribution of power in American industry.[21]

Meanwhile the unions showed themselves increasingly disposed to accept this state of affairs in practice and to concentrate their energies on wage issues, fringe benefits and measures to cushion the effect of managerial decisions. The decisive phase in moulding the unons' approach to bargaining began with the first post-war round of negotiations. These produced in 1945–46 the biggest ever wave of strikes in the United States, and from a long-term psychological point of view the outcome was critical.

It was in the auto industry that the future pattern of collective bargaining was to emerge most clearly. The 1945–46 negotiations between the UAW and General Motors led to a four-month strike, the hardest fought dispute in that round. The union had demanded a substantial wage increase without there being a compensating increase in the company's product prices. General Motors was called upon to 'open its books' and demonstrate its capacity to pay. This was taken as a direct challenge to management's freedom and it clearly influenced the outcome of the concurrent Presidential Labour–Management Conference, though the UAW challenge did not extend to managerial prerogative in matters of production. Indeed, the aggressive UAW wage strategy in 1945 was specifically aimed at unifying the fractious membership of the union around basic demands that could be centrally controlled, leaving production control questions – issues over which union members could maintain an effective challenge only at the workplace – largely untouched. The 1945–46 General Motors strike was, of course, an important landmark in the rise to union power of Walter Reuther, whose militant leadership on that occasion helped him secure the presidency of the UAW later in 1946. But the outcome of the strike was not just a landmark for the Auto Workers' Union, for taken in conjunction with parallel developments in the Labour – Management Conference it marked the beginning of a watershed for American industrial relations generally. It paved the way for a stabilisation of industrial relations in terms largely favourable to the employers and set a pattern to be emulated elsewhere. Management's rights were safeguarded, the closed shop was blocked, and the frequency of collective bargaining reduced.

Reuther's 1945 bargaining strategy at GM was intended to take the initiative away from plant union leaders and vest it in the national leadership.[22] Subsequently the extensive shop steward system that had provided the core of the UAW's organising and protective functions in the late 1930s and early 1940s was effectively liquidated under this new regime, replaced by the grievance committee structure of the legalistic grievance-arbitration procedure. In his bid for leadership Reuther had opposed piecework, incentive payments and other potential elements of speeded-up production standards. But in the years that followed, the UAW became party to bargaining relationships in which production standards were rarely subject to effective challenge by the union.[23] In the next two rounds of bargaining General Motors were able to consolidate their advantage. Starting in 1946, Ford also followed suit. In return for a wage increase, management secured a clause detailing the full range of managerial prerogative, especially over production standards. Although the UAW insisted on retaining the formal right to strike over such matters as a last resort, in practice this became a dead letter. Ford set about reinforcing their shop control by investing heavily in new plant and technology, the operation of which denied workers scope for regulating the production process.[24] A more openly co-operative relationship had been forged between the Steelworkers' Union under Murray and the leading firms in that sector. In the 1946 round of collective bargaining, union and management committed themselves equally to the pursuit of maximum productivity. During the next three years labour – management relations were thoroughly stabilised through the negotiation of an elaborate job evaluation plan as a 'scientific' method of determining wage structures. The two sides were on their way to establishing a pattern of co-operation that would preserve peace in steel for over a decade.[25]

The crowning development in this new style of collective bargaining was the epoch-making agreement between the UAW and General Motors in 1950. The company devised the idea of linking wages to productivity and prices in the context of a long-term agreement. The contract, which was to last for five years, gave workers an annual wage increase tied to anticipated productivity gains – the annual improvement factor – and cushioned them against inflation by means of a cost-of-living bonus. From now on the pattern would be firmly established of unions being granted benefits at regular intervals, in return for which management expected its authority at the point of production to go unchallenged.[26] In this way, with the two sides committed to arbitrating grievances, and with production standards effectively unchallenged by the union, the company bought itself five crucial years of industrial peace while a vast programme of capital investment was being undertaken that would fuel the prosperity of the 1950s. The agreement was interpreted as having significance not only for the automobile industry and the American economy but for the Western world's economic prospects. As the *New Leader* saw it, 'General Motors had in effect bet a billion dollars that the United States economy will remain stable for the next half decade. [...] We suspect that General Motors' astonishing faith in the future is motivated, in part at least, by the hunch that our vast foreign aid programme, which is scheduled to terminate in 1952, will be continued in one form or another through 1955.'[27]

In some ways, what was being written and said about this new phase in collective bargaining was as important as what was being done, particularly since propaganda directed at labour was now playing an important part in the Cold War. The ideal of harmonious, pluralistic industrial relations based on elaborate collective bargaining routines under enlightened capitalism became the subject matter of a growing literature even in the late 1940s. A close-knit group of business, labour and academic personnel who would come into their own in the 1950s as evangelists of the new liberal conventional wisdom in industrial relations was already being assembled in 1946–47 under the aegis of the National

Planning Association (NPA). The moving force behind this group and an important link between it and the Marshall Plan was Clinton Golden.

By the end of the war, planning for productivity growth had become Golden's chief interest. Disillusioned by the failure of the President's Commission on Labour–Management Relations to establish clear ground rules for the practice of labour relations, Golden left the labour movement and in 1946 proposed that the NPA institute case-study research in a number of firms with a view to isolating the factors that made for good industrial relations. The project began the following year, two weeks after the announcement of Marshall Aid, under the joint supervision of Golden and Scanlon, who was now at MIT.[28] Associated with the project were industrialists such as Batt and Zellerbach. Among the academics who conducted the case studies were several of the people who later formed the core of the highly influential Ford Foundation-backed Inter-university Labour Relations Programme[29] of the 1950s and 1960s – Clark Kerr, Frederick Harbison, John Dunlop, Charles Myers, Abraham Siegel and John Coleman, together with Douglas McGregor – cutting their teeth here in a field they were soon to monopolise. Publication of the case studies began in 1948 and continued until 1953. The dominant themes of the reports were ones that would become familiar in academic industrial relations in the next two decades: the trend was towards an extension of democracy in industry through collective bargaining,[30] the two sides of industry having it within their own power to mould good or bad relationships.[31] But peaceful, trusting industrial relations were more likely where unions accepted the private ownership of industry and where there were no serious ideological differences.[32] Thus, despite the claimed trend towards democratisation, the norm was for management to strive to prevent unions from interfering with its essential prerogative.[33]

The case studies were widely used in university teaching, as models for further research and provided extensive source material for popularised accounts in newspapers and magazines. They were also widely circulated abroad as part of the Marshall Plan propaganda offensive and helped set the agenda for industrial relations discussions in the various participating countries,[34] despite the fact that union–management relations at the firms studied deteriorated in subsequent years, thus invalidating the general claims of the published reports.[35]

There can be no doubt that significant changes in the power relationship between American capital and labour had come about as a result of early post-war developments in collective bargaining. But the roseate terms in which these were presented to the wider world, especially overseas, lent the developments even greater force in propaganda terms. The 1950 General Motors–UAW agreement which provided 'a moving staircase to prosperity' was a case in point. Though proud of the agreement, the UAW leadership were very conscious that popular understanding of what lay behind it was obscured by the sort of publicity it generated. As a CIO report suggested:

> Pictures of the hand-shaking that accompanied the signing of the GM contract were published, broadcast and the implication was given that the contract was the result of an agreement by two abstractions called Labour and Management to get along together. Little or no mention was made of the actual factors that brought on the settlement – notably the successful strike of the Steelworkers, and most immediately, the long strike of the workers of the Chrysler Corporation while GM negotiations were under way.

From the perspective of the union leadership this was no sweetheart deal but a gain extracted from management against the background of an increasingly threatening labour scene.[36] It was this agreement that first cemented the link between wages and productivity in the United States, but well before it American propaganda in Europe had suggested that the wage–productivity equation was a central and standard feature of US collective bargaining. It was, no doubt, a case of the wish being father to the thought.

Within the Marshall Plan there was a strong sentiment in favour of using every opportunity to advertise the supposed virtues of American bargaining practice. It was regarded as an effective means of rolling back communist influence, fostering higher productivity and exporting to western Europe the American psychology of team work, a valuable antidote to authoritarianism in industry:

> the US drive to extend the scope of collective bargaining is the only one [of the major drives by the common man in the world today] which accepts private ownership, the wage as the worker's share in

a joint undertaking, and the profit motive as the best means of producing goods and rendering services. [...]

In this showdown contest between the US and the USSR for men's minds, we have neglected to involve effectively one of our most telling and cogent arguments, namely that 16 million organised [American] workers get along better and better with their employers; that we have developed a new pattern of human and economic relations that are making industrial citizenship co-eval with political citizenship; that management and union rights and responsibilities move together dynamically.

Looked at in this way, it was the technical nature of collective bargaining that was its virtue. Capitalism itself was not a source of conflict, being regarded simply as a mode of production rather than a political system.[37] As the Chief Labour Adviser to the Marshall Plan, Clinton Golden was to become labour's arch proponent of a model of industrial relations in which productivity growth achieved through labour–management co-operation was a key weapon in waging the Cold War. Presented to the world as the essence of the American system of industrial relations, it often involved a selective borrowing from a number of exceptional experiments and isolated cases. But from these Golden would generalise in glowing terms about a whole new system in the making.

It would be facile to conclude that all the labour officers involved in the Marshall programme accepted unquestioningly the NPA's portrayal of peaceful labour relations or that they shared Golden's ideal of industrial co-operation in the interests of an overriding goal of higher productivity. It was not simply a question of American labour abroad tamely preaching some notion of class collaboration in the wider interests of American capitalism. The adaptation of the CIO to a form of business unionism was itself still in a formative stage when the aid programme began, and American labour's own bitter battle against the restrictive features of the Taft-Hartley Act was in full swing. But organised labour was itself on the receiving end of the pro-productivity propaganda of the period and, in the context of the Cold War, was under much pressure to pass on the message to its European brothers. At the same time the liberal approach to trade unionism displayed by the progressive corporate figures at the head of the Marshall Plan was certainly influential in disposing labour leaders to co-operate with industry in the international programme. The result was that, without a distinct ideological perspective of their own to guide them, trade unions would always be amenable to the blandishments of sophisticated corporate capitalism preaching 'social responsibility'.

Labour in international affairs

The organisational rivalry between the AFL and the CIO from 1936 to their merger in 1955 affected every area of policy, including international affairs. It is tempting to interpret the differences in this sphere as little more than an extension of the struggle for pre-eminence in domestic labour affairs. For the AFL or the CIO to be able to demonstrate that abroad they were recognised as the true voice of American labour would increase their prestige at home and their claim to labour leadership within the USA. Yet there was certainly more to their rivalry than mere organisational jealousy. What was at stake was the question of the role that labour should adopt in a world increasingly polarised between capitalism and communism and the organisational form that such a role dictated. Europeans who dealt in the international field with American labour in these years never encountered a movement with a single, unified approach, even when in the early 1950s the gap between AFL and CIO began to narrow considerably.

In 1945, together with the British TUC and the Federation of Soviet Trade Unions, the CIO had helped found the WFTU. Until the organisation split in 1949 the CIO's international efforts were channelled exclusively through the WFTU: its international policy was pretty well synonymous with WFTU policy. Not until 1950 did the CIO begin to formulate its own distinct line on foreign affairs. By contrast, since the war the AFL had had its own clear perspective on international matters which it pursued with vigour, refusing all the while to have any dealings with the WFTU. The AFL's post-war internationalism coincided with the dawning of America's dominant role in the world economy. The United States was in a position to influence directly political and economic developments in many other countries, and in this context the AFL became the handmaiden of, and at times a significant influence behind, American economic foreign policy.

The post-war international policy of the AFL was, at bottom, a continuation of its traditional anti-communism. Anti-communism was, however, wrapped up in the more even-handed terms of opposition to totalitarianism in all its guises. On this was constructed a theoretical argument that the basic conflict in society was not between capital and labour, socialism and free enterprise, but rather between totalitarianism and democracy. From the early months of World War II this opposition to totalitarianism had taken the form of an energetic programme of relief for the labour victims of Nazism and facism. However, well before the war ended the anti-totalitarian focus of the AFL turned from the threat of Nazism and concentrated on the issue of communism. Here the most influential voices were not those of the traditional apolitical AFLers but of social democrats and former communists.

Undoubtedly the biggest contributor to the moulding of post-war AFL international policy was the former American Communist Party Secretary, Jay Lovestone. He had broken with Stalin in 1929 over the doctrinal issue of 'American exceptionalism' – the view that American capitalism was strong enough to weather depressions for several decades to come. The group organised around him, the 'Lovestonites', operated as an opposition faction within the orbit of the CP (USA) until 1936. Thereafter Lovestone restyled his group the National Independent Labour League and allied himself with those fighting communism within the American labour movement. In particular he helped the former socialist, David Dubinsky, to beat off the challenge to his leadership from communists within the ILGWU.

In 1940 Lovestone confirmed his change in attitude regarding organised labour's role in the world. His starting point was the decline of the libertarian spirit and the emergence of various forms of totalitarianism. Because of what he termed the 'sterility of radicalism' in the United States, with its 'cherished illusions', he was drawn towards the distinctly American 'pure and simple' unionism of the AFL, seeing its approach as an exemplar of the programme labour needed to pursue in a mass-production economy. He envisaged the American labour movement stepping into the centre stage of world labour politics. With the destruction of organised labour in continental Europe, and with Britain in danger of defeat by Germany, he believed that American unionism would become the decisive force in the ranks of international labour. The question then was, what should US labour seek to achieve in its new role, what was its wider perspective? Crucial to his analysis was the challenge posed by totalitarianism: 'Labour cannot go forward without democracy and [...] democracy cannot advance and must perish without labour's conscious, insistent and energetic participation and support.' Thus labour's role was to spearhead the fight against all forms of totalitarianism, within the USA and without. For Lovestone it was a dramatic challenge: 'Here is the great responsibility, the historic task and opportunity confronting American labour.'[38] He now described himself as a small 'd' democrat, promoting a philosophy for labour that gave pre-eminence to the freedom of the individual over collectivist approaches. There was, he said, no longer room for 'isms' in American politics, and he called on all radical groupings to bury their 'European philosophies' and join American trade unions in preparing to defend democracy.[39] By now he was on Dubinsky's payroll and, in that capacity, as the ILGWU leader's window on the world of international labour, he was able to have an influence on AFL policy formulation as it evolved in the crucial war years.

The AFL took very seriously the business of planning for the post-war world. Through the government's Inter-departmental Committee on Post-war Foreign Economic Policy it contributed to the shaping of multilateral trading policies that were to become the lynchpin of America's strategy for peace and prosperity. In labour affairs it was involved in planning for the reorganisation and development of the Department of Labour, stressing in particular the need for a professional corps of labour attachés to service the United States' new world role in labour matters. As a 1944 document of the Federation's Post-war Planning Committee pointed out, 'Essential to this new responsibility is dependable information on the labour movements of other countries'. The labour attachés it sought were to be appointed on the basis of 'experience in the labour movement'.[40] Thus right from the outset the AFL secured for itself an important voice in the development of the labour attaché service, and that came to mean that key foreign-service appointments would be made only on the recommendation of the AFL's international policy elite.

However, more important as a source of the AFL's own post-war international policy was the American Labour Conference on International Affairs (ALCIA), launched by Dubinsky in 1942. Through the work of a number of standing committees and conferences, and in the pages of its quarterly magazine, *International Postwar Problems*, ALCIA helped to formulate the AFL's approach to a broad range of international issues such as post-war currency stabilisation, safeguards against oppressive labour conditions in underdeveloped countries, the future of Germany and the United Nations. But it was on the strategy to be adopted towards communism that its influence was greatest.[41]

With the war in Europe drawing to a close in April 1945, ALCIA's Executive Secretary, Varian Fry, pictured the situation with which the AFL would have to contend. Europe would be divided geographically, and, he argued, there was not a chance in a thousand of independent trade unions or non-communist labour parties surviving in the Soviet satellite countries. In western Europe, too, socialist and democratic labour movements would have to struggle hard to survive. Some unions would be communist-dominated, others would not, and in such cases American aid could be of assistance:

> Substantial financial support by the AFL may strengthen their position in the bitter struggle against the communist onslaught [...]. The duty of the AFL will be to support the democratic side as generously as possible. Even before the final liberation of Germany it will be important to assist materially, financially and morally, the German and Austrian Social Democrats living as political refugees in England, France, Belgium in order to facilitate their very hard competition with the powerfully sponsored German Communists.

A vigorous international policy, then, was envisaged – not just one that would involve AFL activity overseas but one which was aimed directly at intervening in internal labour movement conflicts in European countries. Fry urged that AFL representatives be dispatched to Europe to make contacts with anti-communist groups in labour movements as soon as possible.[42] The delicate nature of the programme the AFL unions were now embarking on was spelled out by Raphael Abramovitch, the social democratic émigré leader who was chairman of ALCIA. Arguing that foreign-language outlets for *International Post-war problems* would have to be found among *political* activists as well as trade unions in Europe, he pointed out that the need was to seek out opposition groups and individuals, since often there would be no reliable official body for the Americans to work with. The task called for quiet perseverence:

> To find such groups takes time. It can be done only through personal contact, since these groups have to proceed with caution so that they do not offend the official bodies too much. [...] We have to *fight* against the resistance of the official circles of the European trade union movement for the distribution of such a bulletin.[43]

However, more important in practical terms than ALCIA was the Free Trade Union Committee (FTUC), which was launched in 1944 by Dubinsky, Mathew Woll of the Photo Engravers' Union and William Green, AFL President, to spearhead the post-war international work of the AFL. The FTUC was sponsored by AFL unions but it was not a committee of the AFL – more a private organisation belonging to a handful of labour leaders. With Lovestone appointed Executive Secretary, there was little accountability of its activities, and as a semi-autonomous body working within the umbrella of the AFL it enjoyed considerable scope for secretive manoeuvring. With the launch of the FTUC an ambitious appeal was made to American unions for a $1 million fund to finance American activities in Europe.[44] Donations began to come in, though at a far lower level than the target set. By July 1945 $112,000 had been collected and a further $94,000 pledged.

The precise projects on which this money was to be spent remained to be determined, and in October 1945 a deputation consisting of two ex-Lovestonites, Charles Zimmerman and Irving J. Brown, was sent to Europe to make a preliminary survey of the situation there. Zimmerman was a vice-president of the ILGWU. Irving Brown, a former member of the Socialist Party in the 1930s, who had secretly retained his membership of Lovestone's group during these years, had held various posts with AFL unions before being seconded to the War Production Board in 1942. In harness with Lovestone after the war, Brown was to become the most influential American trade unionist active in European affairs.

In Europe Brown and Zimmerman distributed a total of $6,850 on behalf of the Jewish Labour Committee to Jewish refugee groups in Scandinavia, England and France. Zimmerman then returned home while Brown set about assessing the long-term prospects for an FTUC-AFL campaign in Europe. Brown's first port of call was Norway, where the Labour Party leader, Haakon Lie, had been seeking American aid for some months. The FTUC had earmarked $15,000 for Norwegian labour, and Brown now urged than a further $10,000 be allotted to them.[45] Lie was to remain a close ally of Brown's in the coming years. In Britain Brown made contact with the TUC General Secretary, Walter Citrine, and International Secretary, Ernest Bell, and determined to his satisfaction that the British were not wedded to permanent membership of the WFTU. But his main contact in Britain was with J.H. Oldenbroek, General Secretary of the International Transport Workers' Federation (ITF), whose anti-communism made him very hostile to the WFTU. Oldenbroek emphasised the need for as many AFL unions as possible to affiliate to their international trade secretariat in order to bolster the anti-communist opposition to the WFTU.[46] Brown responded positively, urging his own union, the International Association of Machinists (IAM), to affiliate to the International Metalworkers' Federation (IMF) and for them to nominate him as the accredited IAM representative in the councils of the IMF. His hope was that other American unions such as the United Mineworkers, the Teamsters and the Railroad brotherhoods would likewise designate him as their spokesman in Europe, and he pressed the idea on the FTUC. As he reported back to Washington, 'It would provide an excellent official function for my presence in Europe.'[47]

Brown soon decided that France should be the initial target of the FTUC's anti-communist campaign. Within weeks of arriving in the country he had made contact with an anti-communist faction in the trade union movement and had arranged to fund them secretly through the office of August Largentier, Secretary of the Paris region of the Printers' Union. He then requested $5,000 from the FTUC to assist the group over the next three months and in the meantime gave them $400 of his own money. As he wrote, 'There are times when a few dollars quickly spent have more value than ten times the value at a later date.'[48] But only a week after his initial request he proposed a far more grandiose programme of support for the anti-communist opposition in the trade unions, with a budget of $100,000 for the next crucial six months to finance organisational activities, literature and personal visits by 'trusted intermediaries'.[49]

However, the early FTUC expenditures in Europe proved to be very modest. Brown asked for $200 to help defray the cost of printing a bulletin for a group of expatriate German trade unionists in Britain led by Hans Gottfurcht, and in February 1946 wrote almost apologetically to Mathew Woll requesting the release of $100 to help Social Democrats in Germany with their printing activies: 'I realise that this is a political request but yet I am convinced that it is in the interests of free trade unionism to help them.'[50] The fact is that the AFL unions were slow to commit themselves wholeheartedly to a European campaign. The FTUC had raised $199,000 by the end of 1945, of which $108,000 was unallocated. But this was insufficient to cover the sort of operation that Brown was contemplating. Back in Washington, Zimmerman had reported to the AFL on the need for a full-time international staff and a permanent representative in Germany, but there was no prompt action on his recommendations and Brown was left cooling his heels in Europe.

Meanwhile he submitted further proposals for an AFL programme in Germany which would involve direct aid to the non-communist unions, food parcels for German union officials, and the publication of a German-language edition of the AFL newspaper. Taken with the request for an AFL representative to be stationed in Germany, the proposals called for a budget of $10,000 for the coming year.[51] However, Brown's expectations of substantial financial help from the USA were soon to be disappointed. In March 1946 his $100,000 six-month programme for France was answered by the allocation of a mere $1,000.[52] Zimmerman complained bitterly on his behalf to Dubinsky. His impression had been that the AFL leadership intended to treat the labour situation in Europe as a matter of crucial importance, and Zimmerman now told Dubinsky bluntly that they should either do the job properly or keep out.[53] Brown's own reaction was to reduce the sum requested for aid to Germany. In March he submitted a revised budget for $3,500 while making it clear to his superiors that he was still keen to stay in Europe and see the campaign through, if only his position could be made more certain.[54] Two months later, with his European contacts multiplying, he submitted further detailed proposals for work in

France, involving the establishment of a co-ordinating centre in Paris for trade union groups opposed to the communists and operations to cultivate oppositionary groups in two dozen industries and towns throughout France. The budget requested was now scaled down to $15,000 for the next six months, and he wrote in a tone of resigned exasperation:

> I do not think it is necessary to add any further appeals [...] I have tried to report faithfully the situation. [...] It is now a question of just how far we intend to go in terms of trying to influence the future which now more than at any other time appears to have possibilities that we didn't dare to dream of eight months ago.[55]

Eventually, in July 1946, the AFL's International Affairs Committee concluded its own official review of the requirements for an overseas programme. It decided to make a positive recommendation to the AFL Executive Board on the question of opening up a European office, appointing a German representative and establishing an International Department to service the committee. Brown was to become the permanent European representative and Henry Rutz, a former officer of the International Typographical Union and until recently an army major on the staff of the Manpower Division of the military government in Germany, was to serve as AFL representative in Germany.[56] By the beginning of 1947 both Brown and Rutz were officially in harness. What this meant in terms of financing the European programme is not clear. Brown remained on the FTUC's books (indeed, he was not transferred to the AFL payroll proper until April 1950), and it is not evident that there was any major new injection of funds from the AFL as such, though some of the FTUC's expenses may have been deferred by the Federation.[57]

The best part of a year had been spent by the AFL in deciding to commit itself to a European programme. However, in the meantime domestic political struggles in various European countries had resulted in lost support for the communists and a more favourable base for AFL activities. The resources made available for the programme were clearly not as great as the FTUC officers had earlier hoped for. But Brown was having no difficulty in finding sympathetic contacts, and the funds at his disposal for France, though not the lavish amounts that have sometimes been claimed for the early post-war operation, were in 1946 and 1947 sufficient to grease the wheels of anti-communist labour group activity, enabling them to publish their literature, their leaders to travel and organise, and generally for them to establish a presence.

More substantial financing seems to have been made available to non-communist labour and socialist groups in Italy through the AFL-dominated American-Italian Labour Conference. Luigi Antonini of the ILGWU was despatched to Italy in September 1944 with $25,000 for distribution to sections of the labour movement. The following year a further donation of $47,600 was made, half of it to the Socialist Party, and again in 1946 the party received $30,000 from the same American source. But what contribution, if any, this made to the subsequent split between Socialists and Social Democrats or even whether some of the money was specifically targeted on the anti-communist groups in the socialist movement is not clear from the records.[58]

In the course of 1946–47 Brown was primarily occupied with building up the anti-communist forces in France. Early in the year he arranged for a special supplementary assistance programme aimed at dissidents in the railway and mining unions, and by the end of the year the French-language edition of *FTUC News*, which Brown edited, was reaching some 30,000 trade unionists.[59] Apart from his main work in France he also made sorties to England, Greece, Austria, Germany and Italy. In Germany at an inter-zonal trade union meeting to consider unification he promised to provide $500,000 to the Western zone unions in order to keep them apart from the communist-controlled bodies of the Soviet zone.[60] Whether such an amount of money was really available to him at that time is perhaps doubtful. It is more likely that he was simply drumming up business and trying to make an immediate impression on the Germans. The FTUC/AFL's known financial dealings in Germany were of more modest proportions. German trade unionists requested 300,000 marks from them to buy two printing presses and to help rent office space for themselves and the socialists in Hesse.[61] By 1947 CARE packages costing $60,000 annually were being sent to 1,000 union officials every two months,[62] and 15,000 union activists were receiving copies of the German-language edition of *FTUC News*. Typewriters were made available and, through Rutz, supplies of thin paper suitable for smuggling into the Soviet zone for use in producing anti-Soviet literature were delivered to anti-communist groups.[63] Meanwhile further aid was being negotiated by the Italian Social Democrats, who had recently broken with the pro-communist Socialist Party. On a visit to the ILGWU convention in September 1947 Giuseppe Saragat requested a loan of $150,000 from the union and obtained promises of $125,000.[64]

Brown was recalled to the United States in November 1947 for a meeting of the AFL's International Labour Relations Committee. It was, in effect, a high-level council of war aimed at taking stock of progress to date and planning for an intensification of the campaign. Lovestone reported that an underground anti-communist German trade union organisation had now been set up in the Russian zone of Berlin and was ready for an active campaign. Brown told the meeting that the AFL had penetrated every country of Europe – so far, in fact, that it had become an army a thousand miles from its supply base. The success of the programme was reflected, he thought, in the responses of friends and enemies:

> in the fight between free trade unionism and totalitarianism, both friends and enemies have elevated us to the top rung in this international struggle, both as a target for attack and support.[65]

But, while the campaign was proceeding well, the FTUC was running out of funds. In January 1948 Woll was forced to pay $25,000 on behalf of his union to the FTUC to keep it afloat, and some of its expenses relating to campaigns at the United Nations were transferred to the AFL proper.[66] Again, a little over a year later, in April 1949, the FTUC's funds were running low,[67] and, with recurrent requests for financial help from the Italian Social Democrats, the non-communist French trade unionists and the French socialists (who appear to have received at least $90,000 from American labour sources between 1948 and 1952 for their struggling journal *le Populaire*),[68] a new appeal for funds was directed at affiliates. The absence of full financial records makes it impossible to say exactly how much was raised and how much was spent. Estimates of expenditure made by outside observers vary, journalistic accounts being replete with rumour and speculation.[69] It seems likely, however, that the FTUC's offical annual budget was not greater than $125,000, though there have also been suggestions, by no means beyond the bounds of possibility, that Dubinsky placed a similar amount again at Lovestone's disposal.[70] But at least until 1948 funding of FTUC-AFL international activities seems to have been overwhelmingly from union sources.[71]

However, from the earliest days of 1948 the CIA was beginning to spend lavish amounts of money in support of anti-communist labour groups in Europe, its newly formed Special Procedures Group (SPG) with an annual budget of $2 million leading the way in Italy with extensive covert financing of centrist political parties and trade unions in the run-up to the crucial general election of April 1948. And when in June 1948 the SPG was replaced by the Office of Policy Co-ordination, with even wider powers to engage in covert activities, it inherited the $2 million budget as well as 'acquiring the ECA's fledgling [Marshall Plan] labour projects and the accompanying funds'.[72]

While a variety of conduits were employed to pass these CIA funds to the target groups in the European labour movement (including at one stage the CIO), the AFL's international programme was the most important intermediary. Since 1945 the FTUC/AFL had invested time and money of its own in attempting to divide non-communists from communists in the labour movement. In the years to come, with the benefit of CIA funds, it was to step up its efforts. How powerful an influence on the labour movement was this support for anti-communist groups as compared with the programmatic appeal of the Marshall Plan and its managerialist values is something we shall return to later.

CHAPTER 5

The WFTU, the Marshall Plan and the labour schism

What we have witnessed for the past eighteen months, even more than before, is a conflict of ideas within the WFTU about the very aims and methods of trade unionism [...]. [It was] idle even to try to reconcile those different ideas within the WFTU. [M.C. Bolle, General Secretary, International Federation of Employees in Public and Civil Services, WFTU-ITS meeting, Paris, September 1948]

The World Federation of Trade Unions had been established in 1945, a global trade union organisation led by the labour movements of the allied powers and intended to continue the spirit of wartime co-operation which had seen them triumph against fascism. The Federation had a larger affiliated membership than any previous international labour body. The one major labour centre missing from its ranks was the American Federation of Labour, which, as a matter of principle, would not entertain the idea of fraternal links with trade unionists from the totalitarian USSR. They viewed the WFTU as a strange amalgam of affiliates, for the most part under the sway of either Soviet communism or the British Empire.[1] From the very foundation of the WFTU the AFL worked to undermine it, and three years later was to play a leading part in splitting the organisation.

Beyond drawing on a widespread sentiment in favour of international labour unity, the WFTU began life with some obvious flaws in its make-up. From the outset it was not altogether clear what the real objectives of the Federation were.[2] The founding conference had been unable to define to everyone's satisfaction what a *bona fide* trade union was: some affiliates were recently established centres in British colonies and under the strong influence of the TUC, others were equally new organisations from countries under Soviet control. The elements of a communist v. anti-communist power struggle were thus present at the outset, waiting to be nurtured by the icy springs of the Cold War.

However, the immediate weakness of the WFTU structure arose from the initial failure to agree on a formula for incorporating the independent international trade secretariats within its fold. On the surface this was a mere technical issue of how to merge separate institutions, the question of transferring funds, of preserving a measure of organisational autonomy. In reality it amounted to a profound philosophical conflict over the nature of trade union organisation – its aims and methods. The leadership of the dominant trade secretariat, the International Transport Workers' Federation, was intensely anti-communist and had no real with to join an organisation likely to fall under Soviet influence. Its public position was that it would affiliate if granted a considerable measure of autonomy.[3] But, in keeping with their centralised, hierarchical concept of union organisation, the Soviet trade union centre insisted on full integration of the trade secretariats within the WFTU and their acceptance of its central authority. More so than other types of international labour body, the trade secretariats concerned themselves with bread-and-butter trade union issues and had well established, direct lines to the grass roots. As the Soviet labour centre clearly intended to use the WFTU to proselytise globally for a form of unionism sympathetic to Soviet communism, they had an interest in curbing the independence of the trade secretariats; equally so if they wanted to avoid the embarrassment of having the secretariats scrutinise wages and working conditions in the USSR.

The early lines of conflict on this were not sharply drawn on an 'East–West' basis. The CIO broadly supported the Soviet position until 1947.[4] The TUC hoped for a compromise settlement, but ties of loyalty with the trade secretariats and the ITF in particular had led to their giving an undertaking in 1945 that continued British membership of the WFTU was dependent on a settlement of this issue satisfactory to the trade secretariats. Reflecting a natural wariness over too close a line-up with the inscrutable Russians, the TUC had, at the outset, arranged an escape route from the WFTU. For the AFL, watching from the sidelines, the conflict over the trade secretariats provided a heaven-sent opportunity to politick against the WFTU and to build a network of international alliances. In the years 1945 to 1948 much of its energy was devoted to gaining influence within the trade secretariats and steeling them to pursue a hard line against the WFTU.

During the first year of its existence there were no major policy differences within the WFTU, though relations between the major affiliates were never totally free from suspicion. However, in the latter months of 1946 and early 1947 the British and Americans became critical of the growing tendency for the Soviet trade union centre and their allies to dominate the organisation. Much energy was spent sending WFTU delegations to various parts of the world to encourage trade unionism, and sometimes these seemed most concerned to boost the prestige of the local communist movement and cultivate political allies for the USSR. The WFTU Executive Board took it upon itself to adopt public stands on purely national issues. Within the Federation the decisions that were taken were often vague and subject to interpretation by the secretariat under General Secretary Louis Saillant, who was increasingly inclined to identify with the Communist Bloc unions.[5] Articles for publication in WFTU organs had first to be translated into Russian before being prepared for release in other languages, and such material had a regular tendency to criticise aspects of Western society while saying nothing that might embarrass the Eastern Bloc states. The lack of evenhandedness in this respect was increasingly evident. The official report of a WFTU conference on colonial trade unionism at Dakar in April 1947 was doctored in the secretariat to favour the Soviet point of view, which led Adolph Germer, WFTU Assistant General Secretary and former National Secretary of the Socialist Party of the United States, to disown it.[6]

Though both the TUC and the CIO had their criticisms of the way the WFTU was being run, they themselves did not always see eye to eye. Yet some serious rethinking of their position was taking place in early 1947. There was now a general recognition that the WFTU was under communist control, but the majority view was that this condition was not preordained and that it was important to remain affiliated and try to steer the organisation along more acceptable lines.[7] The communist response to the announcement of the Marshall Plan quickly helped to dispel such hopes.

For some months after the announcement of Marshall Aid in

June 1947 there were no public pronouncements on it from the major union centres. In August the Dutch NVV asked for the issue to be placed on the agenda of the next WFTU Executive Board meeting but the Federation President, Arthur Deakin of the TUC, was unwilling to do so.[8] The AFL's annual convention in September came out strongly in favour of the Marshall offer and resolved to convene an international labour conference to generate wider support. But the 'Plan' was as yet only a general proposal, and most trade union centres were waiting to hear more details before taking a position. In the CIO and the TUC, where communists were a vocal minority, there was added reason for a cautious approach. At its October convention the CIO avoided a firm commitment to the plan, though President Philip Murray spoke strongly in its favour.

Meanwhile it was the Soviet response to the Marshall Plan, the creation of the Cominform in September 1947, that helped to deepen the division in the WFTU and caused the opposing camps to harden their position. On 5 October the Cominform issued a statement opposing the Marshall Plan as a scheme drawn up by Wall Street and American monopolists for the domination of Europe. The statement signalled the abandonment of 'united front' tactics, the Soviet strategy being to polarise allegiances within the labour movement, with the 'progressives' grouped around the communists and the remainder branded as 'reactionary forces of capitalism'.[9] In November Kuznetsov, the Soviet trade union leader, made a speech to the praesidium of the Russian trade union centre in which he advocated the expulsion of 'all reformist or oppositionist elements from the WFTU', a clear reference to Arthur Deakin.[10] The aim was to discredit the social democratic leaders of the labour movement, and by December the line had filtered down through national communist parties, whose official declarations now called for the removal of right-wing labour leaders from office and for radical changes in domestic policies. Trade unionists were under pressure to disown or rally round their existing leadership. In effect the Soviet trade unions had served notice of their preparedness to split the WFTU over the issue of Marshall Aid.

The TUC were still trying to avoid any step that would antagonise the USSR and embarrass Foreign Secretary Ernest Bevin while there remained a chance of achieving his main foreign policy goal – an international agreement over the future of Germany. The four powers in the Conference of Foreign Ministers were due to make one final attempt to settle this matter in November–December 1947. Not before December would the TUC commit itself on the Marshall Plan. However, the CIO intention was to have the matter discussed at the WFTU Executive Board in late November and Murray wanted the CIO spokesman to follow exactly the line of his convention speech.[11] Deakin was unhappy at the prospect, but since the CIO were determined to raise the matter he agreed not to block them.[12]

After a fierce argument at the November Executive Board the CIO Secretary-Treasurer, James Carey, was allowed to read into the record the text of the CIO convention resolution and Murray's remarks calling for an exchange of views on the Marshall Plan. No discussion was permitted but it was agreed that the matter would be placed on the agenda of the next board meeting. For the labour movement the issue of Marshall Aid was now in the public domain. Meanwhile the Conference of Foreign Ministers had failed for the final time to resolve the central political problem of Europe – the future of Germany – and so, accepting that Soviet intransigence was the root cause of the stalemate, the TUC came out firmly in support of the Marshall proposal for European recovery at its General Council meeting in December. The strategy of the TUC leadership and those supportive of the Marshall Plan within the CIO was to have the matter discussed in an international labour forum where there would be an opportunity to concert a position of general labour support before the legislation governing the programme was voted on in the United States Congress in mid-March 1948. There was, as yet, no groundswell of enthusiasm for the Marshall offer in the United States, and without a strong, positive response from the Europeans the prospects of the legislation being passed were uncertain.

Timing was of the essence. The WFTU was the appropriate forum for the debate, and the next Executive Board was expected to meet in February 1948. But if there was any delay in convening the board the TUC were prepared to convene an international labour conference outside the structure of the WFTU. It was just such a conference that the AFL had been campaigning for since September. They envisaged such an event going beyond mere discussion of the Marshall Plan but also providing a base on which to establish a rival international organisation. Irving Brown of the AFL had been lobbying for this with some success among the Benelux unions, and on two visits to London in November–December he held talks with right-wing leaders of the TUC and the Foreign Secretary, Ernest Bevin, hoping to persuade them of the merits of the idea. Over Christmas 1947 AFL and Benelux union calls for a Marshall Plan conference became more insistent.

However, the TUC were very wary of being drawn into an AFL power play. If the WFTU should split it was important that as many affiliates as possible should identify with the TUC, and that meant placing the blame for the outcome on the Soviet trade unions and their allies. The TUC were determined to have the Marshall issue discussed in the WFTU if at all possible. To flout WFTU protocol and conspire with an unaffiliated union centre in convening an *ad hoc* conference would be to risk losing allies among sister organisations in the Federation. The Foreign Office was now brought into the picture as an intermediary between the TUC and the AFL. Bevin told Secretary of State Marshall to advise the AFL to 'go slow' for the moment, and he asked the British ambassador in Washington to approach the AFL and tell them that the matter could not be rushed if the TUC were to secure the support of other WFTU affiliates. He was betting that the WFTU would refuse to discuss the Marshall Plan, in which case a schism in the organisation looked likely. The ambassador was asked to reassure the AFL that the difference between them and the TUC was not one of objectives but of tactics.[13]

The Foreign Office and the US State Department shared the view that the break-up of the WFTU was desirable and inevitable, and in the subsequent months they each kept a close watch on their respective labour movements, helping to smooth relations between them and, where necessary, guiding them discreetly towards a rupture with the Soviet Bloc trade unions. The American labour attaché to Britain, Sam Berger, was concerned that the TUC and the CIO would be outmanoeuvred within the WFTU and was particularly worried about the lack of firmness in the CIO position.[14] So on 20 January 1948, two days before a CIO Executive meeting, Marshall met Murray and Carey to discuss the CIO position. Murray observed that he could not tell

how long the CIO would continue to be part of the WFTU.
Though he had been an early proponent of the Federation he
recognised that it was now polarising over basic questions of
principle and practice. Still, he thought it was important to hold
the WFTU together if possible, since there was a great advantage
for American interests in having a forum in which opposing
labour movements could meet and talk things over. He felt that
a discussion of the Marshall Plan in the presence of those
movements who were opposed would be more beneficial than a
discussion carried on only with those who were of like mind. Two
days later the CIO Executive firmed up their position by declaring
their support for the Marshall Plan. And for the time being
Marshall himself accepted the 'wait and see' approach towards
the WFTU, contenting himself with the observation that discussion of his plan by the Federation's executive should not be
delayed beyond Februrary.[15]

However, there was to be no Executive Board meeting in
Februrary. Throughout January the TUC had tried unsuccessfully
to secure a February date for the board to meet. They were
informed that 'difficulties' had arisen, Saillant was conveniently
away from his Paris office and could not be contacted. (It turned
out that he had gone to Prague, allegedly for a 'Marshall Plan conference' of Eastern Bloc trade unions. He may even have travelled
to Moscow).[16] Meanwhile, between November and February,
the WFTU *Bulletin* published a string of statements from
organisations opposed to the Marshall Plan, but none from those
supporting it. The *Bulletin* accused the TUC and CIO leadership
of seeking to destroy the WFTU, and the Soviet trade union
journal *Trud* accused Deakin personally of collaborating with the
Foreign Office to achieve this objective.[17] At length, in reply to
a TUC demand that the Executive Board be convened by mid-
February at the latest, Kuznetsov cabled that because of 'an
important collective bargaining campaign' not a single responsible trade union officer could leave the USSR for a board meeting
in February.[18]

With no prospect of an early board meeting the TUC proceeded
to convene in London an international labour conference on the
European Recovery Programme for early March. Union centres
from fifteen European countries were invited along with the
AFL and CIO. Though the AFL had been pressing for such a

development this was a TUC initiative, not an American one. The conference forced wavering European labour centres to choose sides. The French CGT boycotted the meeting, as did, with considerable misgivings, the Italian CGIL – both dominated by communists. However, the CGT's break-away, Force Ouvrière (FO), then in the process of formation, attended, as did representatives of the non-communist fractions within CGIL. Representatives of the labour federations of the Western zones of Germany were present at their first post-war international gathering, and the Scandinavian centres declared for the plan – though the Swedish LO had argued for a delay in making a decision until it was clear whether or not there were any strings attached.[19] Taken together with the support of the Christian trade unions, the effect was to provide a solid enough demonstration of western European labour's approval of the Marshall Plan. A follow-up ERP trade union conference was scheduled for July; meanwhile the March gathering established a Trade Union Advisory Committee (TUAC).

The American ambassador in London was confident that this marked the first step in the break-up of the WFTU and the creation of a new trade union international.[20] In fact, for tactical reasons of their own, and as part of their ongoing skirmishing with the AFL, the TUC had no intention of allowing TUAC to develop into a new international. Such a new organisation would need to be planned far more carefully. However, from this point on the WFTU ceased to have any vitality. The final break-up did not come for another ten months, and during that period it seemed at times that the TUC and the CIO might be having second thoughts about leaving the WFTU – but Foreign Office and State Department officials were always on hand to help steer them towards that end.[21] Although the TUC would claim that failure to reach a settlement over the status of the trade secretariats was the major point of dispute, the truth is that it was the Marshall Plan that brought out the deeply rooted ideological differences between the WFTU's affiliates. Those ten months were marked by an extended game of cat-and-mouse, each side waiting for an opportunity to attribute blame to the other for the deteriorating situation in the Federation. In consequence the WFTU was virtually paralysed.

Meanwhile international crises followed one another in rapid succession, making it almost impossible to separate cause and effect. The temperature of the Cold War dropped sharply with the February 1948 *coup* by the communists in Prague, even as the ERP trade union conference was in preparation. In the ensuing weeks there was widespread talk in British and American government circles of the imminent prospect of war with the USSR. In April the European flashpoint shifted to Italy, with a critical general election held against a background of threatened and anticipated insurrection. Two months later the insurrectionary moment seemed to have arrived, with the assassination attempt on Palmiro Togliatti giving rise to a general strike, which in turn led to the first major split in the post-war Italian trade union movement. Meanwhile an even more dangerous situation threatened in Berlin, with the city's western zones blockaded and the United States embarked on its dramatic air lift. And in October a general strike of French miners had assumed insurrectionary proportions, the CGT's opposition to Marshall Aid constituting a significant part of the hidden agenda in this confrontation.

The effect of all this was to sharpen the lines of division between communists and non-communists in the various national labour movements. The TUC annual conference in September 1948 saw a drastic shift in the mood of delegates. Whereas in 1947 the AFL fraternal delegate had been extensively heckled for remarks critical of the WFTU, this time Arthur Deakin received a rousing ovation for his fierce denunciation of that same body. The climate was ripe for the TUC leadership to launch a vigorous campaign against communism in the labour movement. Similarly, the CIO convention in November saw the anti-communist forces, led by Walter Reuther and Emile Rieve, in the ascendant. Political differences in the American labour movement had been honed as a result of the 1948 communist-backed presidential campaign of Henry Wallace and the Progressive Party, a campaign that much of labour interpreted as an act of treachery. On the crest of an anti-communist wave, both the CIO and TUC leaderships were now free to withdraw from the WFTU as and when necessary. In the polarising situation of 1948 there was no longer any hope of accommodating the international trade secretariats within the WFTU: that was always sufficient excuse for the TUC to quit the organisation. The fact that they, the CIO and the Dutch NVV led the walk-out at the January 1949 Executive Board in the midst of an unseemly procedural debate over whether a resolution to suspend the Federation was in order was really of minor importance. As a unified body embracing communist and non-communist trade union centres the WFTU had come to the end of its short, fragile life when European labour found itself forced to make a choice over the Marshall Plan.

CHAPTER 6

Labour and the administration of Marshall Aid, 1948 – 50

Labour occupies a strategic position in the affairs of nations and by reason of its strength is wooed as it has never been wooed before [...]. The conventional diplomat will fail miserably in these revolutionary days unless he understands the rise of labour governments of the world [...]. Only those who have an insight into these forces, who share in heart as well as in mind an understanding of the labour struggles throughout the world, are equipped to interpret correctly and faithfully what they see.

Yet knowledge and understanding of both American and European labour movements is the essential tool of modern diplomacy that is unfortunately missing from the equipment of our conventional diplomats. It is in this precise respect that American labour can render a unique service, whether it represents the government in particular missions, or sits as an observer of the European scene, or acts as an educator of the rank and file of the people. [Supreme Court Justice William O. Douglas, address to CIO Convention, 1948]

American union leaders were involved in the campaign to generate public and Congressional support for aid to Europe. In late 1947 a special Citizens' Committee for the Marshall Plan, organised to inform the American public of the facts and issues involved, included on its executive committee James Carey, Secretary-Treasurer of the CIO, and David Dubinsky of the International Ladies' Garment Workers' Union. George Meany, Secretary-Treasurer of the AFL, and Carey were both members of the Harriman Committee, and the same two were appointed members of the Public Advisory Board which maintained a watching brief over the work of the ECA. But it was also politically expedient to grant labour a role in the administration of the aid programme. Why?

There were several factors. The spread of communism in Europe was of paramount concern to the United States government, and since communism sought to exert its influence through organised labour it was *within* the labour movement and *through* the agency of labour personnel that communism had to be fought. The aim of the ECA was to rationalise and modernise European industry. Long-established practices and a resistance to change on the part of employers and workers had to yield to new methods. 'Productivity' was the vogue word, the American policy of 'scrap and build', of willing adaptation to change, had to be sold to the Europeans, and who better to take the message to European workers than representatives of their affluent American counterparts, who had directly benefited from such an approach to industry at home? With the political representatives of organised labour in office in several European countries, the best ambassadors from America were likely to be people from a similar class and organisational background if not with identical ideological perspectives. Side by side with this there was an equally important public relations task to be performed within the United States. Economic aid to Europe was by no means a universally popular policy: large sections of the community, including trade unionists, remained to be convinced. More than any other section of American society, labour would have to make sacrifices in the course of rendering aid, in which case it was unthinkable that organised labour should not be prominently involved in planning and administering the programme. The Truman administration was desperate for all-party support for its aid policy. American trade union leaders were agreeable to the appointment of businessmen such as Hoffman and Harriman to the senior posts in the ECA, but the *quid pro quo* for their active support was a substantial labour presence at every level in the Hoffman-Harriman team in the ECA.

An Office of Labour Advisers working directly with Hoffman and responsible for appointing labour personnel to Marshall Plan missions in Europe was established in ECA headquarters in Washington. 'They are part of the first team,' declared Hoffman, and, theoretically, were to be involved in the whole range of ECA policy-making, not just labour affairs.[1] In the European head-quarters of the ECA in Paris – the Office of the Special Represen-tative (OSR) – there was a Labour Advisory staff and a Labour Information staff, each headed by men picked by the AFL and CIO in conjunction with the ECA's Washington Office of Labour Advisers. One of these two also held the official title of Special Adviser to Harriman, the Special Representative. Then again, in most of the sixteen participating Marshall Plan countries the ECA mission included on its staff American trade unionists as Labour Advisers and Labour Information specialists. In Norway and Sweden trade union officials actually headed the local ECA missions. By 1950 the mid-point of the four-year Marshall Aid programme, the ECA employed no fewer than sixty-five union people in advisory and information roles. If one includes in the calculation Labour Attachés in Marshall Plan countries (also appointed on the advice of the American labour movement) and US embassy officers with responsibility for reporting on labour affairs, the total diplomatic force directed exclusively at western European labour movements was 78.[2] The potential influence of such a body of experienced professionals in individual countries where the full-time staffing of trade unions was often minimal, was very great.

Labour advisory staff in the European headquarters – OSR – were required to formulate basic policies, advise the Special Representative on all matters pertaining to labour and represent the ECA on OEEC committees dealing with problems relating to manpower. Within the individual participating countries staff were to liaise with the local labour movements, advise and provide technical assistance to unions, employers and governments on issues to do with manpower utilisation and training, productivity, housing, prices, wages and working conditions. In the field of labour–management relations advisory staff were specifically required to encourage policies for achieving the full co-operation of workers in industry: 'it will be essential to develop industrial relations policies [...] which will reduce frictions to a minimum [...]'.[3] Every aspect of American aid was potentially a subject of consultation with nationals of the participating country, representatives of unions, management, government and civil service. As Price comments, 'Contacts developed within each of the participating countries were far wider than the traditional communications between embassies and foreign offices. [...] What developed was, in effect, a new and greatly broadened pattern of diplomacy [...].'[4]

A great deal of Marshall Aid work was of a high-profile nature: American help needed to be seen to be given. The sudden appearance in Europe in the late 1940s of a plentiful supply of American goods, all carefully labelled as products of the generous aid programme, was a valuable advertisement for the American way of life. But in a more direct way the Marshall Plan allowed the United States to mount a huge, explicit propaganda campaign in favour of American values. Staff were recruited from American newspapers, radio and the film industry, and the Madison Avenue advertising firm of J. Walter Thompson was hired to carry out an extensive propaganda drive on behalf of the virtues of Marshall Aid and American capitalism. In consequence the budget for information work rose from $500,000 to $20 million during the life of the ECA, with up to $17 million more coming from counterpart funds. As John Hutchison, Deputy Director of the OSR Labour Information Department, later observed, 'The Marshall Plan information programme in Europe was a rather free-wheeling, large-spending operation [...].' Even at this level of spending it was always the Americans' contention that they were only matching the large expenditures on propaganda by the USSR. Harriman told a Senate committee in 1949 that such activity in the ERP countries was costing them $20 million *per annum*. He admitted later that the figure was plucked from the air, but anyone familiar with the level of Comintern financing of world communism before the war would know that the amount was quite within the bounds of possibility.[5]

In this context the information and propaganda aimed at European trade unionists was always regarded as a crucial aspect of the whole programme. At its peak 224 Americans were employed by the ECA in information work in Europe, equivalent to half the staff of OSR, with at least 10 per cent of them professionals specialising in labour affairs. At one level the Labour Information Department fulfilled a basic public relations function for the ECA, the ERP-TUAC's weekly *Labour News Bulletin* being the mouthpiece through which the department spoke to trade unionists. In countries such as Britain, France and Italy the Labour Information staff helped produce a regular embassy bulletin for the use of editors of labour newspapers. In addition a Special Media Section of OSR produced pamphlets, posters, exhibits and radio programmes for broadcasting to America and Europe. Side by side with this standard public relations role the Labour Information staff were also responsible for co-ordinating the collection of information on anti-ERP propaganda and developing counter-attacks. Communist propaganda was to

be combated either through ECA's own outlets or indirectly
through material prepared for release by European labour organisations. As Alfred Friendly, chief of the Information Division in
Paris, noted, the division in OSR and the country missions 'are
to be something far different from the traditional, accepted
information office of a Federal Agency. They must be recognised
as having a specialised aggressive role to perform [...].'[6] Looking
back on the programme, a former acting chief of ECA operations
in Europe reflected:

> In everything we did we sought to change or to strengthen opinions
> – opinions about how to build free world strength, about America's
> role, co-operative effort by Europeans, investment, productivity,
> fiscal stability, trade measurement, industrial competition, free
> labour unions, etc.[7]

In short, going beyond a mere information programme, it was a
vast exercise in economic and political education aimed at all
segments of the community in the participating countries.[8]

The labour input to the Marshall Plan was thus substantial,
but its early record of achievement was slight. Labour operations
under the Marshall Plan got off to a most inauspicious start. Part
of the reason was poor co-ordination between different tiers of
administration in the ECA, and a good deal of that was attributable to the rivalry between the AFL and the CIO. It is hard to
overstate the debilitating effect on the Labour Division of the
ECA due to the antagonism of these two organisations for each
other, even when after 1948 they were both animated by a strong
spirit of anti-communism.

The State Department's candidate for senior Labour Adviser
to the ECA was Clinton Golden of the Steelworkers' Union
(CIO). While his talents were widely recognised, the AFL were
strongly opposed to having a CIO man in the post. William
Green, President of the AFL, informed the State Department that
his preferred nominee was Irving Brown, who since late 1945 had
been a roving representative in Europe for the Free Trade Union
Committee.[9] Even at this stage Brown had already emerged as
a controversial figure in the international labour field and, as
such, was unacceptable to the CIO. The *impasse* was resolved
by appointing two men to head jointly the Office of Labour
Advisers in Washington, Golden and Bert Jewell, an AFL nominee

from the railroad brotherhoods. The compromise prefigured the way that internal union politics would intrude into ECA Labour affairs, with appointments sometimes reflecting the triumph of expediency over sound judgement and the needs of the job at hand. The question of balance between AFL and CIO personnel persisted as a sensitive issue throughout the life of ECA and its successor agencies. Most Labour Information staff were members of the American Newspaper Guild, a CIO union, which left the AFL free to argue for a preponderant share of the more prestigious Labour Adviser posts for its own members. It then became a cause of much resentment within the CIO that six of the top Labour Advisers in Europe were from AFL unions while only three were CIO nominees.[10] But it was not simply prestige that was at stake: an appointee from one federation might be in a position to neutralise the preferred policy thrust of the rival body. 'With Berger in the Embassy and Killen [of the AFL's Pulp and Sulphite Union] in ECA, it means that the AFL is completely running the show in Britain,' Elmer Cope reported to CIO headquarters.[11] And as George Meany was urged in connection with the appointment of a Labour Adviser for Germany:

> A strong AF of L personality as director of [...] labour affairs would be in a better position to ward off the CIO manoeuvres to impose their view on the economic picture [...].[12]

Under the joint leadership of Golden and Jewell, all formal communications from the Labour Divison had to go out under both signatures, suggesting that they operated at the level of the lowest common denominator. Compounding the problem, neither of the two men was in robust health, and by 1950 neither had his heart in the job. From February that year Golden was working only two days a week on ECA business and Jewell was keen to relinquish his post.[13] In the event the Labour Office at ECA headquarters never exuded any sense of dynamism, never gave the impression that the Advisers were having any significant influence on strategic decision-making. Whether this was a reflection of the calibre of the personalities involved, the compromise implicit in the dual leadership of the operation or the persistent complaint that their office was understaffed,[14] Hoffman's claim that the Labour Advisers 'participate in the discussion of all policy questions at HQ and help formulate policy' seems to have been true only in a formal sense.[15] The fact of the matter was that ECA was well and truly under the dominance of business interests and operated consistently according to that logic. The Washington Office of Labour Advisers rarely appeared to be involved in anything beyond the low-level, pork-barrel politics of dispensing patronage to union officials anxious for foreign postings.

Jewell and Golden were appointed on 28 May 1948, a month after ECA had come into being with Hoffman's installation as Administrator. Their first task was to approve a senior labour appointment to the OSR in Paris. A week later Boris Shishkin, an economist with the AFL, was chosen to serve as Director of the Labour Division. The choice was effectively made by Harriman: Shishkin was someone he had worked with previously. Golden and Jewell were not in favour but in the circumstances felt obliged to go along with the appointment.[16] Immediately, however, the CIO protested at what it saw as discrimination in favour of the AFL. Carey told Hoffman that this breach of a previous understanding on the equal treatment of the two federations would force him to withdraw from participation in all aspects of ECA work. He even hinted at a complete withdrawal of the CIO from any involvement in the programme. However, he indicated that he would settle for the appointment of a CIO man of equal status to Shishkin in the Paris office. The compromise was agreed, and within three weeks Harry Martin, President of the American Newspaper Guild (CIO), was appointed Director of Labour Information for OSR. He was given the additional title of Special Adviser to Harriman, though the significance of this was never clear and all indications are that it was merely a gesture to smooth ruffled feathers. Martin, a Texan and a newspaper reporter by profession, lacked stature in the labour movement and never really managed to establish himself as Shishkin's equal in the counsels of the ECA.

The haste with which these various posts had been created and appointments made was soon apparent.[17] There was no clear understanding among those involved of the relationship between the Labour offices in Washington and Paris or between the two Labour divisions in the OSR. There was no close supervision from Washington of Shishkin's operation nor of the Labour staff in the various missions. Golden believed that he had no responsibility there, the task being that of Harriman and the mission chiefs. Consequently, with no firm directive to the contrary, Shishkin assumed responsibility for the entire labour programme abroad. Within a few months of arriving in Paris Martin was complaining that he was not being treated as Shishkin's equal. Communications were being received from Washington and policy decisions taken without his even knowing about them.[18] Early in 1950 a Labour staff member of the London mission commented on the 'not too good liaison between the Mission and OSR and the much graver lack of liaison between both OSR and the Missions and Washington'.[19]

The personal animosity between Shishkin and Martin added an extra dimension to the rivalry between the AFL and CIO for a dominant voice in ECA affairs. Both men lobbied continuously within the ECA to undermine the other's position. The clash of personalities persisted until the end of 1950, when Shishkin returned to the United States. Empire-building was much to the fore. In the early days Shishkin pressed to have a staff of sixty-five, four-fifths of whom would be in the highest-paid posts.[20] It was his constant complaint that he was being starved of adequate staff to do a proper job.[21] Martin complained, with some justification, of Shishkin's attempts to centralise all the ECA's European labour operations through his office, a policy that had a deadening effect on labour initiatives in different countries. As Special Assistant to Harriman, Martin felt entitled to a higher status than Shishkin, and in the early months of the ERP the CIO's pique at what it regarded as the inadequate status of its people lay behind its refusal to invite either Hoffman or Harriman to its annual convention in 1948.[22] Shishkin countered by claiming that Martin was intent on building up his Labour Information empire throughout Europe in breach of an agreement that such staff would be appointed to only four countries, and that the Labour Information staff were issuing slanted material aimed at enhancing the prestige of the CIO in Europe. He pointed out, too, that the CIOer Alan Strachan, ECA Labour representative in Greece, was a personal friend of Golden and reported direct to him on Greek matters, with the result that Shishkin's office knew little of events in that country.[23] But the identical complaint was put even more strongly and with more justification by the CIO, who protested at the AFL's monopoly of Labour appointments in Italy and the fact that staff there reported directly to the AFL rather than to ECA head-quarters.[24]

The problem in the OSR was not simply bad personal relations between Martin and Shishkin and their contribution to low morale among Labour staff. The real cause of the low morale was frustration due to an inability to make any impression where it was deemed to be most needed in Europe, and this had more to do with the structure and policies of the ECA than with personalities.

The truth was that there was no high-level Labour input into ECA policy-making, and this stemmed from the vacuum at the top. The position was summed up by Ted Silvey, Executive Assistant to Golden and Jewell, in April 1950 in a private communication to Philip Murray:

> At the end of two years, the labour movement has not obtained proper fruits of the authority it was granted. This is true largely because Mr. Golden and Mr. Jewell have been indifferent to the responsibilities of their office, and less than competent in carrying out this work [...]. Because Golden has insisted he is only an 'Adviser' in ECA, the great volume of work that the Labour office should have accomplished in this first two years has largely been left undone. [...]
>
> Essentially, Golden wants peace and quiet. In seeking it, he has [...] allowed important questions to go unmet [...]. When men overseas do write good reports and get into real projects, their papers are merely read and filed, and often their suggestions ignored.

In Silvey's view the Labour operation to date had been a qualified failure.[25]

In and around ECA there was a basic confusion over the nature of the role of Labour staff. They were often referred to as 'labour representatives' and it was common for American unions to think of their staff on secondment to the ECA in just those terms – the representatives of labour in the ECA. Of course, a major purpose in employing union officials in the aid programme was to win the confidence of European labour and so ensure support for the Marshall Plan and related aspects of American policy. The problem facing the ECA was a real one: many European trade unionists feared the prospect of American economic imperialism. The job of ECA Labour personnel was, therefore, to go among them and speak as fellow trade unionists. ECA staff advertised their labour background to good effect. An *entrée* to union organisations and events was sometimes to be gained on the strength of their American labour or socialist credentials. In Britain, for example, William Gausmann of the Labour Information Department would write reviews or articles in the left-wing press in which he might, when it was thought propitious, disguise his ECA role and be identified as a former member of the National Executive of the Socialist Party of the United States, or simply write as an individual – 'unlabelled goods' as he would say. Similarly, it was Gausmann the socialist rather than the foreign service officer who arranged the itinerary for the visit to Britain of the American Socialist Party leader, Norman Thomas, and who chaperoned him at his various meetings with representatives of the labour movement.[26] If Labour Advisory and Information staff were to be effective they had to be prepared to operate in ways that were unorthodox for conventional diplomacy. This they did. Yet the Labour programme was felt to lack dynamism. What was the explanation?

Golden was unable to accept that his staff were 'representatives' – freewheeling agents of their unions in the United States – but he wanted them to work on a loose rein, to be free to act as catalysts within the ECA, stimulating positive action and scrutinising with the eyes of experienced labour officials the policies proposed by other Marshall Plan divisions. All this required a measure of independence on their part. But if they were to agitate vigorously within the ECA for pro-labour policies they needed to be free from worries about job security. None started with a permanent position in government service, and so job security could come only with a clear-cut assurance from their sponsoring union that they could return to their previous position after leaving the ECA. In other words, they could 'keep their hat on the rack'. Yet in many instances there were no such guarantees. Thus Golden blamed the American unions in large measure for the sclerosis in the Labour Division.

However, no guarantee of future employment in the labour movement could alter the fact of their subordinate position in government service. Labour staff were required to work within the policy framework laid down by the ECA. If they brought with them the dynamism of union organisers and stimulated more self-criticism among ECA policy-makers and programmers or utilised their labour background and contacts on an unofficial basis to get things done, so much the better. But ultimately they had to operate policies over which they had no control.

Traditional rules of diplomacy involved dealings on an official government-to-government basis. Marshall Aid operated more flexibly, allowing a considerable amount of direct contact with sectional interest groups such as trade unions in the participating countries. As the American unions saw it, *their* 'representatives' in the ECA were dealing direct with their labour counterparts in Europe. Through this link aid could be used directly to strengthen non-communist unions in various ways. But such aid would be of diminished value if not complemented by national government policies that gave meaning and purpose to a strong, democratic labour movement – policies of economic growth, social re-distribution and, crucially, support for a full negotiating role for unions in allocating the rewards of a fast-growing economy. To secure such policies in countries such as France and Italy with conservative administrations the ECA would have had to make aid at national level conditional on a change in attitude to questions of social inequality. But the ECA's selective 'non-interventionist' stance generally precluded this. The ECA might apply subtle or informal pressure to encourage the adoption of more progressive domestic policies, but as long as more important objectives of the Marshall Plan to do with capital investment programmes and sound money policies were being pursued the ECA was unlikely to put official diplomatic relations at risk by intervening in national affairs in an area guaranteed to cause offence.

By and large the ECA was prepared to forgo the leverage that could have been brought to bear in securing more progressive social measures in Europe. It was in this sense that the Labour staff were prisoners of a policy they could not control. Mutual recriminations were of no avail: the problem was beyond the capacity of the Labour Division to resolve. The idea that Labour Advisers were trade union 'representatives' carrying the full weight and punch of the American labour movement was a myth. It was part public relations exercise and part 'cover', and as such could be very valuable – but it was irrelevant to the policy-making process within Marshall Aid.

Golden further explained the ineffectiveness of the Labour

Division in terms of the personal inadequacy of the staff. He complained that the AFL and CIO regarded ECA positions as a way of dispensing patronage or getting rid of second-rate people whose services they no longer required. He later observed, 'Bert Jewell and I had a very unhappy time to say the least, refusing to recommend for appointment some of the characters passed on to us by both AFL and CIO.' He went on:

> Trade union people had an *opportunity* to assume a large measure of leadership in the administration of the Marshall Plan [...]. They neither grasped the opportunity nor provided except in a very few instances, men of sufficient calibre and stature, to influence policies and procedure.[27]

For this reason he came to regard his period as Labour Adviser as 'pretty much a case of love's labours lost'.[28]

In terms of size the ECA Labour staff may have looked impressive but qualitatively it left much to be desired and organisationally it was rudderless. The relationship between the Labour Division and other sections of the ECA was not clear. Unlike other ECA divisions, whose Washington-based chiefs closely directed the work of their subordinates in the field, Labour staff in Europe were often left to fend for themselves.[29] In part what was lacking was top-level leadership in the Labour Division ready to insist that they be involved in the development of all major ECA programmes and that they should have the final word at least on all labour aspects of the programme. What then was the nature of the Marshall Plan organisation within which labour was required to work, and what was the basic emphasis of its programme? This is the subject we turn to next.

CHAPTER 7

Marshall Aid as a programme for business

If we still insisted that we were not interfering, all that it would mean was that our interference was unconscious and random instead of conscious and directed toward a specific social objective. The Russians were shaping our policy, not by direction but by indirection. We listened to what they accused us of doing and then insisted we were doing the opposite. The result was that we never thought out at the top policy level a definite set of social objectives. We were too busy pretending that we were not interfering in the internal affairs or economies of our European friends. [William Gomberg, 'Labour's participation in the European Productivity Programme: a study in frustration', *Political Science Quarterly*, LXXIV, No. 2, June 1959]

The Marshall Plan agency, the ECA, was in all major respects a business organisation run by businessmen. The most important force in shaping the concept of Marshall Aid had been the Harriman Committee, nine of whose nineteen members were leading businessmen, five of them prominently involved in the highly influential Committee for Economic Development. Averell Harriman himself went on to become the No. 2 man in the ECA under Paul Hoffman, while the committee's executive secretary, Richard Bissell, became Deputy Administrator. Senator Vandenberg, the Republican chairman of the Senate Foreign Relations Committee, whose brokerage had been decisive in securing bipartisan support in Congress for the ERP, had insisted that the ECA be headed by a businessman: 'the business side of this essentially business enterprise shall be under the effective control of adequate business brains'.[1] In fact Vandenberg had vetoed President Truman's first two nominees for the job of Administrator, thus ensuring that former car salesman and President of Studebaker, Paul Hoffman, secured the appointment.

Hoffman liked to be thought of as a leader of a new band of 'businessmen-statesmen' standing 'above politics'.[2] The ECA's national programmes were presented as economic rather than political — their legitimacy projected in terms of the perspectives of business management and economic rationality.[3] As Hoffman claimed, in denying any involvement in politics, 'I think that the State Department has an agency set up to deal with the political field. I think that we can do our job with the economic field [...].'[4] When, during the early years of McCarthyism, he and other liberal businessmen were accused of being among the most dangerous men in America, his response was characteristically 'apolitical': 'I think it is very important that we as a group think of ourselves not as right, left, conservative or radical, but as responsible.'[5] He gathered around himself at the highest level a policy-making staff of businessmen like Harriman, William C. Foster of Pressed & Welded Steel Products, Maurice T. Moore, President of *Time* magazine and Thomas McKittrick of Chase National Bank. In fact, at every level in the burgeoning ECA administration, businessmen were preponderant. And among its senior spokesmen overseas were leaders of the business fraternity such as William Batt of SKF, David Bruce of the Aluminum Company of America and David Zellerbach of Crown Zellerbach, who became heads of mission in Britain, France and Italy respectively.[6]

In the first year of the plan, aid to Europe was mostly in the form of foodstuffs, fertilisers and raw materials. These were needed to cope with the economic and political 'emergency' and, as such, they performed a vital function in holding the line for the United States against communism. The earliest shipments to Italy, for example, were sent very much with a view to shoring up the electoral prospects of the Christian Democrats in the general election held a mere three weeks after the passage of the Foreign Assistance Act.[7] But, having met the initial challenge, subsequent phases of the aid programme became successively more interventionist and were aimed at reshaping the political economy of Europe.

The ECA and economic policy

A prime objective of the ECA was to promote multilateral trade, which meant vigorously challenging the sterling area with its barriers against American entry to extensive markets. But the Marshall Plan brought with it a range of protectionist measures of its own designed to give an advantage to American business. American shipping was protected by legislative provisions requiring 50 per cent of aid consignments to be carried in US vessels. The legislation required that at least a quarter of wheat shipments to Europe should be in the form of flour already processed in the United States. And while there was a huge demand in Europe for tractors, the legislation imposed a $75 million limit on the amount of farm machinery that could be purchased in the United States with Marshall Plan dollars. The clear intent was to protect American as against European agricultural interests.[8] The Americans protected their steel industry by refusing to allow exports of scrap and pig iron to Britain on the scale that they had before the war, while finished iron and steel exports from America flooded Europe. The reciprocal Trade Agreements Act of 1949 contained a clause preventing American tariff reductions in any product as soon as the United States felt the pinch of competition and, in consequence, America cut its imports from Europe by a third in the first half of 1949. Yet import controls by Europeans met swift retaliation. The Marshall Plan facilitated a large expansion of sales by American oil firms to Europe. But when the British government reduced dollar area imports of oil in 1950, American oilmen complained and the United States cut off dollar aid for building British refineries.[9]

The Cold War element in the aid programme led to a severe restriction of trade between east and west Europe, impinging upon western hopes of economic revival. The OEEC's initial plans for European economic development under the Marshall Plan had assumed a steady revival of trade with the Eastern Bloc. Purchases of timber, grain and coal from this source would have helped conserve precious dollars. However, the ECA had the power to refuse aid deliveries to Europe if they were likely to assist production for export to eastern Europe of goods having a military value. Asked in a Senate committee whether American steel exports to Britain were being used to make jet engines for Russia, Hoffman was adamant: 'If it is true [...] they have got to stop it or we won't furnish aid.'[10] As a consequence, trade with the East was gradually reduced to a trickle, and one result was to deprive OEEC countries of much-needed non-dollar supplies of coal in 1948–49 during a period of particular shortage.[11]

The ECA sought to use its position as creditor to the participating countries to influence national economic and industrial
policies. The Europeans were committed by bilateral agreements
to expand their production capacity and to maintain monetary
stability. Inadequate performance in these areas inevitably
invited more American pressure to achieve the objectives. But
while at an early date Hoffman proclaimed increased production
as his primary objective, in practice the ECA expended much of
its energy in pressing for the deflationary policies that would
achieve monetary stability. As Finletter, the ECA mission chief
in London, told an American Chamber of Commerce meeting,
'The key standard of economic recovery is financial stability.'[12]
Deflation, of course, tended to conflict directly with the aim of
increased output. The tension between, on the one hand, the
need to expand demand and stimulate large-scale investment
and, on the other, to stabilise finances was never fully reconciled
under Marshall Aid. The recession that finally hit the United
States in 1949, combined with the deflationary policies in Europe
for which the ECA was substantially responsible, greatly retarded
European recovery. During 1949 United States production fell,
unemployment rose swiftly and imports from the participating
countries were reduced by 30 per cent. The dollar shortage in
Europe was almost as serious as it had been in 1947.

Italy. The application of banking criteria in economic management had a direct effect on organised labour in Europe. The
objective was to encourage investment through high profits and
to discourage consumption through restraint of wages. Low
standards of living would allow a surplus for exports while
keeping imports down. The Italian government seized the opportunity presented by Marshall Aid to integrate its economy into
the Western capitalist trading bloc. Industrial activity was to be
generated through the forces of international demand rather
than domestic demand arising from high national wage levels.
Squeezed by intense deflationary policies at home, Italian firms
were required to compete on the international market to survive.
A low-wage economy was an essential part of this strategy and
by 1950 Italian consumption was only 47 per cent of the United
Kingdom level and 64 per cent of the German level.[13] In this
climate there was little scope for ECA Labour staff in Rome to

work for policies of social reform or pro-labour measures. Yet the ECA's Industry Division had been able to strike a blow for American business and against the Italian public sector. They had effectively blocked oil exploration in the country, which was an activity under Italian government monopoly control. The ECA was hoping to allow private exploration, in the knowledge that this would open the door to the American oil companies.[14] Meanwhile among ECA Labour staff there was concern over the fact that the two most senior figures in the Italian government agency responsible for Marshall Aid were men who had served in the Italian embassy in Berlin under Mussolini, one of whom had voluntarily joined a German SS unit after the fall of the Italian fascist regime.[15]

France. Whereas in Italy Marshall Aid was accompanied by extreme deflationary measures, in France inflation was rampant for at least the first year of the aid programme. Common to both countries, though, was the fact that the labour force was unprotected from the harsh effects of government economic strategy and regressive social policies. In France early post-war price controls were mostly lifted by 1948 and prices doubled in the fifteen months to October 1948, before credit control and budgetary measures began to halt the rise by spring 1950. By this point the Monnet Plan had achieved a considerable amount of reconstruction and modernisation and production was some 20 per cent above pre-war levels. The traditional business classes were once more in the ascendant and the values of capitalism were being reasserted. The emphasis of the Monnet Plan was on modernisation through heavy capital investment – consumption being downgraded in the interests of industrial restructuring. Although in the earliest phase the plan gave priority to investment in the basic nationalised industries, it was soon geared to the private economy and market forces. The socialist approach to rationing was being replaced by rationing by income.[16] Real wages averaged well below the pre-war level. Only when family allowances were added did labour income approach pre-1939 levels, but only a quarter of all families received them.[17]

The emphasis on capital investment for industry left few resources for social welfare programmes. There was an acute housing shortage which the French government largely ignored. In 1949 only 20 per cent of houses had water, gas and electricity and were connected to the sewerage system. A million and a quarter new houses were needed, yet in 1949 only 40,000 were completed. France had attempted only one-tenth of what Britain had accomplished.[18] Although Marshall Aid counterpart funds were available for use in house-building, the French government showed no interest in using them and by early 1950 the mission was prepared to concede that nothing could be done to induce it.[19] Not until September 1950 was $30 million of counterpart released for a housing programme and even then the French government used some of it for other purposes.[20]

Britain. Britain's indebtedness to the United States as a result of Marshall Aid really represented but another phase of an ongoing post-war relationship in which the Truman administration sought to influence the direction of Labour's domestic economic and social policies. Though totally committed to the Marshall Plan, the Foreign Secretary, Ernest Bevin, was extremely hostile to the American insistence that the CEEC should visit Washington for further negotiations in September 1947 after having completed their report on Europe's economic needs. He firmly believed that this was an infringement of national sovereignty, a view that, as Henry Pelling observes, Molotov would have rejoiced to hear.[21]

The prospect of American opposition to the proposed nationalisation of the steel industry hung over Labour's protracted inner-party debates on that question. Hoffman had told the Senate Appropriations Committee in May 1948 that he might not approve of the British government taking over the industry. The issue of the public ownership of steel had become a test of Labour's commitment to socialism. Hoffman's intervention now added to the pressure for Labour to moderate its approach, and several Cabinet Ministers began to waver in their support for the policy, including Bevin, who suggested a postponement of any action, rationalising that in that way it would not appear that the government was being subjected to American pressure.

Cushioned by Marshall Aid, the British economy recovered well in 1948, largely as a result of the government's successful export drive. However, the 1949 recession in the United States was to curtail British exports to America and create another dollar crisis. By the second quarter even Marshall Aid was inadequate to cover the balance of payments gap. The Americans were disappointed with the early results of Marshall Aid. They explained it in terms of Britain's large expenditure on social welfare programmes, which, they argued, made her a high-cost producer and hence a poor performer in United States markets.[22] American pressure in favour of the devaluation of sterling now built up in the spring of 1949. Yet the truth was that British export prices were not seriously out of line, the value of exports was only slightly below target and some measure of temporary relief from the American recession, even the prompt payment of Marshall funds in July 1949, might have prevented further dollar losses and avoided the currency crisis.[23]

However, the Americans insisted that Britain submit to the 'natural laws' of competitive economics rather than be allowed to insulate herself from external pressures in order to indulge her extravagant socialist whims.[24] Ultimately the pressure for both devaluation and deflation succeeded. In the intergovernmental talks that preceded the September devaluation the American ambassador, Lew Douglas, advised Acheson to play down the ideological differences between the two governments so as not to give Labour's leaders the impression that America was intent on bringing about the downfall of the government.[25] The Labour government devalued by rather more than was necessary, hoping thereby to impress upon the Americans that deep public expenditure cuts were not required. But public-sector economies still followed, the burden falling on the shoulders of the less well-off, an outcome that ECA Labour staff felt unnecessary. The housing programme was cut by half as much again as the already bloated defence budget.[26] But the ECA mission in London was still not satisfied with Labour's post-devaluation pruning of public-sector spending, pressing for further reorganisation and demanning of the nationalised railways and an acceleration in the closure of uneconomic coal mines.[27]

Britain, more than any other Marshall Plan country, was successful in resisting the pull of American 'strings': the use of counterpart for debt retirement neutralised its potency as a vehicle of American interference. But Marshall Aid and the American influence in Britain that accompanied it certainly contributed to that mix of forces that was leading Labour to lose its sense of socialist purpose and self-confidence as a radical reforming party in the late 1940s.

Germany. As an occupied country, even before the Marshall Plan Germany was more effectively under American influence than either France or Italy became under the ERP. By the time Marshall Aid was introduced the voice of Germany's conservative business class was already being heard strongly, whereas Socialist Party influence in bi-zonal administration was on the wane and organised labour was increasingly disregarded by the military government. The long-term reconstruction plan for Germany which was adopted in 1948 under the Marshall Plan, with the aim of restricting living standards by 1953 to only 85 per cent of the 1936 level, was prepared without trade union participation. The Wurttemberg Trade Union Federation denounced the 'private viewpoints' and 'class interests' of its authors and observed:

> ... it is highly important to know for whose benefit the workers – who by taxation on consumer goods – are required to renounce a decent living standard in order to achieve the reconstruction of Germany.[28]

The event that proved decisive in restoring the fortunes of the German business class was the currency reform of June 1948. This measure enhanced the wealth of property owners, allowing them to make vast profits on hoarded goods. Price controls were now removed and, as in Italy, real wages fell sharply while unemployment rose astronomically from 1948. Inflationary pressures were countered with new regressive taxes and other deflationary measures. Production slowed, bankruptcies soared and meanwhile employers seized the opportunity to reorganise and re-equip their plant. By the end of 1949 industry would be able to produce 25 per cent more than a year earlier with no increase in manpower. The Americans gave full support to the Economics Minister, Ludwig Erhard, and his free-market economic policies. The military government decreed that the central bank was not subject to any political body but responsible to the market economy. The Basic Law also made government deficit financing illegal except under the most extreme circumstances.[29] As Victor Reuther of the UAW claimed in an American radio broadcast shortly after meeting the American

Military Governor, General Clay, in summer 1948, the military government was using Marshall Aid to 'force the energies and hopes of the European peoples into the mould of American free enterprise [...]'.[30] After the federal elections of 1949 which restored civilian rule Erhard continued to be the architect of economic policy in the Christian Democrat government, opposing the concept of full employment as a threat to the 'free economy'. By early 1950 the government's goal was to allow unemployment to rise to over 1·75 million in the succeeding eighteen months and then to continue at that level. Germany most definitely was not to become a welfare state.

Regressive tax policies benefited the rich, taxes on luxury buildings being reduced while the house construction industry was starved of resources. The programme of integrating refugees was cut by half, while the government allocated 50 per cent more aid to the tourist industry.[31] A low-cost housing project started under Marshall Aid early in 1950 was soon brought to a halt as a result of government refusal to allow the unions a role in administering it.[32] ECA Labour staff proposed withholding counterpart withdrawals unless the house-building programme was doubled, but this conflicted with the primary aim of 'dollar viability'.

By 1950, eighteen months into the aid programme, unemployment was 2 million and conditions reminiscent of 1933 were reappearing. But the West German government's strategy continued to be to maintain high prices – so as to enable industry to finance capital improvements out of current sales – while insisting on further tax reductions for those with high incomes.[33]

As in France and Italy, there was a need for tax reforms, blocking the loopholes for the rich and shifting the emphasis from indirect to direct taxation. The ECA might have applied pressure to secure these objectives but its real priorities – the pursuit of balanced budgets and dollar viability – were rather different. In the early months of the ERP direct intervention by the ECA to achieve its priorities risked bad publicity and the Americans therefore exercised a measure of self-restraint in the initial phase. But, as Harriman told a meeting of the Council on Foreign Relations in April 1950, the interference had now increased: 'we have put on pressure – a great deal of it aimed at forcing sound fiscal policies'.[34]

The ECA Labour Division in Europe

It was only from mid-1949 that the Labour Division was fully staffed and operational and by then the Marshall Plan had, in an important sense, achieved its immediate objective. The availability of ERP credits from spring 1948 onwards helped western European countries bridge the dollar gap, thereby relieving several national economies of the prospect of immediate collapse and the possibility of a major communist advance in the wake of the resulting economic and social privation. The immediate threat of communism was thus substantially contained. A wave of communist-inspired strikes in late 1948 against Marshall Aid had reinforced this process. The strikes were frequently unpopular and largely unsuccessful and caused the communists to lose much support. The dramatic impact of early Marshall Aid shipments and the fierce opposition to them by the communists had led in the space of a few months to a major shift in the contours of labour movement politics. By 1949 neutralist tendencies among many non-communist labour movements had been transformed into support for the American alliance and the North Atlantic Pact. In countries such as France and Italy where communists dominated the labour movement break-away unions had been nurtured by the Americans. Elsewhere steps had been taken to marginalise the communist minority. On a global scale the WFTU had split and plans were in hand for the formation of a new non-communist labour federation, the ICFTU. The first labour appointees of the ECA played a useful supportive role in helping to engineer some of these developments. The initial phase of the Marshall Plan had thus been successful. Most of the ECA's Labour staff now entering the field did so at the point where these early successes had to be reinforced and extended. For the most part it meant cultivating the anti-communist forces in the French and Italian labour movements in their opposition to the communist-dominated centres.

France and Italy. ECA Labour staff in Paris acted as nursemaid to – even as an extended arm of – the break-away Force Ouvrière. From the outset FO had been dependent on modest financial aid channelled through the AFL. According to the American ambassador to Rome, Harriman had obtained some

early funding from US industrialists operating in France, money
that was used to pay strike-breakers in Marseilles. The donors
evidently included firms such as Standard Oil, General Electric,
Singer, National Cash Register and Otis Elevator. During the
autumn and winter of 1948 FO had received a loan from the AFL
totalling approximately $20,000, paid in instalments every few
weeks on a drip-feed basis.[35] An attempt was also made by
Clinton Golden to raise substantial funds from American business
sources for FO, hoping that this would prompt American labour,
and especially the CIO, to be more generous. In December 1948
he arranged a meeting in New York with David Rockefeller,
Frank Altschul, the Chairman of General American Investors
Company, and others who were known to be sympathetic. The
businessmen were keen to help, but Philip Murray told Golden
that the CIO would not support efforts to raise funds from such
sources, and the effort foundered there.[36] By late 1949, with
dues income covering only a quarter of outgoings, FO was all but
insolvent. The French government had closed off further financial
help because of the militant demands being made by FO, and once
again the Federation turned to Irving Brown, who, with a new
source of CIA funding now available, was willing to assist.[37]

In Italy the ECA Labour Division was even more preoccupied
with the task of fighting communism and the communist-led
CGIL. As in France it worked closely with the AFL but also
deployed its own extensive resources. Labour staff were engaged
in widening the fissures in the labour movement that had appeared between the announcement of the Marshall Plan in 1947
and the passing of the Aid legislation in spring 1948. The split
became real in June 1948 as a result of the general strike which
followed the attempted assassination of the Communist Party
Secretary, Togliatti, when the communists disregarded the call
of the non-communists in the CGIL to limit the strike, turning
it instead into an insurrectionary event and insisting on the
inclusion of the Communist Party in government. Colonel Tom
Lane, soon to combine the role of Labour Adviser with that of
labour attaché in the Rome mission,[38] immediately met the
Christian union leader, Pastore, and urged him to form a break-
away organisation, the LCGIL. The following month a party of
senior American labour officials, including Dubinsky and Luigi
Antonini of the ILGWU and Lovestone and Brown of the FTUC,

descended on Italy following the second ERP trade union conference in order to further the split and, in particular, to secure
agreement on the need for this from trade union members of
the Social Democratic and Republican parties. A devout Catholic,
Lane argued with Vatican officials the case for a secular non-
communist labour organisation, only to be ticked off in person
by the Pope.[39] Meanwhile the American embassy in Rome
sought funds for Pastore's organisation in the United States.
Estimating that he needed $1·5 million for administration over
the coming nine months – including wages for 1,430 staff! –
the ambassador cabled, 'We trust that the State Department will
explore all possibilities of obtaining the required funds for this
group,' and, suggesting that the matter be discussed with ECA,
'We believe we could handle financial transfers here discreetly
[...].'[40] The LCGIL embarked on a major organising drive in
forty-five Italian towns and cities in December, with the
American embassy's labour and consular staff attending many
of the public meetings.[41]

Initial failure to attract Social Democratic and Republican
members from the CGIL to the LCGIL forced the Americans to
pursue collaboration between the various groups by means of a
Marshall Plan trade union advisory committee for Italy. The
committee established a bureau with a paid staff. Meetings of its
officers, conducted under American auspices, were held at the
ECA mission headquarters in Rome on a weekly basis from
October 1948.[42] In effect these were a valuable preparation for a
top-level visit to the USA in spring 1949 by Pastore, and the
leaders of the Social Democratic and Republican factions in
the CGIL, Giovanni Canini and Appio Rocchi. Accompanied
throughout the trip by Lane and the Labour Information Officer
Jim Toughill, the three leaders were feted by American labour and
came under intense pressure to reach a basis for trade union
unity. Before they left for home on 9 April they were able to
announce an agreement acceptable to the Americans.[43] A
merger of Social Democrat and Republican trade unionists
with Pastore's essentially Christian Democrat centre would be
effected by the end of the year. The ECA's Rome mission circulated half a million copies of the report of their trip by the three
leaders in which they stressed the support there was in America
for a non-communist form of trade unionism.[44]

Money and organisational help were now required. The Labour Information staff in Rome were publishing a monthly trade union journal, *Nel mondo del lavoro*, broadcasting five programmes a week over state radio and releasing at least one documentary film per month for commercial distribution in cinemas.[45] As Toughill recalls, 'I had a fairly substantial budget.'[46] The ECA appointed two additional labour consultants from the American labour movement to work in Italy with the mission and embassy staff for three critical months in autumn 1949.[47] The Italians had asked the FTUC for a considerable amount of financial assistance. Dubinsky realised that it would not be possible to raise the full amount, though he was confident of being able to provide enough. But by July 1949 it was apparent that large sums of American money were flooding into the coffers of the Social Democrat and Republican trade unionists, payments which had not passed through nor been authorised by the FTUC. Dubinsky regarded the amounts as being beyond the needs of the situation and, assuming that the ECA was the source of the funding, was disposed to tell Harriman of his intention to wash his hands of the operation and its consequences.[48] He also asked the AFL's International Affairs Committee to issue a statement dissociating themselves from any use of pressure tactics in connection with the irregular financing of the Italian unions. But he was successfully opposed by Meany on the grounds that to issue such a statement would be to cast doubt on the legitimacy of the Italian programme.[49]

Faced with considerable doubts among Italian Social Democrats and Republicans about the soundness of the merger policy, the AFL and ECA used their financial leverage to force it through to a conclusion. In September 1949 Lane and Brown convened a meeting with the wavering Italian leadership in the Grand Hotel in Rome at which the Americans urged that the merger be concluded in November and threatened to cut off funds in default of this. 'We are insisting on unity this year [...] not another penny will be forthcoming until clearer understandings and agreements are made [...]',[50] Brown reported to Lovestone. However, the power play backfired and although Social Democrat and Republican labour leaders, together with a rump of their membership, joined Pastore to form the new Confederazione Italiana Sindacati Lavoratori (CISL), the majority of their followers remained outside. In September Norman Thomas sent a telegram to Secretary of State Dean Acheson criticising this blatant American interference in Italian trade union affairs, particularly the activities of embassy officials such as Lane, whose clumsy intervention had served to drive a wedge between non-communist trade unionists.[51] Thomas's telegram itself had a dramatic impact when it was publicised in Italy and helped prepare the ground for a new, third labour federation, the Unione Italiana del Lavoro (UIL), created in spring 1950 and consisting primarily of Social Democrats and Republicans.

ECA officers in France and Italy had achieved a measure of success in helping to launch and keep anti-communist rivals of the CGT and CGIL alive. But when it came to the task of constructing a more acceptable economic and political order in Europe the problems were often rather more intractable and it was at this point that Labour Division staff began to experience serious frustrations.

In Italy they could make no headway against the reactionary policies of the Italian regime. In Paris, from the outset, the Labour Division pressed for a fairer distribution of incomes, advising the French government as early as summer 1948 that they might reasonably permit wage increases without undermining the long-run aims of budgetary stabilisation and financial equilibrium.[52] However, they were up against not only a French administration pursuing conservative policies but also a mission led by men who accorded social reform a lower priority than financial orthodoxy. The Finance Division of the mission wielded far more influence. In spring 1949 the Americans did put pressure on the French government to reform the inequitable tax system and even threatened to withhold counterpart as a sanction, but eventually they were prepared to settle for the minor reforms introduced by the government.[53]

The Labour Division's calls for more liberal wage policies, improved social conditions, and their warning of social unrest and even communist gains if improvements were not made, were all largely ignored. In the second half of 1948 labour militancy was on the increase and finally broke out in the northern coal-fields in a general strike in September–October led by the CGT and supported initially by both FO and the Christian CFTC.

Widely held industrial grievances over wages, speed-up and democracy in the management of the nationalised coal industry now mingled with communist denunciations of Marshall Aid. The strike turned into a violent confrontation against the French government before the action collapsed with the miners near starvation. The CGT had received upwards of $1 million in foreign assistance, overwhelmingly from the USSR and eastern Europe, while from the United States, in a calculated bid to embarrass the government, the miners' leader, John L. Lewis, had cabled the AFL demanding that they ask President Truman to request the French government to stop making war on its own miners by organised strike-breaking.

Indeed, there was sympathy for the miners from some strange quarters, given that the strike had cost France the equivalent of an eighth of its allocation of Marshall Aid for the year. At a dinner in October 1948 Hoffman, Harriman, Thomas Finletter, the ECA mission chief in London, and Lew Douglas, US ambassador to Britain, all told the Labour Cabinet Minister Hugh Gaitskell of their sympathy for the miners and their shock at the failure of the French government to attempt a more egalitarian distribution of essentials.[54] The fact was, of course, that the ECA had it within its power to insist on such a policy, but no attempt was made to do so and the chief of the Labour Division offered no strong protest. Among the criticisms of Shishkin by his staff in the Labour Division was that, while he enjoyed excellent relations with his superiors in the ECA, his influence was not deployed to the benefit of European workers. In contrast, during his short spell as Labour Adviser to the French mission, Michael Harris of the Steelworkers' Union was more boisterous in his support of pro-labour measures. He was hostile to Monnet's approach to planning, which allowed little participation by labour; he argued strongly against ECA support for wage restraint, and he identified closely with those in the leadership of FO who were pressing a more militant wage policy in 1949. And it was precisely these close relations that led to his removal from Paris and his 'promotion' to ECA mission chief in the quiet pastures of Sweden.[55] The fact that Harris had become a mission chief was not, as American labour liked to think, a sign of their increasing influence: it was a result of labour's eclipse within ECA.

In August 1949, echoing a view that had been expressed by FO,

Labour Information Chief Harry Martin called for the reinstitution in France of free collective bargaining. Without it, he argued, the non-communist unions risked being wiped out in a wave of communist-led political strikes. His proposal generated a vigorous debate within the Paris office of the ECA. Some Americans had reservations about a return to free collective bargaining on the grounds that, to be effective against the employers, non-communist and communist unions would need to adopt a united front, and that would undermine one of the main purposes of the Marshall Plan. They argued that a safer policy would be to secure wage increases by means of government decree. However, at a top-level ECA meeting involving Harriman, Barry Bingham (the Acting Chief of Mission) Shishkin, Martin and Kenneth Douty of the Textile Workers' Union (CIO), the recently appointed Chief Labour Adviser, it was unanimously agreed that wage increases of some description were necessary and that this view be represented to the French government. The Labour staff believed that they had finally achieved recognition of the fact that the Marshall Plan lacked social conscience in its emphasis on balanced budgets and the balance of payments. But it soon became clear that Mission Chief David Bruce was not in favour of this approach and the Labour Division's victory proved to be pyrrhic.[56] Returning from a field trip, Douty waxed enthusiastic over the possibilities of positive work with French labour, but on meeting Bruce he was read a long lecture on the need for financial stability.[57]

The ECA Labour staff recognised that any decline in the influence of the French Communist Party between the creation of the Cominform in 1947 and 1950 was, in essence, due to its own unpopular tactics, its support for sabotage at home and anti-colonial movements abroad, rather than to the positive achievements of the ECA and the French anti-communist movement. And by 1950 there were already signs that communist fortunes were improving as a general result of the continuing critical economic state of Europe.[58]

Germany. In Germany, under military government until 1949 and with the labour movement in the Bi-zone virtually cut off from direct contact with General Clay, there was little that American trade union personnel could do to alleviate the

desperate hardship experienced by the labour force, let alone help
the unions achieve their wider policy goals. The Marshall Plan
and the measures of economic liberalisation that accompanied
it contributed significantly to undermining the prospects of
developing a socialised economy. In the months preceding the
introduction of the Marshall Plan the German sub-committee of
the House of Representatives Committee on Aid to Europe (the
Herter Committee) had called for the direction of German
industry to be returned to its 'rightful owners', with them granted
complete freedom to use raw materials and foreign credit. The
German trade union leader Hans Boekler complained to the ERP
Trade Union Conference in Paris in July 1948 that the Americans
aimed to prevent the nationalisation of coal, to which both the
Christian Democrats and the Socialists were committed.[59] The
official American position on socialisation was conveyed to
Mathew Woll, chairman of the AFL's International Affairs
Committee, by General Clay:

> as a representative of the US government, it is my duty to uphold the
> advantages of free enterprise in restoring a normal economy. [...] A
> very large percentage of the members of the German trade unions
> repudiates the theory that free enterprise is possible in a democratised
> economy. I cannot accept this theory which perhaps to some extent
> accounts for German labour feeling that we are not in full sympathy
> with its aims.[60]

But American business interests made it abundantly clear that
there would be no private American investment in Germany
unless the demand for socialisation was dropped altogether.
German labour was effectively faced with a choice between
solving their domestic economic problems through socialisation
and an extended period of privation or building up their economy
more speedily on the basis of private enterprise, foreign investment and American aid.

At American military government insistence the issue of
socialisation was to be deferred until Germany became self-
governing: in effect it was dropped altogether from the political
agenda. Meanwhile, in an interim settlement Military Government Law No. 75 of 10 November 1948 provided for the breaking up of the heavy industrial concerns of the Ruhr and for the
shares to be held by German trustees appointed by the military
authorities. There was no provision for consultation with labour

on the appointment of the trustees nor for the inclusion of labour representatives among their number. Yet among the twelve trustees appointed nine had played a prominent role in German industry under Hitler, the most prominent being Heinrich Dinkelbach, the vice-chairman of Thyssen's giant steel concern, Vereinigte Stahlwerke, during the Nazi years. As Harvey Brown of the Machinists' Union, the newly appointed Labour Adviser to the American High Commission in Germany, observed in 1950, 'There are too many top Nazis in top positions in business and management.'[61]

Not only did the Americans rule out socialisation on the grounds that it was a decision that needed to be taken by all the German people at a later date, they also blocked legislative moves within the different Länder to establish co-determination. By autumn 1948 such laws had been passed in Hesse, Baden Wurttemberg and Bremen as well as in the French zone and the British-controlled area of North Rhine Westphalia. The American military government overruled their provision for co-determination in economic matters, contending that it was up to a future German state to decide on this fundamental principle. In October 1948 the Hesse and Baden Wurttemberg legislation was finally allowed to pass, but with the clauses on economic co-determination omitted. Though not themselves enamoured of co-determination, the American unions strongly questioned the right of the military government to block state legislation on social and economic matters. Woll pointed out to Clay:

> Our country does not and must not seek to impose any type of economy or economic policies on any country. [...] We think that the aim of American policy should be the consolidation of democracy throughout the world. Therefore, we must avoid creating any impression that we want to compel other peoples [...] to adopt one or another form of Americanisation.[62]

Part of the American strategy in reforming the German currency and freeing industry from wage and price controls was to allow more scope for collective bargaining. To military government officials and American labour representatives, this was far more acceptable a method of advancing trade union aims than reliance on government agencies and the political process. The Labour Division of the military government was under instruction to assist unions, employers and public agencies to find effective means of co-operation. Collective bargaining in a free-market context was to be the chosen vehicle for this. With the replacement of the military government by a civilian High Commission in 1949 the remit became more explicit. The Trade Union Policy and Relations branch was to encourage:

> the adoption of collective bargaining as the basic technique for improving wages, hours and working conditions instead of the legislative process, and discourage reliance upon the State and its agencies for protection in any area where the same end may be achieved through collective bargaining.[63]

Prior to 1948 there had been virtually no bargaining, though Law No. 35 of August 1946 had established procedures for voluntary conciliation, mediation and arbitration. When, following currency reform, David Dubinsky had complained to Clay that uncontrolled prices were rising much faster than wages, the Military Governor undertook to remove the remaining restrictions on wage movements, though the Germans themselves would have been far happier with renewed controls on prices.[64] Clay reasoned that the German unions were not aggressive enough in the wage bargaining field, but a visiting British delegation from the TUC clearly identified the logic of German labour's position: 'The Trade Union movement of the western zones take the view that a simple presentation of successive demands for increased wages would only start a prices spiral with wages following a long way behind.'[65] The enactment of legislation on collective bargaining in January 1949 was therefore of no great immediate value to the German unions, having little apparent relevance to their preferred ideal of a planned, socialised economy.

By 1950 it was evident that German labour felt no enthusiasm for the Marshall Plan. As one American Labour officer in the High Commission for Germany wrote, 'It is indeed difficult to counter the propaganda from the East that ERP has done nothing for the common man [...].' Labour Director Harvey Brown observed, 'government and employers take the position that the Marshall Plan is there to unleash builders and move men, the welfare of the Western German workers is secondary'.[66] And because of the absence of any direct relationship between the American military government and the German trade unions in the past, the problems facing ECA Labour staff in Germany were now, perhaps, greater than elsewhere in Europe.

CHAPTER 8

The reappraisal of Marshall Plan labour policy

[...] hitherto anybody could do anything because there was just no policy. Every official would improvise his own policy in the name of vague anti-Communism. [William Gomberg to Irving Brown, 29 January 1953]

It took eighteen months from the inception of Marshall Aid before US trade union criticisms of the operation of the ERP became very vocal, with ECA Labour staff lending their support to complaints made by delegations which visited Europe from the American labour movement. In December 1949 Americans for Democratic Action published an anonymous article in their journal complaining that labour was only a junior partner in the Marshall Plan organisation.[1] Undoubtedly written by a member of the ECA Labour staff, and reflecting the view of most members of the Division, it was the first public criticism of the ERP from an American labour source. But the weakness of the Labour operation within the ECA had been noted within the first six months of the ERP by a junior official of the CIO, Jay Krane, who in autumn 1948 was the newly appointed aide to the American Assistant General Secretary of the WFTU, Elmer Cope. Based in Paris, and in daily contact with ECA Labour staff, Krane kept a meticulous diary of events and impressions. Early in December 1948 he had reached a conclusion that was to be widely shared five years later – that the American trade union approach should be either to insist on a high-level policy-making role in the ECA, or to setle for complete independence with freedom to criticise the ERP.[2] As for the substance of the programme, he was convinced that mistakes of tremendous importance were being made in ERP policy orientation. The preoccupation was already entirely technical, the emphasis being on increased production, no attention being paid to the need for social reform.[3] Striking a note that would be commonplace in the closed confines of American labour personnel in Europe over the coming years, he observed that it was difficult to be positive about the ECA: the most labour could do was to stress how bad the situation would have been but for the ERP.[4]

What general perspective did American labour personnel bring with them to Europe? They saw themselves engaged in economic reconstruction, work that required a social conscience. They wanted to export to Europe the values and material benefits of vigorous American business enterprise – not necessarily because it was capitalist, but because it was efficient. At the same time they hoped they would be laying the foundations of a more democratic and, perhaps, socially just Europe. Labour staff always stressed the importance of aid as a support for increased democracy. The logic of their position was to support administrations and policies that were broadly social democratic or progressive capitalist in perspective, favouring to a greater or lesser extent social welfare reforms and a mixed economy as against the economic liberalism and free enterprise that was part of the rhetoric of American business and the main thrust of much ERP policy. American labour unions were not unanimous on this point. Those from a CIO background – some former socialists, a few still members of the Socialist Party – were perhaps more committed advocates of government welfare programmes, whereas the AFL tradition was inclined to be wary of government measures to protect workers when those workers might be protecting themselves. Nevertheless a sufficiently broad spectrum of American labour saw the practical benefit of private and public welfare policies and an altogether greater concern for the interests of labour as a bulwark against communism. The frustration that Labour staff experienced within the ECA stemmed from the gradual realisation that the aid programme accorded social justice a lower priority than economic revival and that in the ECA's internal debates labour counted for less than business.

By late summer 1949 the success of the Marshall Plan in extending support to pro-capitalist forces in Europe was reflected in election results in various places. In some countries a clear rightward swing was discernible, with socialists being eliminated from coalition governments. At the same time policies aimed at achieving another ECA objective, the establishment of sound money by means of devaluation, threatened to depress the living standards of workers still further. In view of these trends the Labour Division of the OSR warned of the real possibility of an increase in militancy among non-communist unions, which would no longer be restrained from taking industrial action by the presence in government of labour or socialist spokesmen. Such industrial militancy over genuine economic grievances appeared unavoidable to the OSR's Labour Advisers. It might push the non-communist unions into a common front with communist unions which the latter would then seek to exploit. The communists would once again have an opportunity to put themselves at the head of popular agitation, and their fortunes, depressed since the beginning of the Cominform's ultra-sectarian line and the flirtation with insurrection in France and Italy, would begin to revive. The Labour Division's general advice was, therefore, in support of conciliatory policies on the part of employers and governments. Employers should be prepared to meet workers half way and make concessions before strikes forced them. Governments should act impartially and encourage the two sides to negotiate their own solutions in the interests of minimising the impact and duration of the strikes.[5]

The main problem areas in Europe for the ECA were France, Italy and Germany. Eighteen months after the start of Marshall Aid vast amounts of dollars had been poured into those countries. But while the aid had proved a boon to the employers it had left the working class almost untouched. This condition began to be generally recognised in the Labour Division in autumn 1949. Sol Ozer, an economist in the OSR, observed that 'ECA is running out of steam after [an] initial period of creativity,' and spoke of the development of 'fundamental ideological conflicts' that it would have to face up to, such as that between the goal of financial stability on the one hand and the achievement of an acceptable standard of living on the other.[6] Outside the ECA the critical note was sounded during the founding conference of the new International Confederation of Free Trade Unions (ICFTU) in December 1949. From the conference Harry Martin reported on the

> increasing emphasis on Labour's conviction that American aid money must be used more effectively in the future for the economic betterment of the living conditions among workers in Europe and elsewhere. [...] the Administration must take positive action in this

connection in fairly short order if that criticism is to be prevented from shaping into actual opposition.[7]

Within the ECA the sharpest criticisms of the effects of existing aid policies were contained in a series of reports written in early 1950 following field trips in France, Italy and Germany by Harry Turtledove and Lemuel Graves, two Labour Information Officers on the staff of the OSR. The reports told of unenthusiastic support for Marshall Aid even among the non-communist trade unions. It was not a question of the message not getting through, nor could it be solved by more propaganda:

> Marshall Plan propaganda is ubiquitous. Hardly a day goes by without a good blurb in the papers, and even shop windows are loaded with subtle US propaganda. Marshall Plan literature is distributed by the bale. In all, one feels that the workers have been exposed to our propaganda and have absorbed a certain amount of it – the anti-Communist angle, for instance. But the fact remains that this propaganda must be in effect negative [...] we can't tell them how well off they are, thanks to the Marshall Plan, because they are not well off and they know it.

Their material conditions had to improve before they were likely to believe in the Marshall Plan. But for their conditions to improve there would have to be a major shift in Marshall Plan priorities and, in all probability, far-reaching political change in the recipient country. As one of Turtledove's reports pointed out, the sceptical worker was not likely to be convinced 'unless we choose to disassociate ourselves publicly from the government and its action'.[8]

Concurrent with the Turtledove–Graves despatches, Kenneth Douty, Chief Labour Adviser to the French mission, drew attention to the imbalance between high levels of production and low levels of consumption in France. Production was up a fifth over 1938 while real hourly wages were 35 per cent down. Underconsumption was the basis of the problem, as it had been in the USA in 1929. The answer was surely for the ECA to intervene more directly to secure better social provision and higher levels of income for workers.[9] In a separate letter to Golden he reviewed ECA policy in this respect:

> the stated ECA policy of non-intervention would seem a sound one. Perhaps labour people would be inclined to intervene in a country like France with a right-of-centre government, but the other side of

the picture is the right to intervene in a United Kingdom with a Labour government. Given the complexity of forces in the American political scene, I would feel that non-intervention is the safer policy for labour [...].

But, the next question is, aren't we intervening now? Aren't we insisting in France, for example, on a balanced budget and certain fiscal policies? And aren't we using our control over counterpart to enforce them? [...] Presumably the Mission could, without going to a concept of intervention, press on the French Government policies that would serve the social needs of French workers and the political needs of American policy. To influence the Mission to make such represenation should be one of the efforts of the Labour people in the Mission.[10]

The question of how interventionist in domestic European politics the ECA should be had never been far from the surface in internal discussion.[11] Briefed by the State Department in 1948 on US policy towards France, Hoffman had been told: 'We should support any non-Communist French government by all reasonable means short of direct interference in the internal affairs of the country.'[12] However, as Douty recognised, non-intervention was an elastic concept, more to do with public relations than with practical politics. The architects of the aid programme were well aware that the sheer weight of economic forces that they had unleashed would compel a brand of politics in participating countries compatible with the economic imperatives of free enterprise.[13]

The immediate outcome of this internal debate within the OSR's Labour Division was a formal proposal, submitted by Turtledove in April 1950, that the ECA should bring over to Europe large numbers of American labour union officials who would work with trade unionists at the local level, stiffen their backbone and lead to a greater appreciation of the relevance of Marshall Aid.[14] This proposal – Operation Bootstrap, as it was called – was to provide the background for much of the internal discussion and programming that went on in the Labour Division of the ECA for the next six months. It was the ECA's one positive response to a widespread feeling among the Labour staff that it was neither sufficiently large nor free and flexible enough to combat the problem of disaffected labour in the ERP's trouble spots. The proposal chimed with an increasingly critical note being sounded in American labour's own discussions of Marshall

Aid, and this would eventually lead the CIO to distance itself from the Marshall organisation in pursuing its own programme in Europe.

In early May 1950 a resolution highly critical of the ERP labour programme had been passed at the convention of the Textile Workers' Union of America (CIO), causing some consternation in the ECA, since Philip Murray was present at the convention and was known to favour the resolution. It charged that the national labour movements in Europe were hardly involved in the administration of aid in their own countries although this was something that the participating governments had committed themselves to. It further maintained that there was little reflection of labour thinking in the application of Marshall Aid and that in the absence of a spirited labour point of view in the administration of the ECA there was a strong danger of labour 'representatives' becoming mere adjuncts of the State Department.[15]

Shishkin was forced to admit that there was much truth in this. The lack of effectiveness of the French non-communist unions in relation to the Marshall Plan was, he argued, due to their own lack of cohesion, but elsewhere the criticism was well founded. In Germany the American High Commission's Labour Division lacked influence, and the prospects of any improvement under the Adenauer administration were doubtful. And in Italy the trade union committee established to co-ordinate Marshall Plan work had been greatly weakened because of the reluctance of the Italian government – especially the Ministries of Finance and Foreign Affairs – to co-operate with it.[16] The preponderant strength of the communist trade unionists in both Italy and France led governments and business in both countries to continue dealing with them, rather than to follow their anti-communist instincts and risk the wrath of the communists by extending recognition to their smaller rivals. This tendency was to dog the Labour Division throughout the life of Marshall Aid.

The Textile Union convention debate served as a curtain-raiser to a top-level conference of twenty-five union leaders and senior ECA administrators held in Washington only a few days later to review labour's role in the Marshall Plan at its half-way stage. The conference saw an emerging consensus that what was needed in the Labour programme was not more activity by agencies of the United States government but a greater direct role for American labour under the aegis of the ECA. The unions were invited to shoulder the cost of such activity as a sign of their commitment to the programme, though Marshall funds would be available in the last resort.

There was a conflict of opinion within the Labour Division as to how large such a programme should be. Harry Martin, who had pushed the idea from the outset, favoured an ambitious scheme with up to 100 union officials coming to Europe. France would be the first target, but the operation would be extended to Italy and Germany soon after.[17] Golden requested that $1 million be put aside from the ECA's technical assistance budget to pay the dollar cost of sending American trade unionists abroad. Clearance was given to the use of Italian and French counterpart funds to cover the non-dollar cost of the scheme.[18] And on top of this $50,000 was made available from the 'Administrator's Fund', that secret portion of the 5 per cent counterpart fund intended 'to finance without indication of source' projects approved at the highest level of the ECA.[19] The significance of these amounts was noted by Barry Bingham, deputy chief of the French mission: $100 per month would pay the wages and expenses of a full-time organiser, and a hundred additional organisers strategically placed at that crucial time might change the whole picture of French trade unionism within a year.[20] Though there was no firm agreement on the details of the scheme, the Labour Information Department boldly announced that 100 American labour organisers would go to France, Italy and Germany over the next year, and on top of this American labour would make available, at their expense, the services of twenty people ready to visit Europe as trade union consultants if invited by European labour organisations for a specific purpose.[21]

Some field staff were appalled at the prospect of such a large number of people with no immediate appreciation of the situation at hand being turned loose in Europe. 'A trained, well-disciplined crew of infiltrators makes sense in some situations, but it can't be done this way. This is no time to play cops and robbers,' commented one member of the division.[22] Shishkin and Douty concurred, and argued for a small pilot project involving around a dozen officials to be tried out in the autumn of 1950. The Washington meeting of labour leaders and ECA staff had considered a proposal under which both the French and the Italian missions would be allowed to expand their Labour staff so as to have two or three extra American trade unionists attached to them as consultants. They would be expected to travel extensively and work as closely as possible with the local non-communist labour movement, promoting ideas of increased productivity, liberalised trade and the part that organised labour could play in such programmes.[23] And it was, indeed, in this more modest format that Operation Bootstrap took shape. The ECA's grandiose scheme for a large-scale invasion of Europe by American labour organisers never materialised, for by now the more sober view of the American trade unions was beginning to be heard.

The Washington meeting of labour and ECA leaders had agreed to sponsor a joint AFL and CIO delegation to Europe to report on conditions. A trio of middle-ranking officers – William Belanger, Harold Gibbons and Carmen Lucia – visited France for six weeks in July–August 1950, and the report of their trip strongly reinforced the criticisms of Marshall Aid that had already been expressed internally within the ECA:

> Our productivity programme in France carries serious threats to the welfare of the workers and does nothing to protect them – as the Communists so accurately charge [...] temporary unemployment caused thereby is ignored [...]. There is no protection against wage cuts [...] [resulting from] the adoption of machine methods [...]. There is nothing to prevent the direct benefits of increased production made possible by Marshall Plan aid from going entirely to the employer.

The delegation repeated the call for counterpart funds to be earmarked for low-cost housing as part of a vastly increased propaganda programme at grass-roots level. But there were also very specific proposals to introduce aspects of American industrial relations practice as a means of aiding the non-communist unions – legislative changes designed to strengthen free collective bargaining and efforts to encourage practices such as the granting of exclusive bargaining rights, the union shop, adequate dues paid by check-off, written contracts and more union activity at local and shop level.

It concluded by calling for a stronger American union presence in Europe, the point being addressed more to the labour movement than to the ECA.

Instead of one or two men stationed in Europe, a half dozen competent representatives of the American labour movement should be available in France alone for advice and counsel to the French labour movement. In addition, American labour should assign and maintain full-time American labour technicians and specialists such as accountants, organisers, publicists and research people in every region and/or national union to aid and assist French labour in its day to day task.

In general it called for a much more concerted effort by labour. There was need for immediate financial assistance on a far greater scale than ever before, and funds earmarked for special purposes ought to be made available, with expenditure supervised by special committees of the ICFTU.[24]

The effect of this report was to help convince the American labour movement that the ECA was not an adequate vehicle for pursuing trade union policies in Europe and that they would have to be more self-reliant. The AFL were, of course, already well established in Europe, with headquarters in Brussels and, latterly, generous covert funding from the CIA. After some indecision the CIO now made their first substantial move in the direction of developing their own distinct international programme. They had created an International Committee in February 1950, and in October Victor Reuther drafted a concrete proposal for a CIO programme in Europe, to be directed from a permanent office on the Continent. The proposed European office would serve as the vehicle for distributing ECA resources, money and supplies to free trade unions and ensure that this assistance was properly used by the recipients. It would help with 'pilot plant projects', conceived under Marshall Aid and meant to encourage European unions to break down employer opposition to higher wages, lower prices and sound labour – management relations – in effect to encourage the adoption of the American approach to labour relations and productivity. Pilot plants would become an important part of the next phase of ECA labour policy. The proposed CIO operation would encourage labour organisations in Europe to initiate representation to their government on projects which would then be supported by the ECA. The office would also provide assistance, encouragement and advice to the ICFTU (in a way that it had not in the years of the WFTU) in the fight to build strong, democratic labour unions and against the world-wide communist challenge. Equally it would directly assist the democratic unions in Europe by developing and providing techniques for winning away membership from communist-dominated unions and in combating communist propaganda.

As envisaged by Reuther, the programme was to be a long-term one and it was to be presented in a way acceptable to Europeans rather than launched as a hard-sell American project:

> The representatives must attempt to see their operation through European eyes, and understand and accept the aspirations and interests, including national interests, of the various European labour movements, and make their contribution on this basis.[25]

The CIO tended to be more sensitive than other American groups to the traditional values of European labour and cautioned government representatives against the blanket export of American labour relations norms and practices. In particular Reuther criticised American labour attachés for defining their function too much in terms of exporting US collective bargaining techniques:

> We must [...] start from the premise that most unions are going to have a political identification and tailor our efforts to this fact. [..] Collective bargaining may well be one of the tools in our kit – just as it is with the Communists – but to give immediate priority is an oversimplification [...].[26]

They emphasised the importance of direct contacts between American and European trade unions, not relying on government agencies as intermediaries. The CIO wanted to see a more systematic use of Marshall Plan funds, but only for labour projects which had been specifically approved by them and which would bear their imprint.[27] If ERP programmes could be devised that enabled non-communist unions to play a more prominent role in their country's economic and industrial life while helping them to improve the material conditions of their members, the basis of a progressive union movement might be laid. Such thinking was central to the CIO's commitment to the pilot plant schemes.

 The CIO opened their European office in Paris in 1951 with Victor Reuther as Director and a staff of two – Helmuth Jockel in Germany and Charles Levinson in France. As with Brown's AFL operation, the CIO were primarily engaged in resisting communist influence in the labour movement or, in the not altogether helpful term of the day, promoting 'non-political' trade unionism. But there were important differences in the two approaches. For the AFL the simple objective was to give material support to those European labour elites who demonstrated in ideological terms the most consistent anti-communist line. On the other hand, the CIO sought to distance itself from what it saw as the crudeness of the anti-communism practised by the AFL. The latter had not so much challenged political unionism as simply substituted one form of political alignment for another:

> Largely because of the political preoccupation of the national leadership, the non-Communist unions have relied to a dangerous extent on a too-simple and too-negative anti-Communism. They have, therefore, had some marked success in frustrating Communist political strikes, but have lost their own ability to use the strike weapon to further economic demands, and have saddled themselves with a reputation for breaking political strikes [...]. It is not too much to say that in Italy, American policy is paying a rather heavy price for the electoral victory won again Communism in that country in April of 1948. We too are the victims of a negative anti-Communism.[28]

Despite the Cold War rhetoric that crept into CIO statements in the early 1950s, ideologically and in practice their approach was more flexible than the AFL's, more adaptable to European conditions, less insistent on trying to force foreign labour movements into a rigid mould. Sterile anti-communism was never so pronounced in the CIO as in the AFL. Walter Reuther's dictum 'Neither Standard Oil nor Stalin' reflected a feeling of unease at being forced to choose between distasteful alternatives.

They were critical of the AFL and American government policy in Europe, which had been to favour some labour factions and not others, according to whether or not the AFL found their leadership acceptable. In France FO was favoured by the AFL over the Christian CFTC – and the ECA was encouraged to render aid accordingly. In Italy the AFL, in conjunction with the State Department and the ECA, had attempted to force a premature merger of non-communist labour groups under the banner of the AFL's preferred group, the CISL. The CIO strongly disapproved of this whole approach. The Italian operation had produced an artificial 'top-level merger consummated under remote pressure in New York'. The CIO recognised the importance of financial aid to European labour, but claimed that previous assistance rendered without adequate control had had positively harmful effects. Referring to the glut of money that had entered Italy, and had apparently angered Dubinsky, a CIO delegation to Europe remarked:

> We regret the manner of American support to Italian labour, where the corrupting influence of aid unwisely granted and poorly super-vised is sadly in evidence. Too much of that aid has gone to acquire and maintain physical properties, such as national headquarters [...].

The CIO approach was thus interventionist without being crudely manipulative in the AFL manner:

> It is unwise to play favourites in the complicated movements of European labour. Our task is not to unify but to galvanise; to provide some of the raw materials of a more vigorous life on the level of economic action. Out of that new vigour can come new victories, new insights, new confidence, new impulses towards functional, if not organic union.[29]

It was not, then, a question of master-minding the policies of other labour movements by pulling strings in Washington, Brussels or Paris. The CIO argued that Americans needed to display more humility than they had in the past when intervening in countries such as Italy. They were entitled to espouse unity among Italian unions, but they had no right to force it. What was needed was a flexible and practical policy capable of building up the economic muscle of European labour and so drawing strength away from the communists.

Their strategy was to find an organisational focus and a form of activity that would enable a vigorous trade unionism to develop and flourish in the different countries. Without ruling out or attempting to undermine political activity by labour – indeed, as Director of the programme Victor Reuther found himself much at home with European social democrats – the primary emphasis was on economic and industrial activity. If workers could begin to see the scope for improving their own lot by their own endeavours in this field they had a chance of over-riding the ideological and religious differences that kept them apart and thus kept them weak. So, unlike the AFL, whose approach was to buy support among union leaders in promoting non-communist unity, the CIO hoped to realign and reinvigorate trade unionism at the level of the non-communist rank and file by helping unions provide for the economic needs of their members more thoroughly than communist-led organisations were capable of doing. As redistributive social policies were not on the agenda in France, Italy and Germany, the strategy came to emphasise the need for productivity growth and plant-level collective bargaining over the division of shares from increased output. CIO policy therefore fed in directly to the ERP's growing concern with increased productivity achieved through the techniques of scientific management. In the FTUC Brown and Lovestone saw this as a product of the CIO's naive belief that communism took root only where workers were hungry – 'belly communism' was their dismissive expression for it. Consequently they had little interest in the productivity training programmes for trade unionists – 'hair-brained schemes' as Brown once referred to them – that came to dominate the Marshall Plan labour programme.[30] These were just an ineffectual response to the misguided concept of 'belly communism'. In their view something more than economic and social gains for workers was needed in order to eliminate the evil of communism.[31] What was required was a more direct ideological campaign.

The CIO's approach to the development of the non-communist labour movement in Europe was a long-term one. It would encounter many obstacles before being discontinued as a result of the merger with the AFL in 1955. Meanwhile the ECA Labour Division was in desperate need of some more immediate improvement in the social and economic climate in Europe. Labour Information Director Harry Martin strongly supported the call for a more vigorous Labour policy. In spring 1950, against a background of rising industrial militancy in various parts of Europe, he advised Milton Katz, Harriman's deputy, that Marshall Plan policies risked alienating European labour:

> we face a grave danger of losing completely the support of European Labour *at the worker level* [...]. My opinion is that it has become absolutely *imperative* that the very top echelon of ECA leadership come out openly and boldly with statements that will offset this dangerous threat [...] in the propaganda field.[32]

He persuaded Katz to make a strongly worded speech along these lines at a ERP-TUAC Executive meeting in Rome in May 1950, called to mark the half-way stage of Marshall Aid. Katz spoke of the need for high and stable employment, higher productivity (whose importance Harriman had not always recognised) and positive steps towards European integration. Martin regarded the episode as a major triumph, marking a decisive and necessary change in emphasis if the ECA was to reclaim the waning support of European labour.[33]

Of course it was no such thing, as events were to prove. A two-day conference of OSR Labour personnel later in May 1950, attended by Harriman, Katz, David Bruce, the Chief of Mission to France, and several US labour attachés, provided an opportunity to discuss the situation and air frustrations. James Killen, Labour Adviser to the UK mission, summed up the view of the Labour staff, pointing out during a discussion of the production drive:

> Lip service has been given to these safeguards [i.e. policies for full employment and retraining] by Ambassador Katz and others in public statements, but I am perhaps not fully informed. I have not seen in any country ECA action specifically designed to insist on the provision of funds for public works and housing or these other things to take up or to aid in taking up the slack.[34]

Three of the most senior Labour Advisers, Killen, Douty and Wesley Cook of the Austrian mission were asked to prepare a joint statement on behalf of the Labour staff in Europe. It called for a restatement of ECA objectives combined with effective programmes on employment, prices, consumption and housing. So far, it pointed out, ECA objectives and accomplishments had been stated in terms of trade liberalisation, economic integration, European payments union, all crucial to European recovery but having virtually no direct and positive meaning to European workers. The authors therefore called for a 'ringing declaration' from the higher ECA authorities that full employment was the prime aim of the Marshall Plan. They called for the governments of the participating countries to re-examine their programmes to provide an improvement in real incomes, for the ECA to initiate a complete re-examination of country programmes and for it to make 'direct and forceful representations' to European governments on matters of housing, protection against unemployment and the sharing of increases in production and productivity. Finally they called on the ECA to encourage and initiate broad programmes to safeguard workers against the dislocating effects of trade liberalisation and the productivity drives.[35]

However, the reaction of the ECA's policy planners to proposals for more direct action to safeguard living standards was a foregone conclusion. Richard Bissell had recently rejected Douty's proposal that substantial wage increases be urged for French workers. That would be inflationary, and instead he pinned his faith in competition policy to increase the supply of goods and services and thereby lower consumer prices.[36] Hoffman had already cabled Harriman:

> Full employment therefore cannot be overriding objective but is only a legitimate goal to extent that it does not conflict with measures essential for viability. In particular reiteration of goal of full employment is not sufficient answer to any and all criticism of domestic monetary policy, balance of payments situation, investment programmes and consumption levels [...].[37]

On living standards the Administrator would not budge from the position agreed by participating countries in 1948 that *per capita* consumption should not rise above 1938 levels before the end of the aid programme in 1952. Consequently the joint statement by the Labour staff cut little ice. Harriman told Katz, '[...] it is an unbalanced statement and it would be fatal to hold out hopes which could not be realised.'[38]

The year 1950 was very much a time of truth for the Marshall Plan labour programme. Hitherto the Labour Division had failed to make any real positive impact on national policies for labour–management relations and social programmes in the trouble spots of Europe. However, they had played a significant negative role in helping to divide the labour movement. The politically fragmented labour groups in France and Italy were either too weak to attempt revolution, or too weak to insist that Marshall Aid be made to benefit them directly. It was not the outcome American labour had bargained for, but it had facilitated the achievement of other Marshall Plan goals. A mood of cynicism was now discernible among the Labour staff where formerly there had been enthusiasm. In October 1950 the State Department convened a conference of government officials presided over by Ambassador-at-large Jessup on future American goals in international policy. Once again participants heard the by now ritual statement that labour was the most important target of

American propaganda in support of democratic ideals. Robert Oliver of the Oil Workers' Union (CIO), and recently appointed executive assistant to Golden and Jewell, asked just what was meant by this. Did it mean that labour in overseas countries was to be the target of propaganda designed to make dissatisfied people more compliant, or was the purpose to help them win their grievances, convincing them that the democratic nations had an interest in their welfare that transcended the requirements of military expediency. To William Foster, Hoffman's successor as ECA Administrator and a former steel magnate, he wrote, following the conference:

> By economic support and clever use of propaganda techniques we may be successful in a short term operation of keeping a reactionary government in power merely because it is anti-communistic [...].

But, he concluded, 'You can't establish a propaganda substitute for a decent standard of living and simple justice.'[39]

With the militarisation of Marshall Aid accompanying the outbreak of hostilities in Korea in June 1950 there was a new urgency in the ECA Labour programme. No substantive changes in policy of great value to labour occurred, but there was a more systematic approach to combating communism. Assistance to non-communist trade unions had to exceed what had gone before, and as Shishkin indicated, this was to be 'intimately related to organisational, informational and propaganda activities'. Success depended on the ECA's ability to assemble 'a competent staff able to act as a disciplined and anonymous task force in the work of development of effective personnel and organisation within the European non-communist trade unions'. Apart from maintaining current contacts and liaison with European trade unions the ECA's Labour Division would need to launch what Shishkin termed 'aggressive' and 'confidential' programmes.[40] At the Labour staff conference in May 1950 the French mission chief, David Bruce, had talked of the importance of subversion as an anti-communist weapon. During the war he had been head of OSS activities in Europe and was responsible for espionage. Now he advocated the use of black propaganda techniques, or 'sabotage', as he regarded it, in addition to routine ECA public relations and information work:

I think our tendency is in letting our civilisation speak for itself. It has not worked [...]. I do not think we can simply accept as a fact that truth under all conditions will prevail [...].

In the black [propaganda] field it would be possible to revive some of the things that happened in the war [..]. let me call it 'subversive propaganda' [...]. I address myself only to the question of what you, I and everybody in this room might be doing in regard to it [...].[41]

This was the theme that Shishkin emphasised in summing up at the close of the conference: the need to subvert the enemy, the need to formulate a basic propaganda strategy going far beyond the standard information and publicity programme to all aspects of trade union work.[42]

ECA Labour staff were formally divided into two departments – Advisory and Information – but in practice the two were hard to separate and there was a considerable overlap of functions. Labour Advisers were expected to monitor labour and manpower developments in the participating countries while the Information section engaged in public relations/propaganda work. In fact it was more realistic to view them as complementary parts of an overall intelligence-gathering/opinion-moulding exercise. But the point about this intelligence role was that it was not simply desk work such as embassy staff might be engaged in; it involved active intervention.

A clear indication of the role that Labour staff were expected to play in the Korean War phase of Marshall Aid is apparent from general guidelines drawn up by Glen Atkinson, Labour Adviser to the UK mission in January 1951. The threat of communism was not regarded by the ECA as very serious in Britain, yet Labour staff had to make a special effort to capture hearts and minds in the labour movement. '[...] the largest and most important basic group in any democratic industrial society is the wage-earning group. It is to them above all that our foreign policy and defence aims must be secured. *This cannot be done solely through informational channels'* (emphasis added) Consequently Labour staff were to contact and cultivate members of the Labour government, Labour members of Parliament, members of the party's National Executive Committee, local Labour and trade union leaders and influential rank-and-filers, all with the aim of furthering acceptance of American foreign policy and defence aims. It was their broad responsibility to discover and influence British attitudes (and especially trade union attitudes) on manpower questions relating to the defence effort. More specifically they were required to gather intelligence on possible trouble spots in defence industries and to screen workers and plants where defence contracts had been placed so as to pre-empt the danger of sabotage or politically inspired strikes. In doing this they were to exchange information with the TUC and its affiliated unions on actual or possible industrial disputes. And through personal contacts within the TUC and individual unions they were responsible for imparting 'techniques and strategy for eliminating CP influence in specific trade union and trades council situations with particular emphasis on areas where CP strength is greatest or most strategic with reference to the defence programme'.[43]

What this actually meant can be seen in a small way in the work of William Gausmann, the mission's Labour Information Officer. Gausmann was a very able, energetic official and a perceptive student of British labour affairs. He travelled widely around the country, attending union conferences and Labour Party gatherings, lecturing at labour movement weekend and summer schools, and in the process became one of the best informed observers of the labour scene. He was familiar with the personalities and their politics and his reports on internal developments in particular unions or sections of the movement tended to be highly detailed compilations of valuable intelligence.

Under instructions to intervene to secure American defence interests, Gausmann became directly involved in anti-communist campaigns as the Marshall Plan moved into its militaristic phase. In May 1950, for example, he began discussions with a section of the leadership of the Clerical and Allied Workers' Union on how to eliminate communists from the union, a campaign that was to prove successful. He cultivated the leadership of the Birmingham Labour Party, whose journal, *The Town Crier*, closely supported Atlanticism and American foreign policy objectives in general. He took the initiative in convening a group in South Wales which was brought together to launch a Labour-oriented newspaper, *The Democrat*, so providing a challenge to the Communist Party in this, one of their strongholds. His department worked closely with the TUC, gaining privileged access to sensitive information and being able to report to Washington, for example, on the TUC's plans to purge communists from the London Trades Council before the event. Gausmann briefed Labour leaders attending a communist-backed peace conference organised by the Scottish TUC. He liaised with the international trade secretariats in London, advised the International Transport Workers' Federation on their public relations and, on their behalf, hired a specialist to work in their information section.[44] As an ECA official he had close contacts in the Foreign Office and he assisted with the publicity for and distribution of a collection of anti-communist writings, *The Curtain Falls*, edited by Denis Healey and published by Ampersand, an imprint established and subsidised by the Foreign Office's secret Information Research Department, which specialised in grey and black propaganda.[45]

From the outset he had good contacts with people in the labour movement grouped around the magazine *Socialist Commentary*, whose editor, Allan Flanders, he had met at Oxford just after the war. Gausmann worked unofficially on *Socialist Commentary*, acted as American correspondent and sometimes wrote editorials.[46] He also arranged for the ECA to subsidise the distribution in Britain and America of a pamphlet collection of its articles on trade unionism. Drawn to the magazine's particular brand of Fabianism, he became a founder member of its offshoot, the Socialist Union, which served as a think-tank for the emerging Gaitskellite wing of the Labour Party, and even acted as chairman of a Socialist Union working party on Labour Party democracy – despite the fact that Labour Party membership was supposed to be a condition of belonging to the Union.[47] Interestingly, this partisan political activity in Britain brought him into conflict with the embassy's labour attaché, Joseph Godson, whose own direct involvement in internal Labour Party affairs even extended to participation in secret caucus meetings of Gaitskell's supporters during the plotting to expel Aneurin Bevan from the party in 1955.[48] There was evident rivalry between the two wings of the American labour movement for the ear of Labour's rising leader – Gausmann's contacts were with the CIO and especially the Reuther group; Godson was an ILGWU protege of Dubinsky. And it was through these channels that Gaitskell was invited by Dubinsky to the United States in 1956 to address the Jewish Labour Committee and for which he received an inflated expenses cheque of $3,000 which helped him to underwrite the costs of *Forward*, the struggling journal newly acquired by the Gaitskellites.[49]

Gausmann's record demonstrates the opportunities that existed for energetic, capable ECA Labour staff to operate with some effect on an individual basis. But on a programmatic level the Labour Division had great difficulty in making an impact. From 1950–51 the ECA's main hope of remodelling the European labour movement lay in its productivity campaign, which was first developed in Britain and subsequently exported to the Continent. We must now turn to this important aspect of the programme.

CHAPTER 9

Productivity and the Marshall Plan: the Anglo-American Council on Productivity

The true revolutionary principle is the idea of mass production. Nothing ever recorded in the history of man equals, in speed, universality and impact, the transformation this principle has wrought in the foundations of society. [Peter Drucker, *The New Society*, 1950]

At home, belief in the American way of life becomes more fanatical with every Communist attack; abroad, countless ECA officials, businessmen, and visiting trade unionists preach the doctrine of mass production for mass markets and a rising standard of life – essentially, in American eyes, a capitalist ideology. [...] Trade unions are at one with business men in believing that mass-production private capitalism offers the world's best answer to poverty and unrest – and believing too, that it is a progressive and revolutionary system compared with many of the backward class-ridden regimes they find in Europe and elsewhere. [C.A.R. Crosland, 'Transition from capitalism', in *New Fabian Essays*, 1952]

With the Marshall Plan nearly half over by 1950, and lasting European recovery still nowhere in sight, various policies were pressed into service by the ECA in an attempt to find a permanent solution. In the course of 1949 it came to the view that Marshall Aid would succeed only if the European countries' balance of payments problem could be solved. This would require the creation of new institutional arrangements and relationships, with bilateralism replaced by a free-trade area.[1] It was in this context that American pressure for the devaluation of sterling built up. Devaluation of the pound was meant to facilitate a general revaluation of European currencies, making them freely convertible and thereby encouraging free trade and profitable investment.[2] To give the new trading and currency relationships the necessary institutional support, the ECA pressed for the establishment of the European Payments Union (EPU) in 1950. The EPU was also the product of a parallel thrust in

ECA policy – the intensified campaign for European integration. By 1949 there were doubts within the ECA as to whether the recovery of autonomous national economies alone would suffice.[3] The Americans now began to press European governments to adopt measures of economic integration, with the ultimate aim of creating a continental economy. The new note was sounded by Hoffman in October 1949, when he flew to Paris to address the OEEC Council, and in a keynote speech told them in no uncertain terms that structural changes in the European economy would have to be made in order to hold the gains already achieved. The ECA, he declared, wanted to see evidence of purposeful moves towards integration. There was strong American support for some form of political union, though again, to avoid the appearance of open interventionism, a State Department document advised a more cautious approach, with emphasis on economic rather than political integration.[4] Two years later that element of caution would be discarded, the Mutual Security Act clearly stipulating that one aim of the aid programme was to encourage 'economic unification and political federation'.

In the meantime the United States was in need of a more immediate solution to its own and Europe's economic problems as the end date of Marshall Aid began to loom. In February 1950 Secretary of State Dean Acheson advised President Truman that America would soon have to take some critical decisions over foreign economic policy. 'It is expected that unless vigorous steps are taken, the reduction and eventual termination of extraordinary foreign assistance in accordance with present plans will create economic problems at home and abroad of increasing severity.'[5] The main option was to regenerate the Western economies through a programme of rearmament. As *Business Week* commented, 'Doubt about future unemployment favours the military [...]. A defence ceiling was set two years ago, when the economic danger was inflation. Now it's deflation that is the economic worry.'[6] Truman duly appointed the Grey Committee in March 1950 to review the needs of the American economy and asked them to consider, in particular, policies for defence planning and their economic implications. In this way the militarisation of Marshall Aid was already a matter of serious consideration before the outbreak of the Korean War in June 1950 made it an inevitability. Thereafter the Marshall Plan was transformed into an economic support programme for European rearmament. It became a fundamental axiom of American economic planners that the first requirement of a national economy was that it should provide an effective economic base for military defence against the Soviet Bloc.[7] It was in this, the most interventionist phase of Marshall Aid that the campaign for increased productivity became the focal point and main hope of the entire programme. Throughout Europe the pressure was on to increase industrial productivity, particularly in arms-related industries. And the model that was held up for other countries to copy was the extensive British productivity programme that had been in operation since 1948. This, the most visible aspect of the ERP in Britain, was regarded by the ECA as something of a success.

British governments had been exhorting workers to higher levels of production since the war years. After the war, as the full extent of the country's economic difficulties became clear, the Labour government called on the trade union movement to throw its weight behind a succession of production drives. For their part the unions responded with vigour. Initially increased physical output was what mattered, but as industrial recovery gradually took shape the focus of attention began to shift to the concept of productivity – the more economical production of output. However, it was not until the Marshall years that the importance of productivity really began to register in the public consciousness, and the agency most responsible for that was the Anglo-American Council on Productivity (AACP), which had been spawned by the Aid programme.

The Anglo-American Council on Productivity

The initiative for creating the AACP came jointly from the Chancellor of the Exchequer, Sir Stafford Cripps, and ECA Administrator Hoffman in July 1948. Irritated by a stream of adverse reports on British industrial practices by American businessmen returning from visits to Britain, criticism which could have jeopardised the flow of Marshall Aid, Cripps secured agreement within the government's tripartite National Production Advisory Council for Industry (NPACI) that such transatlantic visits be officially sponsored in future so that American businessmen would see the real situation in Britain and not a partial and distorted one. Cripps approached Hoffman and they agreed to set up a joint British-American council on productivity.[8]

There was considerable British criticism of this agreement from the outset. Press comment was unfavourable, and British trade union leaders who first heard about the council during the second ERP – TUAC conference were profoundly irritated. The decision had been taken without consulting them and they were irked by the implication that British industry needed the advice of the Americans to increase production.[9]

The reception among union members generally was no more enthusiastic, and a number of communist-controlled trades councils wrote to the TUC to denounce its participation in a campaign to further the use of degrading American methods of scientific management and speed-up techniques.[10]

Their understanding of what the AACP would be doing was more accurate than the line put forward by Cripps when he announced the council's creation. Almost from the outset his idea of an information programme aimed at correcting American misconceptions of British industry was transformed into a quite different scheme under which Britons would learn about productivity American-style.[11] The AACP was later to regard its work as 'one of the largest experiments in adult education ever attempted'. However, it is a matter of debate whether its main impetus really was in generating an informed discussion of the factors involved in productivity growth or towards propaganda support of the 'American way of life'. Reviewing the programme, Hoffman remarked, 'Even more important than what Europeans learn about lathes and ploughs is what they learn about America. [...] They found out for themselves [...] the "American Way" [...].'[12] With a budget of close to £1 million, two-thirds of it provided by the American government, the AACP operated from August 1948 to June 1952.[13] Its main activity was to sponsor study visits to the USA and to publish vast quantities of infor-mational literature arising from them. Its work provided much of the raw material of the intense propaganda campaign waged by the Marshall Plan's own generously funded Information Division in London.

The AACP consisted of twenty people, twelve British and eight

American, who met in joint session roughly once a year. Both national sections were made up of representatives from business and labour, the British side being drawn from the TUC, the Federation of British Industries (FBI) and the British Employers' Confederation (BEC). The TUC's representatives, Arthur Deakin, Tom Williamson, Will Lawther, Lincoln Evans, Jack Tanner and Andrew Naesmith, were the most senior and most powerful members of the General Council. For the Americans Philip Reed of General Electric and Victor Reuther of the UAW acted as co-chairman. The British side of the council met regularly to supervise an ongoing programme of activities administered centrally by a small secretariat. The AACP was formally independent of both the American and the British governments, but its funding through Marshall Aid dollars and sterling counterpart funds necessitated close liaison with government departments.

The TUC leaders soon overcame their initial hostility to the AACP. Early on they agreed terms of reference with the employers and the ECA mission in London under which industrial relations practices would be outside the council's purview. And at the first full session of the council they joined forces with the BEC and FBI representatives in a public stand against any investigation of restrictive labour or trade practices. In essence they denied that there was a problem of overmanning or price-fixing, pointing out that many such practices had been abandoned in the war, and arguing that where they still existed they were beneficial to the community. Both sides of British industry were telling the Americans that these arrangements were a domestic matter, unsuitable for joint British-US consideration. Most of the American members of the council were unhappy with this stand. Philip Reed made clear his own view that competition was an important factor and he reserved the right of his American colleagues to record in any subsequent report 'that we in America do feel that the tool of competition, the fact of competition, has a very much greater influence on productivity than you apparently feel here'.[14] In private the TUC leaders were much closer to the American position than they dared admit publicly. They were all really agreed on the need to eliminate restrictions on the more 'scientific' use of manpower, machines and raw materials. The problem was how to get the rank and file to see things that way.[15] And within months the TUC was engaged in a joint investigation of restrictive practices with the BEC.

The first joint session of the AACP in October–November 1948 had ended with agreement to pursue certain lines of inquiry. Sub-committees would be set up to investigate (a) the degree of mechanisation in various industries on both sides of the Atlantic, (b) different levels of productivity in comparable industries, (c) methods of educating workers and managers in efficient practices. In addition a committee to promote transatlantic visits was established. For some time there were few tangible results. The detailed analysis of productivity performance proved more difficult than some had assumed. By February 1949 the Economist Intelligence Unit was pouring cold water on much of the work of the AACP:

> The project started with rather facile assumptions, based on some highly publicised productivity studies which had already appeared. Only after the American members of the Council came face to face with the facts of British production did they appreciate how complex are the causes of differences in output.

The one beneficial result, according to the Intelligence Unit, was that the Americans on the council could now disabuse their countrymen of such widespread myths as that Britain's difficulties were due largely to sloth.[16] The EIU was wrong on that count. In the early days of the AACP the American Ambassador, Lew Douglas, had told Secretary of State Marshall, 'the only answer to Britain's difficulties is to work harder and, I fear, for less'.[17] In subsequent years popular discussion of productivity in British industry rarely rose much above that level. During the 1950s British employers would join the chorus and, with considerable success, lay the charge of sloth at the door of organised labour.

When the council met in joint session for the second time in Washington in March 1949 a report from its mechanisation sub-committee revealed that American industry had between two and three times more electrical power per worker than British industry. The difference in the supply of power per head between the two countries had not narrowed since the war, and Britain still had a huge backlog to be made good from the pre-war years of inadequate investment. The paper concluded, 'While there are other factors which affect productivity, there is no single limitation so restricting as a shortage of power and capital equipment.' Kilowatt-hour consumption of electricity per head corresponded almost exactly with the relative standard of living in different countries.[18] Very much the same conclusion was expressed by the *Daily Telegraph* after the AACP had been in existence for a year:

> The basic lesson of American industrial technique is simply this: that greater productivity per man hour results from a higher degree of mechanisation, i.e. from more expensive capital equipment.[19]

The AACP's attempt to compare the levels of mechanisation in more detail and to equate the relationship between this and levels of productivity was abortive. It was impossible to assemble data from which comparisons between British and American firms or industries could be made. In 1950 the AACP's mechanisation sub-committee was therefore disbanded.

Meanwhile, in its capacity as an agency of propaganda, the council's most productive role was in arranging a programme of visits to the United States. In all, 138 teams of managers, workers and specialists – over 900 people in total – travelled to America on such trips. Their various reports of findings received considerable media attention – during 1950 and 1951 a new report was issued every week or so – and the sales of these totalled over 600,000 copies.[20] Beyond this there was extensive follow-up activity. For example, within a few months of the Cotton Spinning team's return, its members had attended a total of twenty-nine meetings involving 3,000 leaders of the industry. A popularised version of their report had been issued, with 50,000 copies distributed – one for every other worker in the industry. The result of such concerted efforts was that public attention was constantly drawn to the subject of productivity. It was the general impact of the reports as a whole rather than the specific recommendations of particular teams that was most important in generating productivity consciousness. In a passage whose hyperbole captures the fanaticism with which the productivity crusade was waged, the economist Graham Hutton was later to refer to the AACP reports as 'a set of documents the like of which, on such a scale and of such practical value, has never been seen in the history of international and cultural borrowing'.[21]

The American visits, lasting about four to six weeks, were made by teams consisting of up to a dozen members, drawn equally from management, technical grades and shop-floor workers. Problems of travel and distance in the United States meant that frequently the visitors were restricted to the north-east corner of the country. Consequently they tended to see only the more advanced industrial areas, and, as was subsequently pointed out by many critics, this influenced the kind of comparisons that the teams were able to draw. Confinement to this part of the United States also ensured that the visitors did not see much of the large sections of the country where industry was untouched by unionisation. Indeed, there were cases where non-union American firms refused the AACP's request to play host to a visit by a team that included trade unionists. Clearly those sections of industry studied by the British visitors were not wholly representative of the American economy.

Although the visit programme was ostensibly a joint union–management venture it is quite apparent that management personnel dominated the teams. Each party had its own chairman and secretary, and in almost every team these positions were filled by management spokesmen. Not only did managers fill the key positions, it was often the employers' side that effectively decided the composition of the party. Sometimes the most the union could hope for was to be allowed to approve the names of shop-floor workers who had already been selected by the employers to make the trip. Occasionally the union discovered the identity of the shop-floor members only on the team's return.[22] When the Foundry Workers' Union protested to the employers' association about the composition of the Steel Foundry team and put forward their own shop-floor nominees the employers rejected them, arguing that, since they and not the unions were bearing some of the cost of the trip, the selection of personnel should be up to the employers.[23] In another case a team in the USA were questioned by American union officials about union conditions in their industry and were embarrassed to discover that no one in the party was competent to answer.[24]

The result was that the management side of the teams was often far more representative of powerful employer and managerial bodies than were the worker members representative of the labour movement. For example, the Building team report noted that the shop-floor members had not been chosen by virtue of any official position they held, simply on the grounds that they represented the 'average worker'. By contrast, the balance of the team included the President and Secretary of the National Federation of Building Trades Employers, who acted as team leader and secretary respectively, the President of the Royal Institute of British Architects and various leaders of other building employers' associations. A further restrictive influence on the shop-floor side of the teams stemmed from American government insistence on strict security checks on all visitors. No one believed to have any association with communism could be admitted to the USA. Various shop-floor nominees were vetoed on these grounds, affecting teams such as those from furniture manufacturing, ironfounding and vehicle building.[25] An alleged strength of the reports in general – indeed, one of their most vaunted features – was the fact that they were all unanimous, with very few dissenting views recorded. Given the composition and method of selecting the teams, that is hardly surprising. But what did the reports contain?

The focus of the industrial team reports

They ranged widely over aspects of American industrial life, dealing with technical, commercial and human factors, managerial techniques, labour–management relations and the broad field of American cultural characteristics. The most frequently cited technical factor in high American productivity was the extensive use of mechanisation. Features of American industry that earned praise throughout the reports included: production planning and control; economic handling of materials; good layout of work places, modern methods of costing, and use of work study. But although it was in their discussion of technical matters that the teams were best informed, it was on vaguer psychological elements that they tended to place their greatest emphasis – invoking factors such as the appreciation by workpeople of the need for higher productivity; the progressive attitude of management, and the spirit of competition in order to explain American productive superiority.

As exercises in propaganda the message of the team reports was clearly directed more at labour than management. The teams formed a highly favourable view of American management with its great professionalism but, curiously, then devoted more attention in their reports to the role of trade unions in raising productivity. Throughout, the reports tended to exaggerate the extent to which American unions employed their own industrial engineers and efficiency experts and to misconstrue the purpose for which they sought to avail themselves of such expertise. More generally the reports failed to analyse in any depth the background to the American unions' alleged productivity consciousness. The 'negative incentives' to greater effort, such as the higher level of unemployment in the United States and the anti-union thrust of the Taft-Hartley Act, were rarely mentioned, and then in a non-critical manner. The Building team report noted with apparent approval that a pool of unemployed workers was always present, the effect being that the American building worker 'has never acquired the habit of doing less than he is capable of doing'.[26] Similarly the Letterpress Printing report complained that full employment had reduced insecurity among British workers and that more competitive conditions in the labour market would inject greater efficiency into the industry.[27]

The reports frequently failed to understand the causal relationship between the high wages and standard of living in America and the high level of productivity. Occasionally there was a recognition that the living standard was both cause and effect of high productivity.[28] More commonly the line taken was that high wages for British workers had first to be earned by higher productivity. Commenting on this, one writer noted how such strictures blended perfectly with the prevailing policy of the British government, which was to regard increased productivity as the responsibility of the workers:

> It could as easily have been an extract from the Chancellor's brief or the speech of a loyal TUC member. The standard of living although described as an incentive and a reward is, for British purposes, only a reward. Surely this is less than logical?[29]

The reports missed the point that it was the historically high cost of labour in the United States that had given rise to the high degree of mechanisation. The relationship of wage costs to capital costs was the exact opposite in Britain.

In criticising restrictive practices in Britain the reports were often less forthcoming about similar practices in the United States. There was scarcely any reference to restrictive labour practices among American workers, depite the fact that in many industries they were common. At the very first meeting of the AACP Victor Reuther had pointed out that the American press berated US labour for their alleged restrictive practices in much the same way as the British press criticised the unions. In industries such as printing union restrictions were well documented, yet the Letterpress Printing report spoke of 'the comparative lack of restrictive practices in the United States'.[30] Commenting on this, the General Secretary of the London Society of Compositors observed that American trade unionists were becoming alarmed at the content of some of the productivity reports, which recommended work methods that American employees themselves were trying to resist.[31]

The general impression conveyed by the reports was of a vital United States economy benefiting enormously from the influence of vigorous competition, contrasting sharply with British industry, which was stagnating under cartel arrangements and weighed down by state controls. Yet this happy picture of an archetypal, free enterprise economy flew in the face of many of the facts of American industrial life. The Steel Foundry team reported, 'Throughout American industry competition is a governing factor [...] within the steel foundry geographical groups, competition is intense for the business in the district,'[32] apparently unaware that in 1947 the US Federal Trade Commission had charged the American Iron and Steel Institute with price-fixing and conspiring to kill competition. Among the corporations named were Bethlehem Steel and United States Steel. Likewise the competitiveness of the American construction industry as recorded by the Building team was sharply at odds with other evidence, which showed that no fewer than 25 per cent of all cases dealt with by the Department of Justice's Anti-trust Division concerned the building industry.[33] In 1950 the Opinion Research Corporation reported that over 60 per cent of industrial workers in America believed that monopoly or oligopoly, not free competition, was the predominant condition in most industries.[34] But despite the reality of oligopolistic business practices and increasing economic management by government in the United States, it tended to be assumed in the reports that more competition and less government restriction would create for Britain similar conditions for the optimum utilisation of resources. Several AACP team reports took the opportunity to express thinly veiled political attacks on the Labour government. The Grey Ironfounding report, for example, complained that company taxes and dividend limitation 'deprives management of a powerful and traditional incentive',[35] while maintaining that its line of argument was above politics: 'In our present plight, productivity must override welfare, traditions and ideologies.'[36]

As always, there were conflicting impressions of the relative effort put in by equivalent workers in the United States and Britain. That lack of hard work was Britain's real problem was widely believed by American observers. The US Embassy in London had reported to the ECA's European headquarters:

> Even at this late date many union leaders still do not advocate or know how to devise union–management co-operation arrangements to increase production and productivity and bring down costs without cutting wages. But this would involve such measures as working longer hours and overtime, eliminating unnecessary labour, changing jobs, rationalising wage systems, removing restrictive practices, refusing to support individual workers who shirk on the job, dealing with absenteeism etc. [...] there is still vast room for improvements.[37]

On the other hand, the point was frequently made, especially when trying to sell the virtues of scientific management, that Americans worked no harder than their British counterparts: they simply worked more effectively as a result of method study, the use of power tools and better servicing of skilled labour.[38] Many AACP reports supported this view, but in British union circles there was much scepticism over what seemed to be a deliberate sugaring of the pill. The trouble was that the reports themselves frequently depicted a much more exacting work regime than employees in Britain were accustomed to. For example, the Steel Foundry report described the condition of repetition workers who 'threw themselves into extremely arduous work [...] with complete abandon and disclaim of exhaustion [...] then [on the whistle] they lay down where they worked and fell fast asleep'. The Building report quoted Alistair Cooke on work rhythms in

American construction: 'they haul and hammer and drill and bulldoze with fearful zest. If they work this way they will keep their job. If they don't, they won't. That is the simple, brutal rule of life in America in prosperous times.'[39] Similarly other reports described the efforts put in by American workers in a way that seemed to belie the suggestions that work in that country required no greater effort.

The corollary to this more intense rhythm of work was often an insufficient regard for safety precautions, the onus of which was placed on the operative. By and large the reports failed to emphasise the connection between the intensity of work, the safety hazards and the general trade-off of the welfare of workers. Little if any consideration was given to whether or not workers were content to sacrifice the personal welfare that continuous production, the practice of eating meals at the machine and the absence of safety equipment implied. The tendency was simply to report these conditions as facts.

Overall, according to the reports, it was not so much the technical superiority of American industry or the unique attributes of its continental economy, richly endowed with natural resources, that gave the United States its decisive advantage in productivity: rather it was the result of cultural factors that could be summed up in terms of the 'American way of life'. Americans were found to be 'production-minded' and the attitude derived from a 'climate of productivity'. But this was hard to define and was simply expressed as an intangible. The debate over productivity and its causes was conducted against the background of recurrent economic crisis where it was expedient to find quick solutions. Pending the arrival of the long-term benefits of new investment – the prospect of which in Britain often receded into the distant future – the typical solution involved greater effort by the work force and changes in methods and processes which frequently entailed less agreeable working conditions.[40] Over time a change in attitude on the part of workers came to be represented not merely as a necessary basis of extra effort now but a precondition of capital investment programmes.

It was common to invoke intangible factors in explaining America's relative industrial success. As a Ministry of Labour paper on the team reports noted:

for our purpose it is the psychological factor which most commands attention. Almost without exception, the reports dwell on what is variously called the 'American Way of Life', the 'will to work', the 'stimulating environment', the American 'attitude of mind', the 'climate of opinion' and the 'energising and infective atmosphere'.[41]

In a report following a visit to Britain in autumn 1949 William Kimble, field director of the AACP, emphasised that 'intangible and psychological influences may be even more important than the many tangible contributions in technique and methods'.[42] The theme echoed continuously throughout the AACP documents. In a 1950 submission to the ECA, the British section of the AACP wrote:

> The most important results of the Team visits are [...] intangible, and are hardly capable of measurement except on a long term basis. They derive from the co-operation in a common enterprise of Management and Labour [...]. High productivity results largely from an attitude of mind on the part of both Management and Labour [...].[43]

The tendency for the AACP to explain productivity performance in these terms continued until the end. In one revealing passage of its final report the document conceded that it was 'quite clear that the major improvements in producitivity cannot be achieved without more capital investment' but went on to affirm: 'we believe that the main value of our experiment may prove to be psychological and lie in the improvement to the climate of opinion about productivity'.[44]

In its reports to the ECA the AACP exuded enthusiasm for the programme of visits and the lessons to be learned across the Atlantic. So impressed were the authors with the American system that they wrote of her industrial relations thus:

> [...] the Teams have observed [...] the good understanding that exists between management and workman. [...] The sense of co-operation in a joint enterprise is [...] present in British industry [...] but its different setting in America has indicated possibilities and potentialities that have, through team reports, brought something new to the conception of industrial relations.[45]

It is hard to discern here any indication that only the previous year US businessmen themselves had blamed poor American industrial relations for an estimated 20 per cent shortfall in productivity achievement, or that the average time lost per worker through disputes in the United States in 1949 was 7·67 hours, compared with 0·75 hours in Britain.[46] Warts and blemishes in the American industrial relations system were often hastily skipped over or ignored. Thus the Cotton Spinning report had described American industrial relations as 'generally good' although for over fifteen years the unions in that industry had been engaged in a bitter and frequently bloody struggle to organise the work force. All in all, the AACP visit programme seemed determined to present American industry in the best possible light.

In the course of all this the TUC were caught up in a dual role which necessitated a delicate balancing act. As members of the AACP, senior members of the TUC General Council were keen to generate among trade unionists a greater consciousness of productivity and its causes. Though confident that much of the technical detail in the team reports was valuable, they were anxious not to provoke a membership revolt within the unions over the implications of the reports' findings, and they were clearly uneasy about many of the crude generalisations in these documents. Their approach was not to attack publicly those reports whose contents went against union thinking but rather to shift the focus to the concrete factors central to increased productivity and to restrain the worst excesses of AACP propaganda.

Among TUC affiliates there was much union criticism of the reports, and not only in unions under communist leadership such as the Foundry Workers, who made clear their total rejection of the AACP programme. In situations where unions adopted a strong public stand against the report on their industry – as with the building, printing, foundry and hosiery unions – the pattern was for the TUC General Secretary, Vincent Tewson, to meet the union leader personally and to urge the need for a more restrained position.[47] Adverse publicity for the programme of visits made the AACP very nervous. Following the criticism received from the hosiery workers, the secretary to the British side of the AACP wrote to Vincent Tewson asking him to intervene for the sake of the continuing success of the programme: 'As you know, we are being pressed very strongly by ECA [...] a case like this, of which ECA are aware, is very unfortunate.'[48] In a similar vein the AACP secretary approached Tewson regarding the possibility of conflict over the Brassfounders' report: 'I need hardly say that the last thing we would wish to promote is any sort of controversy over the report, as this might only have the effect of making management less willing to follow it up.'[49]

The TUC's membership of AACP and its restraint in criticising some of the less acceptable reports handed the employers a huge propaganda advantage. A whole series of crude assertions and ill thought out nostrums about productivity had been repeated over and over again and had gained still further publicity as the subject of extensive press coverage. However, TUC reservations were often confined to internal memoranda. Reviewing the contribution of AACP teams as the work of the Productivity Council drew to an end, the head of the TUC's Production Department, Edwin Fletcher, conceded that the technical material in the reports was first-class, but he expressed strong reservations about their generalisations on social and economic issues:

> The fact remains [...] that really substantial gains in productivity can only be achieved by greater mechanisation, powered tools and equipment and changes in factory layout and production organisation and flow processes – all of which are associated with national economic factors.[50]

To attempt to change the 'climate of opinion' was, he thought, the least practical of approaches to productivity. Yet this had been a major emphasis of the AACP and indeed of the whole Marshall Plan programme in Britain and the rest of Europe.

As a final project before being wound up, the AACP commissioned the economist Graham Hutton to write a popular book on productivity, and as a member of the council's vetting committee Fletcher found himself having to insist on extensive revisions of a text replete with simplistic, psycho-sociological notions and political prejudice. Fletcher charged Hutton with treating the central factor superficially – the USA's historically higher rate of capital accumulation. He complained about the repeated and unproved assertion that the high level of taxation in Britain was a major handicap. It seemed to him that the book also exaggerated British lethargy and then explained it in terms of psychological sickness. Hutton's treatment of restrictive practices, Fletcher argued, was partial and incomplete: such practices were criticised without being clearly defined. No analysis of the reasons for their existence was attempted nor any clear indication given of how they might be abandoned or other safeguards provided. The inference was that they originated in a black past when management was exploitive, but this was contrasted with a white present in which management was now perfectly trustworthy, so that the practices were no longer necessary.[51] The TUC demanded extensive changes in Hutton's draft before the text was approved for publication, and even then they recognised that the book, *We too can Prosper*, was a highly 'controversial document'.[52]

The TUC productivity team

The TUC's main positive contribution to this phase of the productivity drive took the form of a special study team of trade union officials which visited the United States from October to December 1949. The ECA's London mission had first proposed the sending of a TUC team in January, at the time of the break-up of the WFTU, but the idea was promptly turned down. There was still too much opposition to productivity initiatives in the General Council.[53] However, in the course of the year, with constant overtures from ECA Labour staff, and with the first industry teams filing their sometimes contentious reports, the case for addressing the productivity question from a strictly trade union standpoint increased. To maintain their independence the TUC team did not travel under AACP auspices, but the ECA still paid the dollar cost of the trip and waived any need for Britain to pay counterpart in respect of it.

There were initial difficulties in choosing a team acceptable to the Americans. The TUC filtered out two nominees thought to be politically unacceptable, one because of his membership of the Communist Party and another deemed to be a fellow-traveller. A third proposed member was a former communist and was refused a visa by the US embassy.[54] In the end the party comprised ten middle-ranking union officials. The American objective was to win over a younger generation of future leaders to the cause of productivity:

> Our project by exposing a rising leadership in the key unions to the best American practices in this regard will contribute importantly to the metamorphosis of thought and attitude.[55]

Among the party were men who would subsequently rise to the highest office in their unions and become influential members of the TUC General Council: George Doughty of the Draughtsmen, George Brinham of the Woodworkers and Louis Wright of the Cotton Weavers. The party was led by Ernest Jones, President of the Yorkshire Miners. Close American involvement in the project did not stop at the vetting of the team and the financing of the visit. An ECA labour economist, Filmer Paradise, from the London mission, chaperoned the party throughout the tour. Later he and the ECA Labour Information specialist William Gausmann arranged much of the extensive publicity that surrounded the release of the team's report. But, more important, he and Gausmann both had a hand in writing the report.

The TUC party's terms of reference required it to examine American union attitudes to scientific management. Behind this lay pressure to assess what positive contribution unions could make to productivity growth. There was a widely held impression in British government and union circles that in America trade unions were very active in this field. AACP team reports had suggested that a large segment of the American labour movement was vigorously co-operating in production through its own industrial engineers, even to the extent of reorganising plants through an offer of assistance by its technical staff.[56] It was, therefore, the TUC team's job to discover what could be borrowed from American practice. The bulk of the team's report consisted of a detailed description of the structure and functioning of American unions together with a close examination of the responses of the leading unions to the adoption by employers of modern managerial techniques. In this respect it was sober, balanced and a useful corrective to the distortions contained in other reports of the period emanating from the United States. With one exception, the ILGWU, the TUC party found little evidence among American unions of any positive commitment to scientific management. The predominant attitude to this development among the leading unions ranged from outright hostility to passive but reluctant acceptance. Lewis Wright of the Weavers' Union concluded that American union interest in time study was 'purely defensive':

I think it is not a question of whether US labour unions accept the steps and changes necessary to increase productivity. It seems to me [...] that they are not in so strong a position to oppose the introduction of such methods. There is ample evidence [that] they are not, so far as I can see, accepted readily. If they could be opposed, in most instances they would be [...].[57]

The one American union that did not conform strictly to this pattern was the ILGWU, the organisation best known for having a production engineering department. Many of its members were pieceworkers in small clothing shops in a fiercely competitive market. The union had originally agreed to the use of time study as a means of stopping the piecework rate-cutting that was endemic in the industry. Having built up an expertise in work study for defensive purposes, the union later developed the practice of offering advice on production techniques to employers who claimed to be unable to pay union wage rates. Firms refusing the offer of union help faced the prospect of industrial action to secure adequate wages, while those that accepted the offer stood a chance of improving their competitive position and so being able to afford decent rates. The ILGWU approach was therefore merely a variation on the standard American union practice of pressing for high wages regardless. Increases in labour costs as a result of the high-wage policy in this and other industries had traditionally compelled American employers to substitute capital for labour, thus securing high levels of productivity. In most industries the unions had little direct concern for productivity – growth came about as an indirect result of their aggressive wage bargaining strategy. Naturally aggressive management policies then ensured productive efficiency. In the unique circumstances of the garment industry the union was prepared to share its production expertise with employers, but only in the interests of securing decent wages, not as a cushion for marginal operators.

On the surface there was little the TUC could borrow from American experience. The basic components – aggressive wage bargaining by unions and thrusting entrepreneurship by employers – were lacking in Britain. TUC policies of wage restraint and a cartel mentality among employers made for a completely different situation, and the TUC were not inclined to change this by challenging the government policy of wage restraint. What the team had learned exploded the myth that American unions were vigorously co-operating in production matters. However, their report was not the negative document that such a discovery seemed to warrant. The climate of the times demanded a positive report, and so by clever argument the report's recommendations re-worked American union practice into a formula that purported to be relevant to the British trade union movement under a Labour government.

According to TUC thinking, Britain's productivity problem arose from poor management: employers could not be relied upon to introduce the measures necessary to increase efficiency. Organised labour, on the other hand, was a responsible body, and as guarantor of the nation's economic well-being it would have to take the initiative in pressing for the efficiency measures ignored by employers.[58] Hence the basic recommendation of the TUC report was that unions should co-operate in the application of scientific management. More specifically they should 'seek to increase productive efficiency through greater use of mechanical aids and application of time and motion study'. Unions were urged to set up their own production engineering departments and, following the practice of the ILGWU, 'be prepared to give technical advice and assistance to firms whose profit margins are falling to the extent of threatening both wage levels and employment security'.[59] The proposals were advanced in terms of a very limited concept of industrial democracy concerned primarily with efficiency:

> The movement towards industrial democracy will be accelerated when unions strengthen the links between themselves and their members on the job by providing the technical assistance which members need to participate fully in promoting industrial efficiency and good relations with management.[60]

Only by the report putting the best possible gloss on ILGWU practice, by inferring for the other American unions studied an emphasis different from that which they themselves proclaimed, and through some highly imaginative speculation as to future trends in American labour–management relations, was American practice made to seem relevant to Britain. In summing up ILGWU practice the report softened the union's hard-nosed approach to wage bargaining and presented labour–management relations in truly florid terms:

The union [...] seeks to co-operate as fully as possible with employers, so that the best interests of all are served.

By participating in management and helping to stabilise the industry's economy, the operative is able to feel himself a part of an industrial community [...].[61]

As the head of the ILGWU Production Department, William Gomberg, recorded following an ECA-sponsored visit to Britain to help publicise the report, 'Despite the accuracy of the description, it was still strange to find oddly distorted views of what American trade unionists actually were doing [...].' Consequently, in his talks with British trade unionists, he had to emphasise that his union's strategy was not to allow marginal producers to pay a low wage and remain in business, but to force such employers to increase efficiency and pay decent wages under the threat of being driven out of business.[62]

But if the ILGWU was the only American union following this particular strategy how did the TUC arrive at the view that it was a model destined to be adopted by US unions generally?

Here the authors of the report made an imaginative leap and conjured up a scenario designed to appeal to a British trade union readership. The report speculated that the American unions would gradually become more powerful relative to management, that managerial aggressiveness in the pursuit of efficiency would decline and that in consequence the unions would become more responsible in terms of the needs of the national economy:

In thus widening their activities the possibility exists that they [the unions] will assume responsibility not unlike that of the British trade union movement in the British economy. The more successful American unions become in influencing their Government to direct or guide the national economy to counteract inflationary tendencies and stabilise the purchasing power of wage earners, the more they would tend to remove the pressure on management to be aggressive and progressive. In such circumstances, unions might have to rely on forces other than competition to maintain increasing productivity.

In these conditions, an environment not unlike that in Britain, American union interest in scientific management techniques would bear fruit:

> We believe that by employing production engineers, setting up
> management engineering departments, gaining valuable experience
> in time study and other 'scientific management' techniques [..]
> a number of unions have already gone some considerable way
> towards acquiring the facilities for [...] bringing effective pressure
> to bear on management.[63]

By deft footwork the report had managed to argue the case
for trade union adoption of scientific management techniques
as an all-purpose kit, with relevance to any pattern of labour–
management relations that might emerge:

> Where managements are progressive and seeking to use 'scientific
> management' techniques in a reasonable manner to step up produc-
> tion, unions should be prepared to co-operate. If managements
> try to be aggressive the need for effective trade union action is
> accentuated – not to the point of resisting new developments
> but to see that abuses are eliminated and that inaccuracies of
> 'scientific management' are not exploited at the expense of work
> people. Where managements are not sufficiently enterprising and
> progressive, are unwilling to step up efficiency or extend markets
> through lower prices, then unions must press them to do so.[64]

As applied to Labour Britain, the proposals of the TUC team
were not to form the basis of a high-wage policy. Yet, that
being the case, there was still no discussion of any mechanism
by which swollen profits would be redistributed or of how
firms would be compelled to reinvest in ways acceptable to
labour.[65] The TUC were, in effect, proposing a responsible
role for the unions in an area where the unions had no legal
responsibility. There was no parallel move by the TUC leadership to seek a democratisation of private industry, to require
a sharing of power between workers and managers such as
might have made sense of a co-operative approach to production.
There was not even a statutory obligation on employers to
consult their labour force. Trade unions were being encouraged
to generate pressure for the introduction of scientific management without having any guarantees of being able to control
its subsequent development. There was always a case for unions
taking an interest in scientific management for their own protection and even advocating selective use of its techniques. But
to exaggerate American labour's own attachment to them in
persuading British workers of their acceptability was less than

honest, and to assume, as they tended to, that scientific management techniques were neutral was naive.

Spreading the productivity gospel

The TUC report was not issued until June 1950, but well before
that ECA Labour staff were working on its production. There
appear to have been no general meetings of the team to consider
drafts of the report: certainly Doughty was not involved in
any such activity.[66] But as early as December 1949, when the
team returned to England, Paradise was able to tell the ECA
precisely what the main thrust of the report would be.[67] During
the spring of 1950 he helped Robert Harle, the team secretary
and member of the TUC Production Department, to write the
document.[68] Gausmann, from the ECA Labour Information
office, was called in to help edit it, and he and Paradise had
a copy with them when they attended an ECA Labour Division
staff conference in May, weeks before it was issued to the TUC
affiliates. Indeed before the official publication of the report
the ECA mission in London distributed a large number of copies
abroad, urged its translation into foreign languages and prepared
numerous press releases and feature articles for planting in
the British and foreign press. There was even an ECA proposal
to have the report reprinted in a popular format with enough
copies run off for every trade unionist in the United Kingdom.[69]

The Americans were quite ecstatic over the outcome of
the visit. Gausmann reported that 'from a trade union point
of view, this is the most valuable document that has been
produced under ECA auspices to date'.[70] The diplomatic staff
in the American embassy echoed the fulsome praise: 'the improvements the report will have accomplished in British trade
union practice and philosophy will be almost revolutionary'.[71]

The TUC report proposed for British unions a far more co-
operative approach than anything witnessed in the United
States. This even raised the prospect of the findings being used
as a means of pressing American unions to adopt a more co-
operative approach, thus standing the original purpose of the
exercise on its head. As Paradise told the European Labour
staff conference in May:

The UK has made about as complete a turn-about on trade union attitudes, I think, as any trade union movement and it is something the American trade unions could emulate. [...] This is as far as they [the TUC] can go.[72]

ECA exuberance and energy in publicising the TUC report contrasted with Congress's relatively low-key response to it. Copies were distributed to affiliated unions in June 1950, well in advance of the annual conference, but there was no debate on it. Indeed, it was hardly mentioned at conference, the General Council's report simply noting that its recommendations would be reviewed by the Production Committee. The main debate on productivity centred on a resolution which, while advocating increased efficiency, called on the TUC to press for full consultation between unions and management on new methods and processes and urged measures to ensure that the inflated profits being made as a result of the productivity drive were divided fairly. The TUC report failed to address itself to either of these concerns.[73]

However, the TUC had begun to act quietly on the team's findings before the report was even written. At the beginning of 1950 Congress established a fully fledged Production Department headed by Edwin Fletcher. As the United States embassy understood it, the Production Department was expected to 'pay particular attention to the spread of the productivity gospel right down to the grass roots and the creation of a key role in the productivity campaign for the shop steward, the foreman and the supervisor'.[74]

ECA Labour staff worked very closely with the TUC Production Department as it developed its programme of work. In February 1951 the department unveiled its first major initiative – a programme of training in managerial techniques for shop stewards, to be taught in a series of week-long courses. The ECA were highly satisfied with this development, which fitted in well with their concept of how the campaign must progress in Britain. It was, in Paradise's words, 'a very pragmatic and satisfactory approach to the problem'.[75] The British section of the AACP remarked:

To those who know the tradition and practice of British trade unions, there is definite significance in the decision of the TUC to set up a new department within its organisation to deal with productivity and kindred questions.[76]

Scientific management techniques were no longer a cause of worry among the TUC leadership. When the Labour MP Ian Mikardo suggested that the purpose of the TUC production courses should be mainly that of debunking management and demystifying their jargon, Harry Douglass of the iron and steel union retorted loftily that he doubted whether his members would be interested in training courses devised for that purpose.[77] The aim of the TUC leadership was to extend quietly but steadily the familiarity of their members with the techniques of management, and to that end the Production Department put more than 600 union officials and workshop leaders through immersion courses during the next four years.[78] This programme was useful in equipping a cadre of union representatives with technical skills, but at the same time the TUC report and the accompanying publicity were also important in desensitising workers to the notion of scientific management and breaking down some of the deeply entrenched barriers to the use of time study and rationalising techniques. In this sense the TUC report complemented well the sheer mass of anti-labour, pro-free enterprise propaganda that flowed from the industry and specialist reports of the AACP teams.

It seemed that to the TUC scientific management techniques were devoid of ideological content. There was apparently no recognition that under capitalism such techniques were, to a large extent, the means of regulating manpower in the interest of managerial imperatives. Overall the TUC seemed to overestimate the degree to which the British economy was being run in the interests of labour, to exaggerate the extent to which Labour had already transformed society. Policies for increasing productivity became a commonsense part of routine, pragmatic trade unionism. James Crawford, footwear union leader and member of the TUC General Council, asked rhetorically at a productivity conference why high productivity was necessary. In replying to his own question he expressed the conviction that the answer 'could not be couched in terms of any political philosophy'.[79] Productivity was politically neutral. Similarly, addressing a conference of brassfounding employers on the theme of productivity in a climate marked by some rank-and-file hostility to the employers' proposals, Victor Feather, Assistant Secretary of the TUC, sought to lower the temperature, insisting, 'Politics should be excluded, and as in the trade union movement, they should first find what they could agree about.'[80]

However, British workers were being pressed to accept not just the importance of the concept of productivity growth but also the American approach to it, rooted in the values of free enterprise to which labour adhered, it was claimed, as firmly as employers. As a widely circulated US Information Service pamphlet, *Consumer Capitalism*, suggested, quoting a European observer of the American scene:

> the secret of the high productivity of the United States is not in the machine [...] it lies in the unreserved collaboration of the worker and the boss.[81]

For the Americans running the Marshall Aid programme the ideological content of the productivity drive was never in doubt. It was, first and last, a strategy for defeating communism and exporting the American way of life. Philip Reed, Joint Chairman of the American section of the AACP, indicated a clear recognition of this function of the productivity campaign in a key note speech to an AACP joint session in April 1949. He spoke of the world's two great problems – one being the status of the individual in relation to the state, a problem at the centre of the struggle between Russia and the West, the other being the dollar shortage, which sprang from a lack of competitiveness in many European economies. In his mind the two problems were clearly linked, as were the elements of their solution – the promotion throughout the Western world of individualism, the competitive ethic and the pursuit of productivity growth. In other words, it was the communist challenge that was likely to bring Western society to its fullest development. The Russian threat had united the West 'to a degree unprecedented in history, a degree which now begins to give the promise of yielding fruits so firm – political, economical and social – that we may yet come to describe the Russian threat to communise the world as a blessing in disguise'.[82] And during the final joint session of the AACP in May 1953 Colonel Chevalier, one of the American delegation, observed that the council was:

something extending far beyond the question of productivity. America and Britain had to continue to work together for an indefinite period, on the political, diplomatic and military front as well as on the industrial front.[83]

The hostile political creed that was thought to threaten the United States called forth a full-scale ideological response, and productivity was, without question, a key concept in that.

CHAPTER 10

Launching the productivity campaign in Europe

A vision seems to capture the imagination of all the countries of Western Europe, looking to a new high productivity record that will raise the standard of living. This fact has repercussions in politics and ideologies. Production has always been the forte of capitalism. The emphasis of Socialist countries has been in distribution. If Socialist countries of Europe now turn to production as a solution, it is a distinguished tribute to capitalism and the American way of life. [Marion Hedges, ECA Labour Adviser's Office, speech to the Society for the Advancement of Management, 25 January 1949]

In France and Italy in particular, and in the rest of Europe to a somewhat lesser extent, the productivity programme was implemented with none of the elementary safeguards that American unions would insist upon for their own members. It was policed in an inadequate and shoddy way that amounted to nothing more than a speed-up programme that undermined jobs and bolstered monopoly practices and prices. ['FOA labour operation', 6 June 1955, CIO Washington Office files]

In the 'problem countries' of Europe – France, Italy and Germany – there had been very little positive work by the ECA aimed specifically at increasing productivity during the first two years of the aid programme: more immediate efforts to resist communism had been all-consuming. In 1949 not a single industrial engineer was employed by the ECA in Europe. The Industry Division simply acted as a screening agency for proposed investment projects, making no attempt to intervene more directly in the organisation of industry and the work process.[1] The ECA spent $2 million on 'technical assistance' to Britain in 1949 – essentially the AACP programme – but that was out of a total technical assistance budget for Europe of less than $4 million. By the end of the Marshall Plan no less than $43·6 million would be spent on this item.[2] However, by 1950 European productivity was already 40 per cent above the 1947 level, far more than might have been expected from the amount of investment undertaken.

A major contributing factor had been the reimposition of managerial discipline over workers which had accompanied the imposition of a conservative, financial discipline on national economies.[3] But in 1950 American thoughts began to turn to a more systematic approach to productivity growth. Within the ECA the debate saw proponents of *laissez-faire* ranged against those who would intervene directly in industry. The former believed in the simple efficacy of larger markets and emphasised the need for European economic integration. The latter argued that specific measures to increase productivity were more important.[4] The first major contribution to that debate from the Labour Divison came from the economist Sol Ozer in a paper calling for a complete reorganisation of the ERP so as to gear it entirely to the problem of productivity. He proposed that the ECA introduce a scheme of loans to firms on condition that a fixed proportion of any productivity increase would be paid to workers as wages and also be used to benefit consumers in the form of lower prices.[5]

Up to 1950 many ECA-sponsored teams had visited the United States from the Continent but in a far less systematic programme than that run in Britain by the AACP. In the early years it was perhaps sufficient for the Americans to introduce deprived French, Italian or German workers to the wonders of consumer capitalism and a world of material plenty. The process of familiarising them with the technical aspects of mass production would be a much more long-term project. For the time being the non-communist unions in France and Italy were organisationally too weak to influence the course of productivity, and their more powerful communist rivals were dead set against any efficiency drive. In the following years there was a big increase in the number of study visits to the United States. Germany received $1·3 million in technical assistance funds, mostly to finance trips. In Italy the bulk of technical assistance went on 'American tourism' as cynics put it – ten Italian trade union teams alone visited the United States in the first year of the productivity programme. And by 1952 nearly 2,600 Frenchmen had crossed the Atlantic in nearly 200 teams.[6]

French employers paid the wages of their workers while they were in the United States and so, as in Britain, employers were largely responsible for selecting team members. Because of industry's fear of offending the more powerful communist unions, leading non-communists were often excluded from the mixed teams and frequently foremen were sent as 'workers'. Between 1948 and 1951 ten union-only teams travelled from France, but the lack of any formal programme for applying the insights and knowledge gained on the trips meant that their effectiveness depended largely on the willingness of individual employers to act on their recommendations.[7] Yet, for experienced trade unionists, the impressions gained while in the United States were not always favourable ones, as Max Rolland of FO indicated to friends on the ECA Labour staff during a 1950 team visit:

> We are discovering the US through the eyes of managers who want to bust the unions or enslave them [...]. For the time being, everybody seems convinced that the high American productivity is the result of two causes: (a) ruthless action on the part of management (b) the gigantic war effort made by this country which led to the complete retooling and modernisation of your plants.
>
> As for the participation of labour unions in the drive for higher productivity, from what we have been shown, the unions are against higher productivity, except in a few sub-marginal companies, where the workers are giving a hand to management to get out of present difficulties encountered by their employers on the verge of bankruptcy.

But, equally, Rolland was sceptical about the chances of that impression being widely broadcast by the team members on their return: 'I am pretty sure that when they come back to France, the members of the team will play up all the good things, and hush as many of the bad ones, in order to justify their trip to the rank and file.'[8] With such unfavourable images being brought back from America and such cynical allies among European trade unionists, ECA Labour staff had their work cut out in pressing the cause of productivity.

Even in Britain, where the ERP productivity campaign was more firmly established, the conditions for productivity growth seemed to be deteriorating just as the Americans were calling for a bigger emphasis on the programme. Following years of government exhortation to greater effort the ardour for productivity that had been demonstrated by trade unionists in the years of the Attlee government had faded. And at the end of the AACP's life the TUC Production Department advised that the word 'productivity' was due for a rest. With the outbreak of the Korean War in June 1950 the ECA had focused its interest almost exclusively on the armaments industry. This caused performance to suffer in other sectors of industry, which were starved of raw materials. As Gausmann and Paradise reported in December 1950:

> rearmament is inevitably going to mean declines in productivity. While this is to be regretted, our resources are too limited to permit us to concern ourselves with serious productivity campaigns in any other industries.[9]

In view of these difficulties there was need for more carefully co-ordinated productivity work. One of the criticisms of the AACP made by British government and ECA officials was that it had failed to do more than publicise the need to increase productivity. Its early efforts at researching the causes of growth in this area had amounted to little, and though it encouraged unions and employers' associations to follow up the recommendations of team reports, it was not equipped to supervise a vigorous technical assistance programme such as the ECA now hoped to develop.[10] But in the course of 1950 plans were already being made to convert the AACP into a permanent national productivity centre – the British Productivity Council – with a professional staff engaged in a long-term programme of work.[11] It was this expanded model of the AACP that the Americans wanted to export to all western European countries, and in the course of 1950 they began to exert pressure in each participating country for the creation of a national productivity centre through which American managerial values and techniques could be disseminated.

National productivity centres

By the end of the year centres had been established in a number of countries, financed for the most part from Marshall dollars. In France, planning supremo Jean Monnet had originally objected to a productivity council along the lines of the AACP since its emphasis was on labour productivity rather than the productivity of capital.[12] However, to organise the visits programme the Association Française pour l'Accroissement de la Productivité

(AFAP) was founded jointly by the non-communist unions and the employers' association with a budget of $1·6 million. In summer 1950 the German productivity centre, Rationalisierungs Kuratorium der Deutschen Wirtschaft (RKW) was launched with a start-up budget of $0·5 million. In Italy the CISL proposed setting up a tripartite productivity centre but met with opposition from both the government and the employers' association, Confindustria, the latter proposing that it alone should be responsible for channelling aid to industry. Again the employers' desire not to antagonise the communist-led unions was a factor, and when the initial Italian plan for a National Productivity Centre (CNP) was unveiled it included a proposal for participation by the communist-dominated CGIL.[13] In consequence the productivity campaign made no immediate progress there and it was not until October 1951 that the Italian government actually established the CNP.

The slow start in Italy was largely due to lack of enthusiasm on the part of the government. Despite its indebtedness to the USA, the de Gasperi government was anxious to restrain American influence on the course of Italian economic development. They were quite unattracted to the idea of low-cost production and mass markets based on increased purchasing power. Unemployment of up to 2 million and harsh government deflationary policies created a climate in which narrow productivity concerns seemed irrelevant. It was symptomatic of the Italian government's attitude that during 1950 and 1951 it spent only 15 per cent of the ECA technical assistance funds available to it.[14] As elsewhere in Europe, the Americans also attributed the limited progress to the lack of enterprise among employers. In Italy this was a particular problem, since under fascism the industrialists had become used to state protection and lacked the independence of mind to initiate efficiency measures. The productivity chief in the Rome mission argued that the immediate need was to secure administrative reform, especially of the tax system. ECA Labour staff saw little prospect of a fully fledged productivity programme there, and instead of stressing the importance of a productivity council which would emphasise technical aspects of efficiency they recommended that the ECA concentrate on developing the correct political and economic environment for productivity growth: 'Without the proper framework a narrowly conceived productivity programme in Italy will merely be a roundabout way of adding to the unemployment rolls.' But with the mission 'hobbled by an oversimplified concept of "free enterprise" versus "socialism"', as one member of ECA Labour staff put it, what chance was there of developing this proper framework?[15]

Both industrialists and non-communist labour in Italy were apt to cite the government's deflationary policies as justification of their own lack of a positive approach to productivity. The two sides accepted that the country was poverty-stricken and must therefore continue to rely on American aid. For the employers, this justified their low-wage policy and lack of investment, since the assumption was that expanding markets were unlikely to develop. Likewise, acceptance of poverty as an axiom helped the non-communist labour federations to rationalise their failure to build up a movement strong enough to challenge the CGIL. How to escape from this *impasse* was a problem to which the American productivity experts had no simple answer. There was no point in trying to conserve manpower, and all the tricks of the industrial engineer were irrelevant.

However, it was not only in Italy that the Americans experienced difficulties in advancing the cause of productivity. German trade union leaders were also naturally cautious when the idea of a productivity campaign was first proposed by the ECA in January 1950. They feared that it would provide an excuse for lay-offs, and indeed, one of the early American proposals for increased productivity which involved reorganisation of the railway industry threatened the prospect of 50,000 redundancies.[16] Nevertheless the ECA launched its productivity programme with a conference of German trade union economists and Marshall Plan staff in February 1950.[17] The German trade union centre, the Deutsche Gewerkschaftsbund (DGB), was formally represented on the RKW's governing body from the outset, but it played no active part in the productivity drive for the first two years, preoccupied as it was with the campaign for co-determination. The result was that the productivity programme which emerged was geared largely to the interests of the employers. Indeed, some aspects of productivity work were being used to undermine the unions' co-determination policy. The American-inspired Training Within Industry (TWI) programme, based on human relations techniques and financed in part by the American High Commission, was being run in such a way as to build up worker opposition to co-determination. Consequently the unions declined to be represented on the regional TWI bodies on the grounds that it would identify them with an activity over which they had no real control.[18]

For the German unions the whole idea of productivity took a back seat while their principal demand for co-determination was still unresolved. Visiting the country in January 1951 when the struggle over co-determination was reaching a climax, Golden assumed that if adopted the system would result in a situation of formal power-sharing in industry but continuing effective employer control, and, that being so, it offered an unusual opportunity to explore the prospects of improving productivity.[19] On the other hand, given the poisoned climate of industrial relations, especially resulting from the intervention of American business interests over co-determination, the ECA Labour Director, Harvey Brown, concluded that it was a waste of time to introduce American productivity experts into the country now. For a long time they could expect a cold shoulder.[20]

The first major initiative in Germany involving the ECA linked the productivity drive to a housing scheme using the $98 million of counterpart made available for this. But it proved extremely difficult to gain the active support of the unions for the project. The focus of the scheme was the coal-mining industry, where 56,000 miners were living in barracks originally built to house Russian prisoners of war. In many cases miners were living three or four to a room and sharing a single bed in rotation on a shift basis. The idea was that new housing would be a reward for achieving agreed levels of output.[21] Ultimately nine major housing projects comprising 600–800 dwellings were built, but only after considerable delay.[22] When Michael Harris was appointed head of the Economics Division of the ECA in Germany in summer 1951 he devoted himself full-time to the mining scheme, which was then still at the drafting stage. At first the unions were reluctant to participate in the ECA's quadripartite steering committee, and by the end of 1952 Harris had to report that little progress had been made. In his first eighteen months in Germany, he admitted, he had achieved almost nothing of any importance.[23]

Beset by these various problems, it was only in 1951, at the height of Korean War rearmament, that the ECA (soon to become the MSA) began to develop an integrated productivity drive for Europe, with American aid geared to social engineering as well as economic growth. The thinking behind the ECA's Production Assistance drive was outlined by Richard Bissell in June 1951. The Americans proposed to devote more personnel and funds to this area (a budget of $330 million was envisaged in the first instance), intending not merely to work through national governments but henceforth, in more interventionist fashion, to deal directly with industries and plants and seek direct contact with individual managements and trade unions. The ECA proposed to offer technical services to European industry in general, while demonstrating the superiority of American practice. The plan was also to carry the productivity drive beyond manufacturing to the basic industries and the service sector. The new focus extended beyond the question of technological improvements and was concerned with customs, habits, attitudes and practices of business and labour relevant to productivity performance. In practice this meant seeking changes in policy of trade unions and employers' organisations and, where necessary, modifications in national legislation. More generally the ECA was thinking in terms of a broad informational and educational programme aimed at a wider European public.[24]

The ECA was to launch the programme but its intention was that European governments would take control in two or three years. Meanwhile the ECA was anxious that it should not be seen as American interference: the national productivity centres were to advertise the scheme as their own brainchild. They would receive Marshall dollars for the purpose of financing the work of European journalists and academics in investigating and publicising the extent of restrictiveness in industry. That way it would be seen in terms of the discovery by *Europeans* of a domestic *European* problem. It was envisaged that the ICFTU would give a prominent lead in promoting trade union training for productivity along the lines of the new TUC programme for shop stewards. Again, ECA financing would be necessary, but as a spokesman for the Productivity Division put it, 'we hope to do it in an unobtrusive way'.[25]

Of course, there was a basic flaw in this stratagem, as Bissell recognised. Increased productivity usually meant more machinery using more materials with fewer workers. And yet the situation in several European countries was one of machine and raw material shortages and substantial unemployment. Indeed, there were already glaring cases where Marshall Aid had led directly to an increase in unemployment, as in France, where Citroen had recently discharged 3,000 car workers following the installation of American equipment.[26] Embarrassing ocurrences like this caused the Labour Information Department to instruct staff not to mention in their publicity cases where capital investment was known to have reduced job opportunities.[27] All this suggested uncomfortable questions about the real nature and purpose of the aid programme. The reality was that defence considerations came first: the immediate aim was to speed up rearmament while supporting only the essentials of the civilian economy. Meanwhile the vague hope was that somehow the foundation would be laid of future improvements in living standards.[28]

The programme as it developed often involved the national centres in crude attempts to sell simplistic notions of productivity based on what was imagined to be American experience – in particular the mythic idyll of American workers and management jointly striving to create a bigger pie and then amicably sitting down to divide it. Such a model often proved counterproductive when presented to European workers. During an inspection tour of Europe as an MSA consultant, and seeing the harm that was being done to the programme, William Gomberg urged the need to 'assure ourselves that our high productivity propagandists understand the dynamics of higher productivity themselves before they attempt to sell it to others'. 'I have emphasised that higher productivity is something that happened to us. We never planned for it.'[29] Indeed, the advisory board to the MSA Technical Assistance Division, with Gomberg a member, spent the first year of its existence in 1951–52 trying to discover why its efforts were constantly meeting with failure and why a programme that would have made complete sense in America ran into one obstacle after another abroad.[30]

Direct benefits from the new approach were therefore slow in coming. American productivity specialists recognised that European trade unions were more disposed than management to accept the logic of the productivity programme, but without the organisational strength to guarantee benefits to themselves from the gains made in efficiency labour was, in practice, reluctant to disturb the 'equilibrium of scarcity' by striking out in a new direction.[31] In effect the drive for efficiency was devoid of that progressive social element that was necessary if workers were not to turn their backs on free enterprise capitalism. It was just such a state of affairs that Conditional Aid was devised to rectify by making aid dependent on a country's willingness to foster collective bargaining.

Conditional Aid

Conditional Aid, or the Benton-Moody programme, as it was commonly known, was introduced in 1952, based on two new elements in the foreign aid legislation. The aim of the Benton amendment to the Mutual Security Bill of 1951 was to undermine the cartel mentality and trade restrictions among European employers and to expose them to the fresh air of genuine free enterprise, the better to achieve higher levels of productivity. Free enterprise was also to be promoted by encouraging American private overseas investment in Europe. At the same time the amendment was intended to inject a progressive social note into the legislation by encouraging the growth of non-communist labour organisations as collective bargaining agents. To help secure these objectives of the Benton amendment the June 1952 Moody amendment to the European Co-operation Act of 1948 set aside $100 million specifically to stimulate American-style free enterprise abroad.[32]

Taking as its starting point the assumption that there was a lack of adequate credit facilities for competitive firms, poor relations between labour and management, and an absence of educational and other facilities suitable for changing prevailing attitudes, the MSA set about spending the Moody funds in an ambitious bid to modify cultural values and industrial practices. By late 1952–early 1953 bilateral agreements had been concluded with most participating countries on establishing revolving loan funds to industry and the promotion of productivity projects.

Britain. Britain provides a good example of the operation of Conditional Aid in what was, for the Americans, a 'non-problem area'. Of the $100 million budget she was allocated $9 million, to be spent on five basic productivity programmes: advice and training for industry; research into efficiency measures; loan aid to small enterprises; general publicity for productivity initiatives, and support by the government for the OEEC's ongoing work in that area. An initial allocation of $1·2 million was set aside for the employment of specialist advisers to industry.

The TUC had some early doubts about the programme, especially over the understanding that in administering the funds the Board of Trade was required to be in regular consultation with the MSA. They were also sceptical as to how more consultants would be made available to industry without bringing in large numbers of Americans, to which the TUC was strongly opposed.[33] Nonetheless a budget of $182,000 was awarded to the British Productivity Council for an advisory service for its 100 or so local associations and to operate a 'circuit scheme' of inter-factory visits to familiarise workers and management with 'best practice'. By 1954 500 companies were involved in the programme, and a year later more than 10,000 factory visits had taken place. A Conditional Aid publicity budget of $500,000 enabled the BPC to commission half a dozen films for television (the MSA had already made available no fewer than 900 productivity films for circulation in Europe, together with dubbing facilities); the production of a monthly bulletin for a readership of 14,000 and tens of thousands of copies of pamphlets expounding the case for productivity, some of which were translated into Italian, French, Icelandic and even Chinese.[34] An equivalent grant enabled the British Institute of Management (BIM) to duplicate many of these activities for the benefit of its local management groups.

However, of more fundamental importance than any of this were the programmes to promote work study techniques in which both the BPC and the BIM were deeply involved. The BIM secured a sum of $134,000 for a three-year National Work Study Campaign, having argued the need for this in terms which echoed the predominant theme of the AACP team reports. As the BIM put the case:

Work Study is, [...] as Taylor said of 'scientific management' (of which it is the principal technique), fifty years ago, an attitude of mind, and it is only by changing the mind of industry as a whole that any significant increase in productivity and lowering of cost can be achieved. All other activities can do no more than scratch the surface of the problem [...].

Parallel with this in 1954 the BPC established a Work Study Unit whose function was to stage week-long 'appreciation' conferences in major towns. The promotion of work study was crucial for the development of a more modern scientific approach to management. As the BIM put it, work study was an activity 'without which other management control and planning techniques, including costing, cannot operate satisfactorily'.[35]

Loans averaging $30,000 for three to four years were made available to small firms from a 'revolving fund' of $2·8 million. The purpose was to help re-equip and reorganise small business enterprises in accordance with the recommendations of the AACP teams, though the TUC cautioned at the outset that many of these recommendations had now been found to be impractical. A similar amount was to be used to promote training and research in the field of productivity. Much of this went to universities and, as such, dovetailed with the work of the projected European Productivity Agency (EPA). Under the bilateral agreement the Board of Trade was required to spend $720,000 over three years as part of its contribution to the OEEC's work in promoting productivity. In effect this amounted to a subscription to the EPA, an organisation almost entirely financed by the United States, and indeed American in all but name. The balance, almost $1 million, was left with the MSA mission in London to use at its discretion.

Whereas Conditional Aid was applied in Britain with few difficulties and minimal opposition, on the Continent the experience was rather different. The main problem was the lack of any precise mechanism to ensure that American aid did what it was now supposed to do – that is, lead to improvements in the social and economic conditions of working people. In short, there was still no way of ensuring that workers benefited from improvements in productivity. Over this opinions in the MSA Labour Division were deeply divided and no satisfactory solution was ever reached. Harry Martin favoured the inclusion of fair labour standard clauses in any agreements to release aid. He was supported by Nelson Cruikshank, the new Chief Labour Adviser in Europe, who argued that technical assistance and credits should be made available to firms only on condition that they undertook an aggressive merchandising campaign, increased their planned output, granted an immediate 10 per cent increase in basic wages and reached agreement with the non-communist unions on a formula for sharing the proceeds from increased productivity.[36] The idea was rejected by the Acting Special Representative in Paris, Paul Porter, himself a man with a background in the American labour movement.[37] Porter believed that the root cause of the productivity problem in Europe was the existence of cartels, but he claimed that it was not feasible to try and use the productivity programme to combat this by attaching conditions to American aid. Labour had benefited more from productivity increases in some countries than in others, but the MSA was not responsible for the unevenness in the strength of trade unions.

Porter was echoing an argument that Shishkin had deployed some months earlier: strong trade unionism could not come courtesy of management. To require the recipients of aid to sign agreements granting – as some were suggesting – exclusive rights for the non-communist unions and providing for co-operation with the unions over productivity, with guaranteed wage increases to match productivity rises, would smack of company unionism.[38]

Looked at in this way it was a circular problem, with the Americans unwilling to break into the cycle. Only a strong labour movement could look after its own interests in the division of the spoils from productivity, but how were the French and Italian non-communist unions to build up their strength without favourable terms attached to the aid legislation? Six months later Robert Oliver in the MSA's Washington Labour Office revived the proposal in a French context, calling for $36 million of counterpart funds to be set aside as a reward for French employers who broke with the cartel practices of the *patronat* and entered into productivity agreements on an equitable sharing of the benefits of increased efficiency.[39] However, the problem was not solved and indeed was to get worse when in 1952 the MSA Labour Division lost control of this area to a separate Productivity and Technical Assistance Division (PTAD).

Germany. The German trade unions were truculent in their approach to questions of productivity. Since 1950 they had effectively remained aloof from the RKW and began to reconsider their position only in April 1952. However, they were aware that any unconditional support for the Centre's existing programme would simply work to the employers' advantage. Before taking up their seat on the RKW's governing body, the DGB, therefore, sought prior agreement within the Centre that a high-powered commission should be established to investigate all prospects for socialising industry and thereby achieving increased productivity in the widest national economic terms.[40] But of course the political tide in Germany had already turned against such proposals. The DGB remained suspicious of the MSA's productivity programme despite the fact that Harris, chief of the Economics Division in Germany, was confident that the employers could be induced to negotiate an agreement covering the sharing of productivity gains and including union participation in the administration of the scheme to ensure there was no speeding-up and no lay-offs. Frustrated, he accused the DGB of being unwilling to put the employers' good faith to the test: 'I am almost becoming convinced that they do not want a successful productivity programme simply because it might succeed and thus prove that some of the sacred doctrines under which they have lived for so long are not pertinent,' he complained to his mentor, Golden. 'They are living in the doctrinal past and in that respect seem at this point to be far more hidebound than the employers.'[41] However, his analysis failed to take into account what the German unions fully recognised – their lack of any right to negotiate over productivity matters at the *plant* level. The CIO's European representatives also saw the productivity campaign in a far less positive light than did Harris. Their view was that the MSA programme had been taken over by American management types and was being used to impose a speed-up on European workers, a charge which Harris himself strongly rejected.[42]

In spring 1953 the MSA mission and the German federal government reached a bilateral agreement on the Moody programme, involving the expenditure of $7 million to assist small and medium-sized firms with measures to improve productivity. This led to a new wave of productivity propaganda just before the federal elections in August 1953 in which Adenauer's Christian Democrats were seeking re-election. Having previously had no funds available for low-cost housing schemes, the MSA/FOA suddenly announced on the eve of the election that a substantial amount would be available for the purpose, tied to the growth of productivity. In Dusseldorf a productivity exhibition was staged, though it evoked little enthusiasm among labour. As CIO representative in Germany Helmuth Jockel reported, 'The whole programme is a programme where the scientists and the time clocks will play the major role.'[43] For this reason the DGB refused to share responsibility for the administration of Moody funds.

France. In France the productivity drive revolved around the concept of 'pilot plants' selected to demonstrate the virtues of modern techniques of production and workplace organisation. The idea originated with an ECA Labour Division working party in autumn 1950, consisting of Victor Reuther, Gomberg, Douty and Harold Gibbons, who had recently returned from leading the joint AFL and CIO delegation to Europe. One of the French productivity teams to visit the United States in early 1950, comprising managers and workers from the foundry industry, had returned with favourable impressions of American achievements in this field. Following up their report, ECA staff had surveyed two dozen French foundries and devised for them a scheme involving American training in work simplification and new personnel practices – notably the introduction of profit-sharing schemes and salaried status for employees. When Golden visited France in the early weeks of 1951 he was told that productivity in these plants had increased by 20 per cent, and he concluded that there were good prospects for wooing French firms away from the restrictive embrace of the *Patronat* and encouraging them to accept the assistance of American management experts.[44]

With the launch of the ECA's Production Assistance Programme and the Benton amendment emphasising the importance of competition and free enterprise, the pilot plant scheme was formally launched in October 1951. Ten foundries were to receive technical assistance in return for adopting a more modern and aggressively competitive approach to production. Part of the original thinking behind the pilot plant idea was that progressive American businessmen like Henry Ford would assist the programme by helping to introduce notions of low-cost, high-consumption production. As a memorandum from the Office of Labour Advisers put it, 'An organised effort on the part of progressive American businessmen, equivalent in scope and imagination to that now being undertaken by American trade unionism, is essential in France if free enterprise is to rise from its present moribund state [...]'[45] The ECA/MSA was hoping to encourage maverick entrepreneurs in the mould of the American steel magnate Henry Kaiser who would buck the constraints of the employers' association and pioneer a new, thrusting form of capitalism. Equally the aid was intended to have a spin-off in fostering non-communist trade unions; it was therefore important that employers should be willing to enter into collective bargaining with these unions in a way that they had not in the past. By letting workers share the benefits of increased efficiency it was hoped to fire their enthusiasm for the cult of productivity.

In practice the pilot plant programme never lived up to expectations and soon provided MSA Labour staff with a veritable nightmare. From the outset the scheme was little more than a sham. Technical assistance was being given to firms without their agreeing to any real concessions in return. American aid allowed the French productivity centre to make Marshall dollars available to the employers while, as MSA Labour staff noted, all the unions had secured was the right to lecture the employers on the virtues of union–management co-operation.[46] The truth was that in all the plants except the Télémechanique works at Nanterre the non-communist trade unions were a negligible force and were afraid of pressing the employers to match Télémechanique wages and conditions for fear that the militancy it would inevitably involve would play into the hands of the communists.[47] The absence of effective collective bargaining machinery also meant that such plant-level negotiations over productivity as there were would take place within the *comités d'entreprise* which were not under union (far less non-communist union) control. For this reason French trade unionists were becoming increasingly resistant to the pilot scheme even in early 1952.[48]

The unions were ill equipped to monitor the results of the project. Under the Production Assistance Programme FO and the Christian trade union federation, the CFTC, had established a labour research centre, le Centre Intersyndical d'Etudes et de Recherches de Productivité (CIERP), with responsibility in this area. CIERP was actually financed by the AFAP, which was itself largely dependent on French government funds derived from Marshall Aid. From the outset, therefore, CIERP was effectively financed by the Americans, which meant that it was, for all practical purposes, independent of the unions it was meant to serve. The fact that it was so closely identified with the United States and at the same time dependent for its continued existence on the good will of the French government soon undermined its credibility in the eyes of the labour movement.[49] The architect of CIERP was René Richard, the high-profile, persuasive general secretary of FO's white-collar engineering union. Richard was also the leading trade union advocate of the foundry industry pilot scheme, and this led to CIERP having a vested interest in the scheme's continuation. Largely autonomous of its trade union patrons, CIERP gave the pilot programme its blessing even as rank-and-file union members were voicing disquiet. Under an arrangement agreed to by CIERP, workers in pilot plants were merely allowed to elect representatives to a committee responsible for *informing* the labour force of the details of wage incentive schemes. They had no prior right to negotiate with or even consult management over implementation.[50] In effect CIERP provided respectable labour cover for what amounted to a unilateral programme of the foundry employers.[51] By summer 1952 the MSA productivity consultant William Gomberg had discovered that as foundry output was increasing the levels of wages and employment were falling. The research and engineering department of CIERP was no substitute for collective bargaining, and he called for an urgent reappraisal of its entire role.

Meanwhile two other pilot projects had been started in the clothing and shoe industries. Here the same problems as in founding were encountered. There was much short-time working, unions were weak and unable to negotiate adequate ground rules with the employers, and the result was that CIERP came to overshadow the unions, providing the vehicle for vetting and evaluating the schemes.[52] Even in these conditions, which were overwhelmingly favourable to the employers, the national productivity centre found difficulty in attracting industry to the scheme. Far from it encouraging the emergence of maverick firms, the employers' federations maintained their stranglehold on industry, deterring MSA efforts to set their member firms in competition with one another. And, to the dismay of the Americans, French union leaders argued that the only way a full-blown productivity effort could become a reality would be with the blessing of the employers' organisations. That, of course, was guaranteed to strengthen the *patronat* rather than weaken it as the Benton amendment had intended.[53] Yet in July 1952, as labour criticism of the schemes became more vocal, René Richard prevailed upon the MSA to approve in principle an extension of the foundry project to cover a further ninety plants.[54]

During summer 1952 opposition within FO to the productivity drive began to build up. Some opposed it for the class collaboration that it entailed, others on the more pragmatic grounds that it seemed unlikely to benefit the labour force.[55] Meanwhile trade unionists were infuriated by the fact that at a recent productivity conference of employers convened under OEEC auspices the foundry programme had been held up as a model for all other industries to emulate.[56] Yet in September even the conservative newspaper *le Figaro* was forced to comment on the one-sided nature of the scheme. On the eve of the FO congress in November 1952 the Americans in the MSA Labour Division found themselves in the bizarre situation of now wanting to end the scheme while Frenchmen with a vested interest in it, especially the staff of CIERP, advocated its continuation. As productivity consultant Gomberg reflected, 'sometimes no productivity programme is preferable to one that will exploit French labour'.[57]

At the FO congress, against the opposition of the federation's leadership, the metalworkers' union successfully moved a resolution calling for withdrawal from the productivity scheme unless it could be based on a negotiated agreement between the unions and the employers. Consequently FO severed its connection with CIERP and AFAP.[58] Although the Catholic CFTC did not follow suit, critical debate about the role of CIERP continued among its members in the ensuing months. Yet, in spite of all this, in December 1952 the national productivity centre requested the MSA to advance a further quarter of a million dollars to finance the foundry project until the end of 1953. MSA Labour Division advice was to provide no more funds to any of the pilot projects until there was clear union support for them, and that meant bringing CIERP under union control and insisting on the firms involved first signing collective agreements with the unions.[59] Yet, as Gomberg noted, the FO withdrawal from CIERP had set back any realistic effort to link the machinery of collective bargaining with the promotion of productivity in France. The whole affair reflected badly on the role of the United States.[60] In the event the MSA took a decision to release funds to the productivity scheme sufficient for only three more months.[61] At that point the American-inspired productivity effort effectively ground into the earth.

Italy. As in France, Italian trade unions benefited hardly at all from Conditional Aid. It was always an afterthought in what was essentially a businessmen's programme. The national productivity committee (CNP), which was set up in October 1951, was a toothless organisation judged in terms of what the Americans and the Italian unions had been calling for. It was neither an executive body nor an independent agency, but rather a branch of the Prime Minister's office. Set up for only three years in an advisory role, it was meant to formulate broad lines of action on productivity, especially in the area of human relations. But, despite its emphasis on labour issues, the unions were granted only eight of the thirty-seven seats on the committee, the largest single block of members being government-appointed 'experts'. The local sub-units that it spawned were mostly outgrowths of the chambers of commerce.[62]

Pilot plants were an even less attractive proposition than in France. The Italian government itself had not warmed to the idea of a pilot project in the car industry, where, theoretically, government investment might have increased competitive pressure on Fiat. All Gomberg was prepared to advocate after visiting Italy as an MSA consultant was the creation of 'development areas', rural equivalents of pilot plants where, for example, small landowners would be encouraged to improve the techniques of food production without contributing to further unemployment.[63] Development areas thus became the central feature of the Conditional Aid programme. The main one, at Vicenza – the location of one of the most important American military bases in Italy – was started in 1952, with others at Pisa, Solerno, Monza and Palermo. As with the pilot plants in France, the object of the exercise was to demonstrate what could be achieved through the systematic application of modern methods of management. At Vicenza the main feature of the scheme for the nine firms involved was the development of an American-style Training Within Industry programme employing a range of modern techniques from time and motion study and work simplification to human relations management and employee education.

Big claims were made for the positive results of the scheme, but the MSA's Productivity Division concluded that the gains were at best minor. The other side of the coin was low wages, productivity bonuses fixed arbitrarily by management, non-recognition of unions and discipline maintained by fear of unemployment. There was no union involvement in the management of the programme and the CNP showed itself to be almost entirely a management consulting agency. Seminars run by the committee were essentially for the benefit of managers, and at best unions were invited to attend only as observers.[64] Training in marketing, accounting and industrial engineering techniques was promoted, while the CNP held back from pressing the case for collective bargaining or even consultation, and the human relations programme that it did sponsor had the effect of eroding worker support for trade unions.[65]

Among the Italian labour federations the CISL was the most enthusiastic supporter of the programme. General Secretary Pastore believed implicitly in the productivity ethic. With American financial help the CISL opened a training school for union leaders in Florence which sought to develop a technical, less ideological style of trade unionism with collective bargaining as its central focus. At Florence students were taught that a union should operate as an association of its members, not, as CGIL unions did, as the general agent of some abstract notion of the working class, and that the factory was the main theatre of activity.[66] The long-term influence of this programme led in a far more militant direction than most expected. Florence graduates came to criticise the CISL leadership for their lack of drive in the economic field, their failure to challenge management and their lack of independence from the Christian Democrats, who were too conservative and essentially a tool of the wealthy classes.[67] However, in the short term the CISL's Marshall Plan-inspired interest in productivity led it into collaborative relationships with employers. As a member of the CNP it failed to secure any arrangement whereby trade unionists would benefit directly from their contribution to productivity increases.[68] Indeed, in the early 1950s the CISL's wage policy was quite consistent with the Italian government's financial orthodoxy: high wage increases were frowned on as a permanent cause of financial instability. After 1952 the CISL began to criticise the government's national economic policy, but still argued that its shortcomings could be surmounted by an effective programme of union–employer co-operation. It was failure to make headway there under Conditional Aid that finally drove it to adopt a more vigorous wage policy from the mid-1950s, with increases tied to productivity.[69]

On the other hand the UIL was always highly critical of the CISL's approach to productivity and of the ECA/MSA role in pressing for such union policies. It attacked the CNP for being full of academic 'experts', for its paternalistic approach and for not insisting on unions and employers negotiating the share-out of productivity gains. And in July 1953 it called for an immediate freeze on Moody funds for the committee until there were substantial changes in its organisation. For its part the CISL attempted to have the UIL excluded from the CNP over this. But the UIL withdrew of its own accord in 1953 in protest at the committee's failure vigorously to defend the sectional interests of workers in productivity projects.[70] Pastore defended the CISL's policy on productivity, insisting that they were following the successful style of unionism practised in the United States. However, the Confederation was undoubtedly a victim of the excesses of Marshall Plan propaganda about American labour's positive role in promoting productivity. Even if American unions had operated as the CISL appeared to believe they did, Italian employers were, by and large, not prepared to reciprocate.[71]

By 1953 it was clear that Conditional Aid had done little to change perceptions that the Marshall Plan was essentially a businessmen's programme. As the ICFTU noted that summer, firms were free in practice to benefit in efficiency terms without accepting social responsibility for the side effects of their policies. There were no sanctions available against delinquent employers who took Conditional Aid and then declared technological redundancies.[72] But the national labour movements themselves were quite at odds with one another over how to tackle the problem. The TUC criticised the ICFTU for characterising productivity as the result of harder work which had to be undertaken as labour's sacrificial contribution to Western defence and European integration. The British trade union interest in productivity, they claimed, flowed from a natural concern with industrial arrangements which largely determined the standard of wages and conditions.[73] This 'commonsense' approach to productivity also highlighted another difference within the international labour movement over how to ensure that workers received their just deserts from increased efficiency and output. Among the French and Italian unions in particular the view was that the national union centres should agree with their own governments the use to be made of Conditional Aid, and this would be followed by industry-level agreements with employers on the division of the proceeds from increased productivity according to some precise formula. In France FO favoured a wage system under which basic rates would be tied to existing productivity levels, with extra payments related to changes above that level.[74] In Italy the UIL wanted the AFL and CIO to intervene direct with the US government with a view to having the terms of Conditional Aid precisely defined and rigidly imposed by the Americans. The TUC rejected this as general approach, reasoning that it contained an inherent risk that the recipients would become dangerously reliant on the Americans.

The British trade union preference was to rely on natural bargaining strength to control both the application of managerial techniques and the gains from increased productivity. They were anxious to preserve an 'arm's-length' relationship with the government and for this reason refused to accept direct Conditional Aid payments to the labour movement. In effect the TUC Production Department had articulated a positive approach to productivity while at the same time distancing themselves from the growing pseudo-science and technicism in management circles. Their 'natural' approach to productivity gave collective bargaining a central role. Techniques of work study and industrial engineering would merely be used to supplement this, not to achieve some theoretical notion of accuracy such as FO hankered for. No more than rough justice was expected from the market system, and as Fletcher told the ICFTU productivity conference convened in October 1953 to review the issue, 'The last thing desired was to leave the direction of the trade union movement to technicians.'[75] For the weaker trade union movements this was no solution and the conference offered no satisfactory resolution of the problem. In 1955 several European countries had not used up their Conditional Aid mainly because employers did not consider the advantages great enough to compensate for the social commitments that acceptance entailed. Yet the suggestion that American leverage over Benton-Moody funds be increased to achieve social policy changes was rejected by the British and Germans within the ERP-TUAC, however beneficial in theory it might seem to other national movements.[76]

The first two years of Conditional Aid had been pretty much a disaster from the standpoint of integrating organised labour into the American-sponsored productivity drive in the problem countries of Europe. By the end of 1952 FO in France and the UIL in Italy had withdrawn from the programme, while in Germany the DGB had not even begun to participate in it. Though stopping short of severing connections with the French national productivity centre, the Christian labour federation CFTC was deeply dissatisfied with the programme. And in Italy the CISL was under strong rank-and-file pressure to redefine its position on productivity. One by-product of labour's disenchantment was that it made the members of FO and the CFTC in France and of the UIL in Italy more prone to succumb to overtures for united action with the communist-led federations in the two countries. In that respect American policy had proved quite counterproductive. As the CIO representative in France, Charles Levinson, warned Victor Reuther, 'If it continues you can kiss FO goodbye in a year.'[77]

European labour's disillusionment with Conditional Aid was shared by the CIO. Indeed, the CIO's European staff had been very active in urging European labour to hold out for better terms under the Benton-Moody programme. In Germany Helmuth Jockel had been highly critical of Harris's handling of the productivity issue for the MSA, telling Reuther bluntly that Harris had forgotten his trade union principles. He suggested that German industrialists were happy with a situation in which the federal government in conjunction with the MSA made the running in the productivity campaign, thereby relieving business of the need to carry the fight to labour. Meanwhile people like Harris in the MSA's Labour Division were used only for the purpose of pressuring the DGB to support the productivity programme – otherwise they were ignored. And German trade unionists themselves went along with the productivity drive only in the belief that they could not disregard American labour and its support for the scheme.[78] In France Levinson had been centrally involved in helping the FO metalworkers mount their successful revolt against the confederal leadership over the issue of withdrawal from CIERP and the productivity campaign. He had also made it clear to French union officials that they were no longer to assume that MSA Labour staff from a CIO background were speaking in the name of the CIO.[79] And Victor Reuther's own damning judgement of the Benton-Moody efficiency drive in France was quite simply that it was 'a disgrace [...] a labour exploitation programme'.[80]

The CIO's success in helping to oppose Conditional Aid as applied by the MSA probably marked the high point of its influence in Europe. But in a positive sense its international strategy made no dramatic impact. The CIO was uncomfortable in the role of an autonomous power broker in the international field and was keen to work as much as possible through the ICFTU.[81] Operating that way meant that the CIO's international activities would be more acceptable to European labour.

Strongly supported by the CIO, the ICFTU had begun to develop an education and training programme in 1951 designed to equip union activists for the new role in collective bargaining that the CIO and ECA Labour staff envisaged for them. However, lack of finance was a grave problem for the ICFTU, and they were forced to look outside the labour movement for funding for this programme. An International Trust Fund for Free Trade Union Education was established, with the aim of attracting money from the ECA, charitable foundations and even employers.[82] However, the AFL was cool towards the project. It had plentiful funds of its own, indeed its own agenda for European labour. It was at odds with the ICFTU on a variety of policy issues and regarded the organisation as only a half-hearted opponent of communism. Consequently it was not anxious to see the ICFTU/ CIO venture succeed. The AFL therefore used its influence to retard the programme, successfully opposing Victor Reuther's ambitious proposal for establishing an international trade union college in Brussels, funded by the ECA. Instead it was agreed to concentrate on a less ambitious training programme for French and Italian trade unionists based at la Brévière, the Swedish labour movement's recreational centre in France.[83] In spring 1952 the first la Brévière courses were held for 250 French trade unionists. To finance the project the MSA channelled $23,000 to the ICFTU through Reuther's bank account without any mention of the original government source of the funds.[84] At this time Walter Reuther also received what appears to have been a one-off payment of $50,000 from the CIA which was used for other training courses in Europe.[85] And it seems possible that the ICFTU education programme benefited from additional funding arranged by Clinton Golden and labelled Ford Foundation money when in fact it came from the Michigan Foundation – a CIA front.[86]

However, the ICFTU's educational work was always a modest operation. The AFL gladly seized the high moral ground to block open ICFTU funding from government sources and dubious foundations. In 1954 at least $90,000 was available from the Marshall Plan for ICFTU educational activities but Brown would not agree to accept it, on the grounds that it was government money.[87] The AFL were also not prepared to take Ford Foundation money: believing that there were 'subversives' at work in the Foundation who might escape AFL efforts to control their activities, they had ruled out any financial help from that source which Clinton Golden, as a director, might have been able to arrange.[88] The result of AFL blocking tactics was that in 1954 the ICFTU began to contemplate abolishing the educational trust fund.[89]

The fund's demise coincided with steps by the CIO to wind up its European operation. The move was dictated by its impending merger with the AFL, even though the latter had no intention of reciprocating by closing down Brown's Brussels office. In the course of its brief presence in Europe the CIO's strategy for helping European labour had hardly been given a chance to work, stymied to a large extent by conflicts with the AFL within the ICFTU. However, in those few years relations with the Marshall Plan administration had been strained to breaking point over the operation of the pilot plant schemes; the CIO had become highly critical of the effects of the productivity campaign and had disowned much of the American government's programme.

The whole Marshall Plan labour programme had turned sour. The administration of Conditional Aid had helped to produce a flurry of anti-Americanism among former friends of the United States within French labour, and this now chimed with President Vincent Auriole's pointed assertion of French independence and his criticism of American policies towards his country.[90] In the United States 'valuation teams' returned from Europe with a generally poor impression of the Benton-Moody programme. Their reports contributed to Congress's hesitant mood in the course of 1953, when it first repealed the Benton-Moody clauses and then re-enacted them.[91] Meanwhile, Eisenhower's new Republican administration was taking a critical look at the performance of the MSA. Though never very great in the past, the influence of labour in the programme was now at an all-time low. Under the new Administrator, Harold Stassen, morale in the Labour Division was at rock bottom and staff were resigning or being weeded out. In the course of 1953 the number of CIO personnel attached to the aid programme fell from thirty to eleven. By the end of that year the top labour advisory and information posts in Washington and Paris were vacant. The Public Advisory Board failed to meet in the course of 1953 and in December Meany resigned in protest. Stassen had embarked on a major organisational shake-up of the FOA, as the Agency was now called. In 1954 a new aid programme would be announced, involving a sharp switch of emphasis away from Europe to the developing world. Of a projected labour staff of seventy only fourteen would be based in Europe. The Americans were beginning to look for ways of handing the productivity question back to the Europeans.

CHAPTER 11

The European Productivity Agency

such techniques as time study, job evaluation, merit rating, the use of psychological tests for promotion and hiring have been bones of contention between labour and management even in highly organised areas. Their use in areas and countries without unions or with weak unions can become the basis of unbridled exploitation. Unfortunately the Americans in charge of the productivity programme continued to advocate these measures with little regard for the collective bargaining environment within which they had found themselves. The productivity drive degenerated into a management cult in which a fixed remedy was prescribed for each country independent of the peculiar problems it faced. [William Gomberg, 'Labour's participation in the European Productivity Programme: a study in frustration', *Political Science Quarterly*, LXXIV, No. 2, June 1959]

Dependence on the USA was massive, to the point where it is hardly an exaggeration to suggest that the leadership function in the collective mind of British industry was *vested* in America. This process, begun during the war, was carried on through the import of [...] Training Within Industry [...] based on group discussion methods. In 1951 Anglo-American Productivity Council teams returned full of glowing and uncritical admiration of the American management education scene [and] Brooke Bros. subculture. [Alistair Mant, *The Rise and Fall of the British Manager*, 1977]

Concurrent with their early efforts to promote national productivity centres, the Americans had been thinking in terms of establishing an agency in Europe to co-ordinate the national campaigns. After leaving the Marshall Plan to become President of the Ford Foundation in 1950, Paul Hoffman had proposed the creation of a bipartite labour–management international agency concerned with productivity to be underwritten by the Ford and Nuffield Foundations.[1] However, in August 1952 the OEEC took the initiative in establishing the European Productivity Agency (EPA), with responsibility for promoting productivity throughout Europe in line with Western defence needs. It was part of a medium-term programme to increase productivity by 25 per cent in the next five years.

The EPA came into being in May 1953. Ostensibly it was a European creation, with headquarters in Paris, a Director, Dr K. P. Harten, drawn from the German iron and steel employers' research centre, and an Advisory Board comprising prominent figures from European industry, organised labour and agriculture.[2] In fact it was funded overwhelmingly from Conditional Aid. It had a central budget of $10 million for its first three years, of which the USA provided $2·5 million in direct grant, the member nations contributing the balance, largely from their individual allocations of Conditional Aid.[3] Indeed, American financing of the EPA exceeded the amounts originally intended. The MSA Administrator, Harold Stassen, agreed that most of the 60 to 100 Americans working in European agencies in 1953 with expertise relevant to the activities of the EPA should stay in Europe for at least another year, funded from an annual budget of $17 million. They were to co-operate with the EPA and the national productivity centres in administering the $100 million of Benton-Moody funds.[4] The Americans hoped that the EPA would foster European integration while permitting the gradual withdrawal of direct dollar aid. In the meantime the MSA/FOA made a special additional contribution to EPA averaging $1·5 million annually up to 1958.[5] After 1956 the general level of American funding began to decline, but even then the annual budget for work among trade unions was only just under $400,000. And when EPA operations ceased in 1960 with the transformation of the OEEC into OECD, the United States was still providing over half the Agency's operating budget.[6]

Generous external funding gave the EPA a measure of independence from the OEEC. However, at the insistence of the British government the Agency was made subject to ultimate control by the Council of Ministers of the OEEC, with the member states entitled to block any aspect of EPA work.[7] This reflected worries on both sides of British industry that the EPA might be too interventionist. The British Employers' Confederation feared that European competitors stood to gain more than British business from the interchange of ideas and experience planned by the EPA.[8] In fact in Europe there was little if any enthusiasm for the

concept of the EPA. As the FOA consultant Clement Watson, of
General Foods, advised, 'There is no ready-made market for EPA.
It must be sold. We should freely admit that EPA is an American
brainchild [...].'[9]

The Agency operated programmes aimed at both management
and unions. Smarting from its unhappy experience in the first two
years of the Conditional Aid programme, organised labour was
anxious to bring a positive influence to bear on the EPA. The
ICFTU's European affiliates held a productivity conference in
London in October 1953 to decide on strategy in this area. As the
conference report noted:

> Latest developments in several countries show that there is a con-
> siderable effort by the employers to negate the principles of the
> productivity programme by refusing to co-operate with the trade
> unions and specifically to utilise the works councils as a means
> seemingly to comply with the spirit of the programme and at the same
> time weakening and discrediting the free trade unions.

It was time to decide whether or not to continue to support the
productivity drive.[10] In fact official union support for the
crusade was never in doubt: the leadership saw it as an integral
part of the Western defence effort, and to this they were fully
committed.[11] An attempt was made to reactivate the ERP-
TUAC's consultative role within the OEEC so as to be able to
influence early policy discussions, but the trade union impact in
the formative stage was weak. The consequence was that organised labour was initially accorded low standing in the administrative structure and the EPA's labour programme evolved as
a subordinate part of the Human Factors Division, whose main
emphasis was on the promotion of human relations concepts.[12]

There were five main components to the labour programme:
the development of trade union information and research services; a training programme for union leaders; an intra-European
technical assistance programme for trade union visits, conferences and seminars; the development of an ICFTU training centre
and support for ITSs. The FOA contributed the bulk of the
funding for each of these. Participants paid only 12 per cent
of the cost, while the Americans contributed 62 per cent, the
balance coming from central EPA funds.[13] And of course, financial control allowed the Americans substantial political control.
The trade union programme was long in preparation and came

into effect only in mid-1954. Unions were initially mistrustful of the EPA Director, coming as he did from the employers' side. Organised labour was also resentful at being excluded from EPA policy-making during the programme-planning stage. The TUC was initially opposed to the whole idea of a productivity programme aimed specifically at the trade unions.[14] Their chief criticism was of the project aimed at training union officials in productivity skills and an understanding of the joint role of labour and management in promoting efficiency. Five American experts were to devise the syllabus for a training programme that each national productivity centre without then administer, with the Americans assisting as peripatetic lecturers. The course was to cover efficient trade union administration; cost accounting for industrial production; production engineering and time and motion study; incentive payment systems, and the role of personnel management.[15]

While the TUC could countenance such a project in a domestic British context and under their own control, this venture would be dominated by Americans. And though the British were willing to invite European trade unionists to attend TUC courses, they were not prepared to have American experts involved. When training for work study by Americans had first been mooted by the ECA in 1951 Fletcher, the TUC Production Department chief, had warned, 'it is quite possible there will be indoctrination rather than work study'.[16] The British eventually agreed to nominal participation – 'cynical co-operation', as Fletcher put it. The TUC always regarded itself more as a disseminator of productivity expertise than as a beneficiary of the superior wisdom of others.

Meanwhile various attempts were made to emasculate the productivity training component of the programme. The British pressed successfully for the establishment of a larger panel of international trade union specialists in productivity matters who might be seconded from their jobs for up to a year to work with national productivity centres on EPA projects and whose mixed national composition would dilute the American presence in the programme.[17] In truth, the TUC would have liked to see this feature of the EPA's work eliminated altogether. When the labour programme was under review in 1955 the Agency's member states, led by Britain, refused to agree to the level of European

funding that the Americans insisted on. Offering to contribute
$100,000 per year less than the FOA/ICA thought appropriate,
the Europeans were, in effect, insisting on a scaled down programme, with productivity training the obvious candidate for the
axe. For its part the ICA insisted that all the elements of the
existing programme had to remain – the politics of productivity
dictated that – though in the end it was forced to settle for a
budget not far in excess of what the EPA had proposed.[18]
However, in 1955 Fletcher was appointed Deputy Director of EPA
in charge of the Labour and Social Factors programme, and from
there he was in a position to restrain what the British saw as the
worst excesses of American enthusiasm for the productivity
crusade.[19]

FOA/ICA Labour staff in Europe also had their misgivings
about the EPA, though the head of the Labour Division, Barney
Taylor of the UAW, thought the Agency would be acceptable as
long as it was watched carefully by a staff of able American trade
union consultants.[20] They found it necessary to maintain constant pressure on EPA personnel to emphasise basic trade union
programmes. The EPA labour programme chief, Vermeulen,
was known to be an uncritical supporter of job evaluation
techniques and formalised national wages policy, with which
he had formerly been deeply involved in Holland. In all their
dealings with the EPA the ICA Labour staff had to impress on him
the need to steer clear of human relations and psychological
research activities.[21]

Yet with the appointment of John Hollister as ICA Administrator in 1955 in place of Stassen there was a hardening of
the American ideological line which created renewed tension
within the EPA and the ICA's Labour Division. Whereas previously ICA guidelines for EPA programmes spoke of support for
activities designed to strengthen free trade unions, new guidelines by Hollister spoke of strengthening 'free *anti-communist*
trade unions'. Likewise a previous reference to American assistance in the fields of trade union training, education and research
was replaced by an umbrella phrase which spoke of assistance
to 'free trade unions to combat communism'. In other words,
it appeared that only where unions were *directly* involved in
fighting communism could they benefit from American assistance. The change in emphasis was quite fundamental. Labour

staff complained bitterly, but their position was now very weak.[22] The Eisenhower administration would brook no opposition within its ranks: Secretary of State Dulles had insisted that all appointments to foreign labour postings were to be cleared with him, and one of the requirements was that applicants be loyal to the administration. By 1956 appointments to Labour posts were even being made from among people lacking a trade union background. Meanwhile trade union influence in the aid programme had effectively come to an end as the Labour Advisory Board, which Stassen had created to replace the Public Advisory Board, ceased to meet. 'The king is dead. It's not my job to keep Walter Reuther informed on how these jobs are filled,' declared the head of the Labour Division.[23]

Education for productivity

Despite the reduced role of organised labour in the FOA/ICA, after its early difficulties the EPA was responsible for generating a significant level of union activity in the cause of increased productivity. The mid-1950s witnessed the growth of a substantial industry in productivity support services: training schemes, study visits, academic research, management consultancy, publications and conferences all proliferated throughout western Europe, thanks to American financing. During the first full year of the trade union programme 700 trade union officials took part in international visits within Europe. British teams were sent from more than a dozen unions. Such visits continued throughout the decade, the largest proportion of them being to Britain and Germany.[24] In all 350 foreign trade unionists came to study aspects of British productivity between 1956 and 1959.[25] During that period a total of 250 British trade union officers participated in one or other aspect of the EPA programme.[26]

By 1957 teams of mixed nationals, including Britons, were visiting the United States at American expense. Six missions lasting up to six weeks and each with eight participants were scheduled to visit the USA to examine issues such as the social and economic aspects of automation, collective bargaining, health and safety and wage payment systems. Ten British union leaders were also nominated by the TUC to attend university courses in the United States. Most went on the three-month trade union programme run twice yearly by the Harvard Business School. Following his retirement from the ECA, Clinton Golden was heavily involved in this programme. In 1950 Henry Shattick, a wealthy Massachusetts businessman, donated $100,000 to launch a Clinton Golden Fund which helped finance the Harvard course.[27] And from 1952 to 1955 Golden was the director of the trade union programme. In 1951 it was expanded to allow for foreign participants. The ECA covered the expenses of Europeans attending – some fifteen on each course. From 1955 the EPA received a $200,000 subvention from the Ford Foundation (of which Golden was a director) to help defray almost half the cost of European participation. Meanwhile a parallel course of similar duration launched at Columbia University in 1957 provided advanced training for trade unionists in production questions, and this was also attended by TUC nominees. In 1959, when the trade union programme was beginning to run down, there were still 4,000 trade union officers and productivity experts taking part in fifty-one national training sessions, exchange visits by 143 experts or lecturers and fifty-five intra-European missions involving 400 trade unionists, all backed up by an extensive publishing programme which produced more than a dozen information bulletins and pamphlets in four languages.[28]

As far as the Americans were concerned the purpose of the programme of visits was 'to sell the ideas of scientific management, good industrial relations practices and practical business unionism to European management and labour'.[29] In general it was necessary to help Europeans develop an understanding of the benefits accruing from the professionalisation of industrial relations.[30] At Harvard Golden always favoured having union and management officials participate in the same training courses. During the 1950s he became steadily more managerialist in outlook, happy that management had responded favourably to his ideas but disappointed by what he saw as the unions' dilatory response to new imperatives in industrial relations. Even some of his closest friends came to believe that he placed undue trust in sophisticated management. As the MSA Labour Adviser Meyer Bernstein observed:

> Phil Murray never trusted an employer. Clint had more respect for them as individuals [...] I think Clint went too far in one direction and Murray did in another.[31]

It is hard to assess the impact of American visits on the European participants. Seasoned British trade union visitors were not taken in by the more extravagant claims of the productivity lobbyists regarding the American unions' compliant approach to scientific management techniques. For them, as for the members of the 1949 TUC productivity team, the evidence was readily to hand. As the Assistant General Secretary of the Society of Technical Civil Servants reported on his return from three months at Columbia University, 'They [the trade unions] do not, so far as I could discover, co-operate with management in any significant sense in productivity drives or attempts to increase efficiency [...]. The idea sometimes hawked here that American trade unions are enthusiastic parties in raising production seems to have little foundation.'[32] Some returned with unfavourable impressions of working conditions in the United States. As Tom Cynog-Jones, Research Director of the Union of Shop Distributive and Allied Workers (USDAW), wrote after leading a European trade union team which studied the American retail industry:

> Sometimes workers are mesmerised by the prospect of earning a high bonus and accept a working pace which is physically harmful and exhausting. There are times when a slower speed and a lower bonus should be accepted. Our group was disturbed to learn of the way in which the American worker is prepared to sell hard-won leisure. It seemed to us that he had an exaggerated desire to earn money.[33]

Inevitably some participants returned convinced that high American productivity stemmed from an indefinable attitude of mind.[34] At a minimum the experience of pleasant sojourns in the United States would have had the effect of bolstering the cadre of British union leaders who were broadly pro-American in outlook: that was always part of the psychology of study visits. It is perhaps significant that the General and Municipal Workers' Union (G&MWU), the British union that most closely approximated the style of American business unionism, provided from among its leading officials half the British participants in the university trade union courses at Harvard and Columbia.

The effect of the visits on continental European trade unionists is equally difficult to divine, though for French and Italian visitors the sharp contrast between the American system of industrial relations and their own and the equally wide gap between relative living standards seems to have had a positive impact in winning influential converts to the American approach to labour relations. There is no doubt that they were under constant pressure from the EPA to view the American system favourably, the assumption being that their adoption of something like it was inevitable. As the EPA outline of the Columbia trade union course explained, 'it is of vital interest for trade unions to have actual experience of the American "shop floor" policy, since the European methods of forming policy at national and industry-wide levels will probably prove insufficient *during the transition period*.'[35]

Parallel with the training of trade unionists, the EPA was heavily committed to developing specialist institutes for management education. It was indeed a most diligent body, working to import American-style business schools to Europe. As one EPA director ruefully admitted, there was a tendency to regard American methods of management as a remedy for all ills. In 1956 the Agency began to mount seminars in Europe on the theme of training for management, led by American consultants. That year fifty-six European university teachers were sent for a year to study management subjects at American universities. Summer schools were also begun for European lecturers in economics, social sciences and engineering to help them deepen their interest in management topics.[36] Again the Ford Foundation contributed to the cost of bringing American experts to Europe. The raw statistics of activity in this area were impressive. By 1958 the EPA had run 340 courses in management techniques for the benefit of 15,000 participants, one study mission to the USA, fifteen training courses for teachers in America and seven international conferences on management.[37] In Britain the Board of Trade allocated £500,000 million to finance training programmes for personnel and work study managers and to endow further teaching posts in industrial engineering at technical colleges.[38] This large-scale boost to managerialism and the sophisticated control techniques at the disposal of employers in turn reinforced the need for the trade union training that the EPA was also engaged in promoting.

A related project which also had the effect of promoting sophisticated managerialism was the EPA's sponsorship of academic research in the social sciences, a new departure in many European countries.[39] Beginning with a few research projects on the 'human aspects of productivity involving human sciences', the EPA went on to develop a long-term action programme, the objective of which was to promote scientific knowledge of the problems of work. Characteristically this involved training young academic researchers in the United States for a year, disseminating popularised accounts of social science literature to industrialists, and acting as a catalyst for research projects to be financed by foundations and national governments.[40]

This programme also had a significant conditioning influence on the world of labour relations. It was launched at two EPA-sponsored international conferences of academics working in the fields of psychology and sociology, held at Florence in 1955 and Rome in 1956. The FOA/ICA were keen to promote enlightened university courses in business subjects as a means of changing traditional managerial attitudes and furthering human relations programmes in industry. In the USA the 'neutral role of the university between labour, management and government' had enabled it to mould cultural attitudes in this way. The ICA therefore decided on the idea of staging these two major conferences on 'The Role of Universities in National Productivity'. The Rome conference would be attended by top European and American academics, including the presidents of a number of leading American universities, who would afterwards remain in Europe for several weeks for consultations and to attend follow-up conferences in different countries.[41]

The emphasis on human relations was something that American trade unionists were very critical of. Returning from a European visit in autumn 1955, Jack Conway, Walter Reuther's executive assistant, reported that European management were intervening more actively in works council elections to secure the return of docile representatives. This was then supplemented by the extensive promotion of human relations programmes designed to delineate a restricted area of industrial relations where union involvement was permitted, but leaving a far larger and more important area under exclusive managerial control. Most of these programmes were of American origin. Conway's conclusion was unambiguous:

> The EPA over a period of years has laid such stress on achieving productivity increases through the use of incentive pay systems, the use of time and motion systems, and other such techniques that

most plant-level leaders who know anything at all about EPA are extremely suspicious and distrustful of it. If EPA now becomes associated in the minds of these same people with the promotion of these human relations programmes which are essentially anti-union in character, EPA might just as well fold up shop so far as the labour movement is concerned.[42]

When the EPA leaders visited the United States in November 1955, ICA Labour staff were swift to broach their worries about the Rome conference and their belief that it might accentuate the tendency for human relations gimmicks to become a substitute for constructive labour–management relations, especially in France and Italy. But EPA preparations for the conference were too advanced for them to postpone it now.[43]

The Ford Foundation, the Marshall Plan and academic research

Even more influential in setting the agenda for discussion of industrial relations was the research promoted by the Ford Foundation, which was in effect sub-contracted Marshall Plan work. The Ford Foundation was rooted in the values of the Marshall programme. It was established in the early months of the ERP and was operational in 1950, with programmes devised to take over where the educational and propagandistic work of the Marshall Plan left off. Henry Ford II envisaged the Foundation contributing systematically to the development of a world order based on liberal capitalism. With its considerable resources dwarfing other foundations – an initial endowment of some $200 million and a planned annual expenditure of $25 million – it was intended to transcend the existing efforts of government, industry and foundations such as the Rockefeller and Carnegie in the field of education and development for industrial society. The basic objective was to advance America's national welfare, but for Ford this was quite compatible with wider philanthropic concerns: 'The people in this country and mankind in general are confronted with problems which are vast in number.'[44] It was the Foundation's task to resolve some of these.

From the outset it had the fullest support of the State Department. With the intention of spending about a third of the Foundation's budget overseas on programmes aimed at 'maintaining peace' and assisting in 'meeting crises' through a Fund for

Foreign Operations, Ford and Hoffman asked Secretary of State Acheson to suggest projects which his department approved of but could not afford to finance. Acheson's suggestions were all for projects related to the overseas promotion of American managerial values and know-how. Since the general thrust of the Foundation's work was to help increase world levels of production, Acheson told Hoffman that he could count on the assistance of the State Department at any time.[45]

The Ford Foundation became a second home for senior Marshall Plan staff. Throughout most of the 1950s it was headed by the banker John McCloy, fresh from his post as High Commissioner to Germany during the ERP years. Richard Bissell was largely responsible for the organisational shape the Foundation took. A former special representative in Europe, Milton Katz, was made an associate director. From the Marshall Plan's labour staff, Clinton Golden became a director while Leo Werts and Michael Harris moved on to field posts with the Foundation. But the closest tie of all between the Marshall programme and the Ford Foundation was through the person of Paul Hoffman, who resigned as Administrator of the ECA in 1950 to become the Foundation's first president. In his new post Hoffman took the lead in founding an ECA Alumni Association, several of whose more prominent members were now on the Foundation staff.

Hoffman identified the organisation's primary concern as being to help 'avert another war', for which the prescription appeared to be the undermining of support for communism. In practical terms this led the Foundation to interest itself in adult education and, in particular, training and education for trade unionists both in the United States and abroad. Early on, American labour leaders were sounded out as to the most desirable emphasis for the Foundation's work, and David Dubinsky concurred that the number one problem in the world was the fight against communism.[46] It was thus decided that the activities of the Foundation 'should be directed to the rapid and extensive education of adults about the world situation, the nature of the struggle in which we are engaged, and the heritage we are seeking to defend'. An Adult Education Fund was created in 1951 with a budget of $5·4 million and a board of directors including Clinton Golden and Philip Reed, the American co-chairman of the AACP. Its remit was to concern itself with 'the problems of labour relations, and problems of the principles and policies underlying the operation of a free economy'.

One of the early projects sponsored by the Adult Education Fund was conducted by the American Management Association and involved a study of the work being done by university industrial relations centres. Entitled 'Management Education for itself and its Employees', and with a grant of $100,000, the project was led by the British evangelist of scientific management, Colonel Urwick. The Association appointed a committee of prominent business leaders who were to make recommendations regarding the content of industrial relations teaching.[47] The AMA took as its starting point the ideologically loaded assertion that 'management's role in the preservation of a free society is putting the real meaning of a free society to work within the organisation for which each individual executive is responsible. *The basic purpose of management is absolutely consistent with that of a free society.* [...] *The basic objective of management is the development of individuals.*'[48] Naturally these values were also intended for export, and by the early 1950s the Ford Foundation was actively encouraging the development in Europe of employer organisations analogous to the Committee for Economic Development.[49]

Of greater importance in terms of creating a global intellectual consensus around industrial relations issues was the mammoth Inter-unversity Study of Labour Problems in Economic Development. Financed by the Foundation, the project began in 1952 and lasted for over twenty years. Based at the universities of Chicago and Princeton and jointly led by John Dunlop, Clark Kerr, Frederick Harbison and Charles Myers – all contributors to the NPA's earlier research on the causes of industrial peace – it was concerned to discover why, despite the huge post-war American investment of money and effort around the world, there was still resistance to the importation of American industrial relations values. Taking as a starting point the supposed universal logic of industrial society, much of the research worked from an assumption that the ideal society was the 'managed', 'open', 'affluent' capitalist society of the Western world which had reached its apogee in the United States.[50] The project provided a framework and a linking theme for some of the most highly publicised research in industrial relations by many of the best-known academics in the field. The major publications to emerge from the project included *Industrialism and Industrial Man* by the principal researchers; Reinhard Bendix, *Work and Authority in Industry*; John Dunlop, *Industrial Relations Systems*, Walter Galenson, *Labour in Developing Economies*; Henry Ehrmann, *Organised Business in France*; Val Lorwin, *The French Labour Movement*; Daniel Horowitz, *The Italian Labour Movement*; Heinz Hartmann, *Authority and Organisation in German Management*, and Adolf Sturmthal, *Workers' Councils: a Study of Workplace Organisation on both Sides of the Iron Curtain*. Altogether the project gave birth to thirty-six books and forty-two articles and papers. No fewer than ninety academic researchers in the United States and abroad were involved at one stage or another. These included other established figures in the world of academic industrial relations such as S. M. Lipset, E. Wright Bakke, Lloyd Ulman, Sumner Rosen, Abraham Siegal, Mark Leiserson, Bert Hoselitz and Frederic Myers.[51]

If ever an academic project established intellectual hegemony by the sheer scale of its operation, this was it. Many of the publications it produced came to be regarded as definitive statements, and those dealing with aspects of foreign industrial relations were often the only major English-language studies available. This output provided a goodly portion of the basic teaching material of industrial relations courses during the 1950s and 1960s, and against such weight of scholarship it was a daunting task to argue against the logic of 'industrial society' and the 'end of ideology', the benefits of a managerial society, or the line that trade unions existed essentially to trim the rough edge off managerial decisions and otherwise to join employers in preserving the stability of pluralist industrial society.

British academic research on human relations in industry had already been greatly stimulated by the availability of Conditional Aid. The extensive programme begun in 1953 was, in essence, a development of the work originally proposed by the Schuster Panel of the Board of Trade's Committee on Productivity, which had been established in 1947 to investigate the role of the 'human factor' in productivity in circumstances where immediate improvements were required and the prospects of large-scale capital investment remote. Inspired by the work of Elton Mayo, whom it consulted at an early stage, the Schuster

Panel's contribution was to propose a series of research projects in the field of applied psychology and industrial engineering focusing on such issues as group morale, the optimum size of work units and social organisation at work. Schuster's own position was to emphasise the importance of the individual in industry and to view trade unions as essentially restrictive. 'Our chief trouble today is [factors] which prevent the individual from giving his normal instinctive response.' Individual unions leaders, he believed, were inclined to be personally soured and suspicious, holding up progress for political reasons.[52] The panel had argued that 'Industrial Productivity needs to be recognised as a subject for scientific research in its own right [...]. We believe [...] that this kind of operational research will be the chief vitalising element in the whole process of productivity research [...],' though it was aware of the danger of 'premature crystallisation of spurious orthodoxies'.[53] The panel urged the development of academic research in the broad field of human relations.

With Moody funds becoming available to finance it in 1952, the Ministry of Labour gave a lead by convening a national conference on human relations in industry which was intended to focus on American experience as described in the AACP reports. As a member of the TUC Production Department noted with not a little cynicism, '"Human Relations" is the new phrase for industrial relations, plus improved productivity, plus anything which might remove some savagery from life.'[54] But this, together with the other specialisms that had aroused the interest of the Schuster Panel – human engineering, personnel selection and work measurement – provided the basis of what would become an extensive programme of British university-based research:

> There is a strong case for putting more effort into the study of these problems. (For example the problems of time and motion study methods for which there has been practically no attempt yet to contribute any scientifically valid foundation.) [...] The Social Science Departments might use their resources much more effectively than at present if they were given some guidance as to what are important problems to study.[55]

Three university Chairs in industrial engineering and related technological fields were endowed by the University Grants Committee, and social science departments were invited to bid for grants to research aspects of productivity from the £178,000 made available from Conditional Aid. From the outset the Board of Trade narrowed down the definition of productivity research to exclude any proposals relating to wider social factors or themes relevant to productivity performance such as income distribution, the economics of underdeveloped areas or 'social accounting'. A more narrowly defined, functional approach to efficiency was adopted, with a focus on issues such as restrictive practices, the operation of work study techniques, factors facilitating the introduction of new production methods and the characteristics of management organisation having an influence on productivity. By 1956, when, under Conditional Aid, the projects were due to be completed, forty British universities or research institutes had been in receipt of grants and the total published output from the research was 110 books and journal articles on topics ranging from equipment design for efficiency to the utilisation of industrial engineering techniques and the effects of incentive payment systems.[56] Taken together, this programme was almost certainly the biggest single fillip yet to British academic research in production engineering and human relations. It helped foster the notion of management as a science, and in boosting the momentum of managerialism in industry it was of considerable benefit to rationalising employers.

With the OEEC due to be transformed into OECD and the focus of its work about the change, the American commitment to underwriting the EPA extended only to 1960. In 1958–59 the European Regional Organisation of the ICFTU attempted, without success, to negotiate with the EPA for the foundation of a European trade union college, to be run by the unions themselves but still offering courses in subjects relating to productivity.[57] Efforts were also made during its final two years to renegotiate the objectives of the EPA in ways acceptable to labour, but without result. To the last the focus of its attention was on narrow technical details of productivity, to the exclusion of wider social and economic considerations. Proposals to broaden the approach were resisted, employers' organisations insisting that the Agency 'confine its activity to principles and methods which are of such a nature as to develop the spirit of co-operation and to make people organisation-minded in their work [...]'.[58] As the EPA's Advisory Board noted in the closing months of its existence, the main priority was unchanged: 'it is still necessary to work with a view to developing the "productivity mind" among people employed in whatsoever capacity'.[59]

CHAPTER 12

European labour and productivity in the 1950s

On the programme side it is difficult to judge the overall plus and minus of labour's seven years in the Foreign Aid Programme. I would make the guess that the positive outweighs the negative by a moderate degree. The tragedy is in the many lost opportunities to make far more significant contributions to free unionism. [CIO Washington office, June 1955]

The Marshall Plan was, at best, a very partial success in terms of its short-run objectives – to restore Western Europe's economic health and political stability and to make it independent of 'extraordinary outside assistance'. Yet, mainly because of the attractiveness of its symbolic meaning, it succeeded for a time in giving [...] a new sense of direction and purpose. [William Y. Elliott *et al.*, *The Political Economy of American Foreign Policy: its Concepts, Strategy and Limits*, 1955]

Britain. If at times the TUC remained aloof from aspects of the EPA programme its involvement in the work of the BPC and the ongoing efficiency campaign in Britain was consistent. Among the inner core of the TUC General Council, especially, support for productivity initiatives was unqualified. All the members of the TUC's Production Committee served as council members of the BPC except for the Boilermakers' leader, Ted Hill, who had attacked the productivity drive at the founding conference of the BPC and was duly censured by the TUC. Congress pressure was put upon local trades councils to support the work of the BPC's local productivity associations.

In practice few unions responded wholeheartedly to the TUC call to establish training programmes in managerial techniques for shop stewards. In 1952 Ian Mikardo hazarded a guess that not more than three unions in the country spent one shilling per annum per member on education for their new role.[1] Most unions relied on outside agencies to provide whatever training was given – often through the National Council of Labour

Colleges (NCLC) or the Workers' Educational Association (WEA), which ran some thirty evening courses on production and management topics for trade unionists in 1950, each of twelve weeks duration.[2] THe G&MWU had by far the most extensive programme of training for its members, utilising in the first instance the facilities of the Birmingham College of Technology and later universities and technical colleges in over a dozen locations at a cost of over £25,000 annually. The syllabus for the programme was devised by the union and involved the teaching of work study, industrial relations and English in equal measure. The courses, some of them residential, began in 1949, and by 1951 were being offered on a one-month basis at each of the locations. Trade unionists were trained at the rate of 400 or more per year, and by the end of the 1950s 3,000 shop stewards and officers had completed the programme. The teaching was not by trade unionists nor even necessarily by people with labour movement sympathies until 1954, when the G&MWU decided to open its own training school and to appoint its own training officer – the future General Secretary, David Basnett. Basnett was one of four G&MWU officials who had been given three months' training in management techniques free of charge by the management consultants Personnel Administration Ltd and Associated Industrial Consultants Ltd, as had a dozen officials from six other unions.[3]

Whether production training was taken seriously or not, the standard line of many union leaders was to issue ringing calls to their organisations to support, and even lead, the productivity drive. The line was moderated only during the recessions of 1952 and 1958, when rising unemployment rendered it politically untenable. Yet the faith of even the most ardent proponents of productivity that workers would receive their just deserts from improved performance was severely tested in the early 1950s when profits and dividends reached record levels against a background of restrained wages. At the 1954 and 1955 conferences of the G&MWU the leadership complained that the benefits of rising productivity had not been equitably shared and the government was accused of taking advantage of the labour movement's reasonableness.[4] This prompted General Secretary Tom Williamson to propose that the TUC should secure Conditional Aid for academic research into what had happened to the proceeds of productivity. It was a poignant comment on the role of TUC leadership that, after eight years of unwavering support for the productivity drive, one of their number should enquire innocently who had benefited from the exercise.

> There are allegations being made that the workpeople are not getting their fair share; and, side by side with these, there are allegations that too much is being paid out in dividends.
>
> It seems to me that this is a matter in which we should interest ourselves, because there does not appear to be any reliable evidence on which these statements can be properly argued or refuted.[5]

However, the TUC doubted whether the narrowly technicist university research programme into productivity which was being financed by Conditional Aid would accommodate an investigation that raised broad questions of equity and social policy, and no action was taken on Williamson's proposal.[6]

In the T&GWU Arthur Deakin seized every opportunity to preach the productivity message to the membership. His reports to the quarterly executive council meetings and editorials in the union journal included regualar sermons on the subject. Productivity was the joint responsibility of unions and management, members were to 'put their best foot forward in connection with the drive'. In international labour gatherings Deakin repeated the line, from time to time using a guest appearance at a union conference on the Continent or an address to the International Transport Workers' Federation to reiterate 'the hard economic facts of life' about productivity.[7] Like-minded union leaders chorused the message. The G&MWU Chairman told his union conference that productivity was vital to Britain's survival as a political power,[8] and USDAW's General Secretary called on the Conservative government to encourage a 'constant sustained drive to increase productivity'.[9]

Trade union arguments in favour of the productivity campaign frequently acknowledged that workers necessarily found themselves on the other side of the divide from management, but nevertheless, despite their differences, they had a common interest in raising productivity. 'Can we, under a capitalist system, obtain a higher standard of life for building workers by being modern Luddites?' asked the editor of the building union journal, the *Operative Builder*.[10] As the General Secretary of USDAW argued at his union conference in 1953:

I recognise that there may seem to be a natural tendency under such conditions [i.e. with a Conservative government in power] for workers to respond less enthusiastically to productivity appeals [...]. If there are some people [...] who have a conception of holding the government and employers to ransom on this question of productivity, then it must be said that the conception is wholly false, because that ransom can only be paid by the wage earners themselves [...].[11]

Yet some of the most prominent union leaders argued the case for productivity in the belief that traditional antagonisms between labour and capital were no longer valid, or at least that the growing ranks of managerial personnel had to be accepted as a neutral force in industry. The Chairman of the G&MWU, Jack Cooper, deplored the atmosphere of suspicion and bitterness between management and labour when much more co-operation was necessary. Recently returned from the Harvard course, he announced that it was to change these archaic attitudes among workers that the union had launched its education programme on management techniques.[12] Responding the following year to a conference resolution calling for workers' control, General Secretary Tom Williamson insisted on industry's need for workers and management to operate for the common good rather than as opposing forces.[13] The T&GWU *Record* lauded the concept of trade unions as partners in management and production engineering.[14] Arthur Deakin berated those who claimed more output would only line the pockets of profit-makers, noting that the profit motive was, to a large extent, a thing of the past.[15] And in welcoming signs of a growing managerial revolution – the displacement of 'finance' directors by working directors which would gradually weaken capitalism – the T&GWU argued that unions should do nothing to undermine the position of the 'functional leaders in industry whose work maintains industrial units as going concerns for the people to take over in good order when the time comes'.[16]

Full support for scientific management in industry was thus necessary for survival, and Jack Tanner claimed that training for productivity would make trade unionists competent for taking on managerial roles.[17] The trouble with such views was that there was nothing in the policy programme of the trade unions in the 1950s that suggested that workers were being prepared to take over the direction of management, nor any evidence that union-trained production specialists who moved over into management altered the basic nature of labour–management relations. More sophisticated union officials maintained that their involvement in discussions about productivity brought aspects of managerial prerogative under the scrutiny of workers.[18] Scientific management techniques might lead to greater managerial control, but this was acceptable if it was exercised in the context of negotiated consent, rather than a unilateral assertion of prerogative.[19]

Enthusiasts for productivity insisted on drawing comforting if misleading messages from American experience. Members of the steelworkers' union were informed in 1952 that American industry was 'rediscovering the individual' and bringing him into harmony with the machine.[20] Bob Edwards, the maverick left-wing General Secretary of the Chemical Workers' Union, expounded the view that the acceptance of scientific management and incentive wage schemes had increased the influence of American unions, though in retrospect it became clear that their influence over the production process had been stemmed and was now in the process of being reversed by management.[21] Echoing the misconception that had been fostered by the AACP reports, the Chairman of the G&MWU told conference delegates that American unions had enlarged the scope of their activities by setting up special departments to 'co-operate' with management to improve production performance.[22] And, ignoring the evidence of relative under-investment in Britain, his successor attributed America's greater industrial success to 'an attitude of mind'.[23]

Amidst all this TUC technicians were quietly worried about the activities of the BPC's Work Study Unit. Its main function was to provide lecturers and seminar leaders for meetings throughout the country, and the TUC were uneasy at not being able to monitor the message these people spread. They were particularly worried that too much reliance was being placed on the work study concepts developed by Imperial Chemical Industries (ICI).[24] More than any other British company ICI had pioneered work study techniques after the war, and by 1955 had a staff of 1,200 working in this field, 370 of them relatively senior managers.[25] The TUC noted that most of the guest lecturers employed by the BPC Work Study Unit, and even the teaching materials used, originated with ICI. For this reason the TUC urged the unit to concentrate less on time study and to talk about productivity in more general terms.[26] Congress did put forward one nominee of its own for inclusion on the panel of guest lecturers, an expert on the Russian machine-tool industry, but after vetting him the BPC rejected the nomination on the grounds that he was 'politically biased'.[27] However, the TUC were still concerned about the Unit encroaching on industrial relations matters, and in 1955 they vetoed an attempt to establish within it an industrial advisory service for firms – a glorified management consultancy.[28]

Against the background of siren calls for trade unionists to participate enthusiastically in the productivity campaign in the 1940s and 1950s, the TUC's Production Department under Edwin Fletcher offered a sober rationalisation of union involvement. Here, at least, there were no suggestions that the divisions between labour and capital were disappearing, no affirmation of faith in the beneficence of a new class of neutral management technicians. It was a pragmatic approach that concerned itself only with the short to medium term and saw no pro-active role for labour in effecting extensive long-term social change. Trade unions, the department reasoned, had a natural interest in productivity, since they were inevitably concerned to raise the standard of living of their members. Fletcher concentrated more on the potential contribution of new capital than on the revamping of the labour process. The basic cause of industrial inefficiency in Britain was the historic failure of employers to invest, a tendency compounded by the fact that in wartime and during subsequent reconstruction employers had been able to make easy profits. Scientific advance was the chief source of greater productivity, and because of this it was argued that unions ought not to oppose new technology. For their own protection they should be involved at the earliest development stage through their role in the research councils.

The Production Department did not concern itself with the question of whether industry as at present owned and controlled could or should continue. The unions' primary purpose was to extract from industry a reasonable share of the fruits of increased output, and to do this they had to be interested in the level of production. While recognising that increasing productivity could not solve all labour's problems, the reasoning was that many of their aims could not be secured without increased productivity. Consequently, it was in the unions' interest to insist that the most effective use be made of labour. That meant increased capital investment backed by adequate research and more efficient management methods. Workers had nothing to gain from managerial inefficiency. All this posed new difficulties for labour, but they had to be faced.

In general, Fletcher recognised that there was a point beyond which unions should not go in the quest for productivity, the point being reached when they risked losing their integrity as free associations of workers for their own protection. What was needed, therefore, was a positive militant trade union interest in the productivity of their own labour rather than a quiescent agreement with the employers. And a more detailed interest in production matters, he argued, did not necessarily lead to a less virile trade union movement.[29]

However, all this fell some way short of the TUC having a coherent alternative with which to challenge the 'common sense' of the productivity lobby. So extensive was the propaganda and so powerful did the managerial logic appear that unions never faced the issue head-on. Confusion abounded over the new managerial methods. Within the trade union movement it was often argued that work study was nothing new, merely old-fashioned time study under another guise.[30] But whereas unions had resisted it before the war, outright opposition was now no longer necessary in a world of full employment and more socially progressive management. For their part management often played safe and claimed there was no connection between work study and time and motion study – though this was belied by the BIM's own pamphlet, *Work Study*, in which the words 'time and motion study' had actually been deleted and 'work study' superimposed on them.

In fact work study built on the techniques of time study and represented a more systematic attempt to gain control over all facets of the labour process. It was indeed not merely a technique of control but part of an ideology of work supportive of managerial values. The MSA actually hailed its own Work Study Training Programme, begun in 1952, as 'the number one technical assistance programme of all time'.[31] The TUC advice to its affiliates was to query the accuracy and objectivity of work study, but, necessary as this was, it still meant that unions would typically by challenging management over the detail of their strategy rather than the strategy itself.

At the level of labour's grass roots, enthusiasm for the productivity campaign was ebbing fast in the early 1950s. Tangible benefits to workers for their past support were not readily apparent: between 1947 and 1951 output per head of workers in all industries increased by a third, without real wages increasing.[32] The mood of the rank and file explains the decision to mark the termination of the AACP and its replacement by the BPC in more low-key fashion than had initially been planned. The original idea had been to celebrate the transition with a big international conference accompanied by much rousing publicity, but in the event it was decided to mark the occasion with the publication of Graham Hutton's commissioned book on productivity.

Within the trade union movement opposition to the productivity campaign took the form of pressure to distance the TUC from the work of the BPC. At the council's foundation Ted Hill of the Boilermakers pointed out that in the past increased productivity had led to bigger profits without improving working conditions. For this outburst he was censured in the TUC's annual report, and at the 1953 Congress the Boilermakers led an unsuccessful attempt by a group of unions, including the engineers, sheet metal workers, electricians, draughtsmen, foundry workers and vehicle builders, to block TUC support for local productivity committees.

Opposition to increased productivity stratagems became highly vocal once again in 1955 and 1956 when fears about the implications of 'automation' first swept over Europe from the United States amidst reports of how American production had increased by 8 per cent in 1954 with 1·5 million fewer workers. Fears were related to previous experiences in the productivity drive: 'The problem,' USDAW's journal commented, 'cannot be seen in isolation but must be related to the present day drive to increase exploitation, pressure for overtime, and signs of "relative overproduction" appearing.'[33] Automation threatened workers, but firms which did not re-equip also posed a threat. Without new machinery, the likely result of the application of the principles of scientific management was that workers would be pressed to operate obsolete machines and processes ever harder as British industry strove to regain its former international industrial dominance.[34] USDAW's conference reflected the widespread acceptance that automation was a logical outcome of technological developments, but pointed out that despite all possible union safeguards it was still a dangerous force in capitalist hands, and delegates went on to pass a resolution calling for renewed pressure for nationalisation.[35]

Among union members, resistance to the efficiency drive was deep-rooted, if instinctive rather than co-ordinated. Yet amidst the barrage of propaganda in favour of the productivity ethic the counter-argument was rarely stated in union debates. In conferences many delegates expressed enthusiasm for productivity in the context of 'socialism', but it was the exception for delegates to discuss the labour process and to announce, as one G&MWU delegate declared in 1953, 'I have not come on this earth [...] to work every minute of my life, I want to be able to understand music, to be able to read and enjoy this life of ours.'[36] It was also strangely rare for someone in a productivity debate to dwell on the brave new world brought about by scientific management and new technology – in this case at Joseph Lucas, but equally applicable to growing thousands of workers elsewhere in mass production industries where:

> the conveyor system is the last word. Not a moment of time is wasted; the work is so apportioned that every operator has to give his or her constant attention and effort to his or her part of the job. The work is completely repetitive – unmeaning task work to a degree. The work people are mere automatons, slaves to the machine. [...] In every office and workshop in the land such streamlined ruthless efficiency is the goal.[37]

Occasionally similar doubts about the blind emphasis on productivity were even voiced at national leadership level. In 1959 Alan Birch, of USDAW and Chairman of the TUC Economic Committee, observed:

> we now have a spectacle of a drive for efficiency in industries, in firms, in trade unions. What for? For its own sake? Where is the sense of direction that will link up this efficiency in our effort and produce the results which Society is entitled to expect? Why is that lacking? It is lacking because we are trying to apply the principles of private enterprise.[38]

But such publicly admitted doubts were a rare phenomenon and failed to deter the evangelists from resuming their advocacy.

While the attachment of many workers to restrictive practices acted as a barrier to the productivity drive, the new managerial techniques were slowly gaining a foothold. As Les Cannon noted in 1955, there were hundreds of thousands of workers who were being covered by schemes agreed by union officials who undoubtedly supported the productivity drive. '[I]n 1955 many militant shop stewards and trade union officials are recommending acceptance of schemes which, however innocuous they might at first seem, will have the effect of intensifying the exploitation of the members they represent.' Work study did not give workers increased wages proportionate to increased productivity but profitability did forge ahead. Sir Ewart Smith, the technical director of ICI, had recently claimed that the results of the application of work study had enabled the firm to postpone for ten years the construction of a factory costing £1 million.[39] Much as the evangelists of the new productivity techniques promised a world free from drudgery, the fact was that workers were often under great pressure, either to work harder or to put in more continuous and consistent effort.

The debate often shifted quickly away from the potential contribution of technological developments to greater efficiency to the need to utilise existing capital more intensively. As a policy this was justified by Graham Hutton in the mid-1950s on the grounds that inflation now prevented the rapid scrapping of old machinery and its replacement by better equipment. Equally the falling birth rate and shortages of manpower necessitated more flexible working patterns among the existing labour force. In effect it meant a more widespread use of shift working. The burden of achieving higher productivity would clearly fall on labour: 'how on earth are we ever going to double ours [standard of living] in another generation [...] without far more utilisation of our machines and an extension of shifts?'[40] Likewise, though from a more sympathetic standpoint, Anthony Crosland considered the case for increased effort at work as against the demand for more leisure. In essence he was in accord with those who wanted to ease the pressure at work and press for greater relaxation. But the country could not afford to be indifferent to growth: the time was not right.[41] As so often, the ideal society promised by industry's enormous potential receded into the distant, uncertain future.

Italy. Productivity rose faster in Italy in the 1950s than in almost any other Western economy. By 1953 industrial production had doubled since 1938. Output in general engineering was substantial and car production had reached record levels, yet unemployment in metalworking stood at 15 per cent and tens of thousands of lay-offs had been declared in government-controlled steelworks. Between 1951 and 1955 the average annual rate of growth in the productivity of labour was 6·4 per cent, more than double the level for Britain.[42] The ERP had enabled Italy to import a considerable amount of American capital equipment and technology in industries such as motorcycle manufacturing, textiles and the oil industry. Mainly through Marshall Aid, conveyor-belt technology made its first significant appearance.[43] Fiat's productivity offensive of the 1950s was based on the use of imported American capital equipment and the application of more rigorous workplace discipline. Capitalisation and vehicle output grew sixfold in the decade. At the Mirafiori plant output per worker nearly quadrupled between 1948 and 1955.[44]

However, for the most part this was not productivity growth along the lines of the American model, with high consumption fuelling the mass-production process. Indices of consumer spending were low. Food alone took up almost two-thirds of average income in the early 1950s. Not until the second half of the decade did consumer durables begin to appear in significant quantities. But even in 1958 84 per cent of Italian families were still without a television, washing machine or refrigerator. It was this lack of consumer goods production for a strong internal market that held back a solution to the unemployment problem.[45] Lacking a domestic consumer market, Italian firms had to find foreign sales outlets. And rather than employ highly paid workers on labour-saving capital equipment, more often than not industry tended to exploit its surplus labour force, paying low wages and increasing output by traditional speed-up methods. A few firms such as Pirelli deviated from this pattern, favouring mass production for domestic markets, but up to the mid-1950s they were still a small minority.[46]

For the most part Italian employers, like their French counterparts, were resistant to productivity experiments and unwilling to relinquish any of their prerogative that agreement with unions over productivity measures might entail. Their instinct was often to forgo profit rather than follow such a route.[47] In these circumstances it was difficult for the non-communist labour federations to carve out a positive role such as the Marshall Plan called for. The private employers in Confindustria were not interested in institutionalised collaboration with unions over productivity. At national level the CISL and UIL had failed to ensure that social benefits for workers derived from Conditional Aid. In 1955 UIL Secretary Viglianesi was complaining to Walter Reuther that after three years nothing had been done with the Moody funds earmarked for low-cost housing, and he urged that $4 million be spent immediately.[48] For the CISL Pastore had to admit that productivity advances under Marshall Aid had not led to any increase in worker incomes.[49] At plant level the unions were too weak and poorly organised to look after their own interests in a direct fashion as the CIO in particular would have liked. The concept of militant, plant-based collective bargaining advocated by the young graduates of the CISL's training school at Florence remained more an ideal than a practical objective for most of the 1950s. Union divisions and the greater relative strength of hostile employers made the negotiation of plant agreements a difficult operation. And a residual tendency for the CISL's national leadership to behave in a collaborative fashion towards employers led to continued moderation in wage demands.[50] Consequently between 1953 and 1957 there were only 750 plant agreements negotiated, covering a total of only 400,000 workers. More agreements would be negotiated in 1960 alone than in this whole period.[51] In these circumstances the communist-led unions remained the dominant force in labour politics, though the challenge from their non-communist rivals increased significantly in the latter half of the 1950s. Until then at least the CGIL always set the agenda, with its ongoing 'production conferences', its White Papers on working conditions and its agitation for civil rights in the factory.[52] Unable to match it in terms of demagogery, the non-communist federations could not, in their bid for labour movement leadership, point to many tangible benefits that they themselves had won.

Attempts to develop a distinctive FOA/ICA labour programme for Italy were at best halting. There were continuing administrative difficulties in the Rome mission, with the US ambassador, Clare Booth Luce, reluctant to release the necessary funds.[53] In 1955 the CISL's research director conceded that the unions could expect little from the productivity programme. And when the CNP Chairman claimed that at least 'productivity' and 'human relations' were beginning to be discussed in Italy, Gomberg cautioned him against having too much faith in them.[54] With little confidence in the demonstration area scheme the unions, urged on by the CIO, now placed more emphasis on training officials at EPA productivity courses on which mission labour and productivity staff taught. These were of particular value to the UIL, since it was unable to match the CISL's well endowed training centre at Florence. In the first two years of the EPA programme over 1,000 French and Italian trade unionists passed through these courses. Meanwhile in 1955 the International Metalworkers' Federation began to finance courses for trade union officials aimed at developing local-level collective bargaining. In the coming years 5,000 officials attended these at a cost of over $200,000.[55] Even so, training in technical aspects of productivity and collective bargaining made slow progress. The ICA agreed in 1956 to set $50,000 aside for an in-depth union leadership training course in the United States for up to thirty people, but the tendency was always for the Italian participants to want to concentrate on the political and legal aspects of industrial relations – the elements which caused them so much difficulty on a daily basis – rather than on the technical concerns of the productivity specialist.[56]

In ideological terms the Marshall Plan had less of an immediate impact than the programme's authors might have wished. A few enthusiasts of scientific management were inspired by the general value system preached by the Americans, but they were the exception.[57] Yet, on another plane, significant technical modernisation was facilitated by Marshall dollars. As D'Attorre says, 'Ultimately the productivity campaign missed the more ambitious general aims, but opened the path to a considerable renewal of industrial and cultural practice in the country.'[58] However, it was not the firms in the demonstration areas that were critical in improving productivity consciousness, but larger concerns like Olivetti and the progressive public-sector management of ENI and IRI, with their use of work study and sophisticated personnel techniques.[59] Though these approaches often disarmed the workers they also provided scope for the new style of labour–management relations for which the CISL and UIL had been preparing. By the end of the 1950s a few employers were beginning to link higher wage payments with improved productivity in a bid to create a more favourable economic environment for continued growth. The process was assisted by a split in the employers' front in 1957 and the formation of Intersind, representing the more dynamic, modernising public-sector industries which were disposed to reach accommodation with organised labour.

Yet it would not be until after Italy's 'turn to the left' in 1962 and under the more modern, reforming political regime it produced that such an industrial relations pattern would really begin to emerge. Not until the 1960s would there be a further flowering of the Marshall Plan ideology, a greater emphasis on managerial as distinct from entrepreneurial values, and a recognition of the importance of managerial planning for productivity in an emerging mass consumer society. Meanwhile, the take-off for the post-war economic miracle had been based on the existence of widespread unemployment, low wages and a divided, and therefore weak, labour movement.

France. The conservatism of French industry in the early post-war years was deep-seated and hard to root out, but by the end of the 1950s French economic performance had become quite spectacular. Although output and productivity had begun to rise in the late 1940s, with 1938 levels of production regained in 1947, total output at the end of 1951 was still below the level set in the peak year of 1928. Until at least 1953 French economic performance did not give much cause for optimism. Deflationary policies in 1952 threatened the prospect of economic stagnation. Not until 1953–54 was the economy able to achieve expansion without inflation.

The country was beset by political problems at home and abroad which successive weak coalition governments of the Fourth Republic failed to resolve. The result was a state of chronic immobilism which seemed to paralyse all efforts to strike out in a new direction. In this climate it was difficult to inject a sense of vitality in industry – as Marshall Plan officials knew only too well. Jean Monnet had attempted to incorporate features of American industrial life in the planning process which he regarded as a psychological exercise: the plan was a 'state of mind'. French industry needed to adopt the American business psychology and particularly its attitude to growth and constant change.[60]

However, the whole idea was outside the cultural tradition of French businessmen and only slowly gained support. They were divided among themselves over the desirability of modernisation and over the sort of political regime best able to oversee it. The entrepreneurial class had flocked to De Gaulle's party in the late 1940s but within a few years big business was shunning him and looking for a more sophisticated alternative. However, the ultra-conservatism of much small-scale business was reflected in its support in 1956 for Poujadism, whose opposition to the ethic of growth and productivity was in part a reaction against the sort of technocratic values that had appeared in the reforming Mendès-France government.[61]

The encouragement of institutions and attitudes supportive of modern, liberal capitalism was thus a daunting task for Marshall Plan staff based in Paris. There was no dramatic progress as they attempted to stimulate a more aggressively competitive approach to marketing by firms; acceptance by labour of a 'scrap and build' economy, with workers adapting flexibly to changing products and methods of production in return for higher wages, and a generally higher level of material acquisitiveness among workers to stimulate demand in a mass-consumption society. The low standard of living – in 1952 real wages were 36 per cent lower than in 1936 – retarded the emergence of a consumer-oriented society.[62] The infrastructure of industry had been rebuilt in the post-war years at the expense of the working class, and inequality had increased. Until more spending power was available to workers there was only limited scope for expansion and growth. As Marshall Plan Labour staff recognised, the weakness of French unions as bargaining agents retarded the process – hence their campaign to make unions productivity conscious and to encourage collective bargaining over this. Efforts to promote bargaining through the pilot plant programme and Conditional Aid were largely unsuccessful. Only in 1954–55 did the first signs of affluence begin to emerge in sectors of the labour force. Indeed, it was not until 1955 that the non-communist unions at Renault signed the first major comprehensive company-level collective agreement guaranteeing future wage increases and the establishment of fringe benefits in return for a measure of labour peace and acceptance by the unions that the pursuit of efficiency was in the interests of both sides. This completely new approach to labour–management relations was something the Marshall Plan had been working to produce for years and it was hailed as a revolutionary development. But though the Renault agreement furnished a model, only about fifty such agreements had been negotiated by 1960.[63] Smaller, traditionalist employers remained hostile, and, even more than in Italy, corporate-level collective bargaining continued to be a frail institution until well into the 1960s.

In the middle of the decade business began to have confidence in the economy and for the remainder of the 1950s economic performance was strong, output per man hour running at double the rate in Britain and the United States. Various explanations have been put forward.[64] France was clearly reaping the benefit of the investment in infrastructure and heavy industry carried out under the Monnet Plan with the assistance of American aid. About half of all counterpart investment in western Europe had been made in France.[65] She had the most modern steel industry in Europe and vast supplies of cheap hydro-electric power. Indicative planning had helped industry develop longer-term strategies and there was a gradual acceptance of the importance of growth and the need for greater competitiveness – elements fostered by the American aid programme.

However, the modernising task embarked upon through various Marshall Plan programmes was only slowly beginning to make headway when the Fourth Republic collapsed in 1958. The post-war years up to that point constitute an intermediate stage in the transition of French industry from its backward condition in 1945 to its dynamic, modern form in the 1960s and 1970s. To advance the process further it was necessary for the political immobilism characteristic of the age to be swept away along with the republic and for it to be replaced by the sense of strong, purposeful leadership under De Gaulle. By 1958 the Marshall

Plan agencies had helped France overcome the economic crises of the late 1940s and early 1950s, resist the challenge of communism and had pointed industry in the direction of modern liberal capitalism. But that job still remained to be completed.

Germany. Industrial reconstruction in Germany was rapid in the late 1940s; war damage to plant had been less extensive then was at first reported. By 1949 steel output was already higher than in France. Once the United States had resolved on a policy of purposeful reconstruction of the economy within the framework of Marshall Aid in 1947 progress was quickly made. All sectors of industry benefited, especially car manufacturing, rubber, paper and precision engineering. By spring 1948 the index of industrial production was 57 per cent of the 1936 level. The currency reform of June 1948 helped business, and by late 1949 industrial production was equal to the pre-war level. At the end of 1950 output was a third higher again.[66] Post-war recovery had been achieved.

In the years 1950–63 the economy grew at an annual rate of 11 per cent, a rate second only to that of Japan. Of course, the starting level was low, and if the effect of a rapidly growing population is set aside the performance was much more modest. Even then the 'economic miracle' was very much a matter of good fortune. Germany had considerable spare industrial capacity just as the Korean War was creating an international boom in demand for exports. An abundance of cheap labour compensated for the fact that her level of productivity was less than the OEEC average up to the mid-1950s. Even then the balance of payments surplus was due less to the margin of exports over imports than to the fact that the terms of trade moved sharply in Germany's favour.[67] Nevertheless recovery and growth were crucial for the strategic designs of the United States in Europe.

For the Americans Marshall Aid meant reintegrating Germany into the Western international economy. But the restructuring of industry would be necessary before her economy became fully compatible with the liberal capitalism of the United States. The cartel mentality would need to change and the accompanying authoritarianism would have to give way to a more flexible style of management. To these ends Marshall Plan officials devoted much energy. And the American labour programme in Germany was largely concerned with developing trade union values and practices that would complement these changes in business life. Yet though the Federal Republic was, *par excellence*, the country where United States influence was most strongly felt there was no immediate or easy transformation of industrial life along the lines desired by the Americans. Subsequent accounts which point to the close relationship between the US High Commissioner, John McCloy, and the Adenauer government and the deep-rooted bonds between German and American industrialists under-estimate the difficulty the Germans had in adapting to American requirements.[68]

American government activity to win the 'hearts and minds' of Germans was extensive even before Marshall Plan technical assistance funds began to flow. Between 1949 and 1952 over 7,600 programmes, many of them study trips, were mounted by the State Department or the High Commission for Germany aimed at opinion formers active in politics, labour, business or the professions. Up to 1956, 1,700 Germans visited the United States on Marshall Plan technical assistance projects, including over 250 trade unionists in the years 1950–51 alone. Meanwhile 160 American industrial and labour specialists travelled to Germany to assist with projects there.[69] In total, Germany received a relatively small share of ECA technical assistance funds – $1·3 million – largely because she had formerly been one of the most progressive manufacturers in Europe and did not need the assistance. Still, the Germans borrowed readily from American industrial practice, especially in relation to methods of mass production, packing and shipping, advertising and marketing. These were the main fruits of the exchange visits. Indeed, the rapid absorption of American technology was a large factor in the rapid growth of the German economy.[70]

However, the immediate barrier to the wholesale importation of American industrial practice was German industry's resistance to the policy of decartelisation which the United States was insisting on and which the Christian Democrat government was pursuing. The architect of the government strategy was the Economics Minister, Ludwig Erhard, a supporter of the American ideology of competition based on high levels of consumption and production. Having visited the United States in 1949 and studied American anti-trust legislation, Erhard set about creating a framework for competitive industry in line with the American model. The main opponents of his decartelisation legislation were the captains of heavy industry in the Ruhr, who dominated the German federation of industrialists, the Bundesverband der Deutschen Industrie (BDI). Their opposition meant that the Bill introduced by Erhard in the first Adenauer government had still not been passed before the 1953 general election. When it was reintroduced in 1954 it again met the full force of BDI hostiliy.

In August 1953 the *Wall Street Journal* had noted pessimistically that the attempt 'to sell American-style capitalism to German big business' would have to be written off as a failure. And in May 1954 a correspondent of *Fortune* speculated that if the anti-cartel Bill were rejected Germany might well slip back into the old pattern of economic authoritarianism. If, however, it were accepted even in a modified form it would mean 'a major victory, perhaps the greatest victory ever won in Europe, for the principles of dynamic American-style capitalism'.[71] Following a revolt of dissident BDI members in summer 1954 over the intransigence of the federation's leadership the hard-line opposition was moderated, but Erhard's Bill, even in a watered down form, was passed only in mid-1957, to come into effect in 1958. It had taken almost nine years for the Christian Democrats – the 'American party' in German politics – to pass a measure essential if German industry were to adopt United States-style oligopolistic competition.[72]

Meanwhile, continuing attempts were made to bridge the wider gap between German and American practice in matters of personnel and work-force motivation. Starting in 1951 at Baden-Baden, the programme of German-American Management Seminars was instituted, aimed at discussing productivity questions and highlighting American labour's 'partnership' role in this area. But here the assilimation of American practice was far less rapid than in the fields of marketing and advertising. The main German proponents of the notion of social partnership in industry were the leaders of the Bundesvereinigung der Deutschen Arbeitgeberverbande (BDA), whose area was employee relations. In pressing their social partnership views they were anxious to woo organised labour away from its traditional attachment to the potentially radical notion of economic democracy. Yet in the early 1950s at least the BDI reflected the interests of the business community more accurately, while

Erhard's own belief was that his American-inspired high production/high consumption strategy would solve the social problems of German labour without employers having to engage in specific welfare measures.[73]

The climate was also unfavourable for the BDA's project as a result of the bitter debate over co-determination. Labour had held its ground in the legislation of 1951 affecting the coal and steel industries but was forced to retreat from its policy demand regarding the rest of industry the following year. The fact that the unions appeared to have won so much in the 1951 legislation ensured that the employers' hard line – in other words, BDI leadership – would be reinforced in subsequent encounters.[74] Without a widely agreed settlement on this key issue it was unlikely that unions would warm to notions of social partnership. As in the decartelisation debate, the absence of a broad national consensus made it difficult to develop the stable industrial institutions and practices that the United States was set upon. In 1950 the German Minister for the Marshall Plan, Blücher, had called for an 'active wage policy' to help increase production.[75] But the employers' associations saw no advantage in changing their approach to national wage settlements, and trade union preoccupation with co-determination relegated wage questions to a lower order of priority. In this context calls for American-style industrial relations did not evoke an enthusiastic repsonse. In 1948 the American zone trade union leader Markus Schleicher had returned from the United States full of enthusiasm for American labour practices and ready to argue that a switch of emphasis from co-determination to plant-based collective bargaining was desirable.[76] But the industrial atmosphere of the early 1950s made the spread of such ideas difficult. Whatever their merit, without a suitable change in employer practices the unions could hardly reciprocate.

In pressing for a new style of labour–employer relations the BDA was therefore cast in the role of missionary. Noting that the word 'management' did not have a respectable connotation – Germans in that role referred to themselves in terms of their specialisation – engineer, lawyer and so forth – the federation advocated American management methods in its journal while its representatives toured the country lecturing on their importance.[77] But when in 1956 the BDA launched a new phase in its campaign for social partnership co-determination was still deeply resented by employers whose position on the subject had recently precipitated a national strike among miners. And now there was also industrial conflict over wage questions to reckon with.[78]

Under American pressure human relations ideas were widely introduced in the early 1950s, though not without misgivings on the part of the Germans. Where the schemes succeeded it was often because their intellectual lineage could be traced to an indigenous German tradition of industrial psychology dating back to pre-war days which had notions in common with American thinking on the subject. Companies like Volkswagen moderated their emphasis on engineering and sought to accentuate the human factor. But by the mid-1950s the fad for human relations had peaked.[79] In-house training of German managers began at this point, stimulated in part by what visitors to the United States had seen. But the influence of American management science was not initially the dominant one in Germany, even when management began to be seen as something more than a narrow technical specialism. People like Carl Arnold and Reinhard Hohn with an approach to management which was rooted in German notions of discipline and leadership were initially more influential. Following this line, the Harzburg Leadership Academy, which was opened in 1956, soon became the most important management training centre in the country, with a staff of 200 and another 100 freelance lecturers. By the early 1960s some 30,000 managers had attended its courses, of which there were 300 in 1962 alone, with 7,500 participants.[80] It was in this context that work study – the engineering approach to management that stemmed from the rationalising movement of the 1920s – flourished. The German Society of Work Study had 15,000 members in 1957, a fivefold growth in half a dozen years. Some 1,500 conferences on work study were being held annually, with 100,000 participants.[81] The result was that Germany had a corps of trained production engineers which other European countries simply could not match.

By the late 1950s the German productivity centre, RKW, had become a formidable organisation with an annual budget of $1·6 million, 130 branches around the country and 13,000 people attending courses in aspects of productivity each year.[82] But only in the latter part of the decade did one or two universities begin to take an interest in management as a subject in its own right rather than as a series of discrete specialisms. This process was assisted by the fact that German university teachers had been able to visit the United States on EPA study visit programmes. By the early 1960s the American influence was finally beginning to be felt as Harvard Business School-type courses began to dominate management training and development programmes.[83] This belated triumph of the American approach was undoubtedly the result of years of endeavour and investment under the Marshall Plan. But it had come about only in the context of a significant multinationalisation of business (led by American interests) and a generational change in the personnel at the head of German industry.

Marshall Plan social engineering programmes had worked no easy miracles in Germany. Although industry had been very successful, neither employers nor unions had readily gone along with American prescriptions for industrial organisation and the pursuit of productivity. Traditional values and practices died hard in this environment. Some writers have traced to the early 1950s the origins of the corporatism that later came to characterise labour–management relations at the end of the 1960s, but such analyses ignore the deep-seated mutual mistrust that existed on both sides of German industry throughout much of the 1950s. If organised labour softened its position and, in time, showed a willingness to negotiate and compromise with employers around a limited range of economic issues – if the spirit of Fritz Tarnow gradually triumphed over that of Hans Boekler – it was not a direct result of any Marshall Aid master plan so much as the end product of a variety of interacting forces in the 1950s, both political and economic, of which Marshall Plan pressures were but one aspect, albeit an important one.

In the 1950s the four main western European recipients of Marshall Aid demonstrated no uniform or consistent pattern of productivity development. Italy, Germany and later France enjoyed more rapid growth than Britain, although they started from a lower base. But the causes of growth differed from country to country. At least up to the mid-1950s there was no clear evidence that the sophisticated managerial concepts being exported through Marshall Aid were having much immediate impact in industry. Certainly there was no sign that trade unionists were joining in enthusiastically or with great effect in the productivity campaign. A more relevant consideration was, perhaps, the extent to which unions were strong enough to *resist* productivity measures. Here British unions clearly had the edge over their German, French and Italian counterparts. Thus the change in direction in industrial practices that the Americans had hoped to promote came only later, and then gradually. Often it was part of a larger shift in political and economic forces, themselves the product of a variety of factors which could not be attributed directly to Marshall Aid programmes.

Early aid shipments had helped secure European recovery. Beyond that productivity propaganda and the psychological boost to industry deriving from the knowledge that the United States was supporting them had encouraged many private employers on the Continent to seize the advantage presented by divisions and weakness in the ranks of the labour movement to restructure industry to their own advantage. In the short run Conditional Aid had largely failed in its aim of drastically changing the operating culture of the employers and allowing some social benefits from productivity to filter through to workers. Likewise it failed to turn European unions into replicas of the productivity-conscious organisations that American unions were often wrongly imagined to be. But an educational programme to change deep-rooted cultural values could not possibly work quickly. In the longer run the cumulative influence of a plethora of Marshall Aid-inspired productivity institutes, business schools, training centres, academic research and the conventional wisdom that they developed was pervasive throughout Europe. Cultural values, norms and expectations in industry were certainly changing by the end of the 1950s, and in this the Marshall Plan programmes must be seen as an important conditioning force.

CHAPTER 13

Conclusion

The idea that the United States sought no extra political or economic gain in return for Marshall Aid is nonsense, [...] the idea that the gains achieved were so large as to have shaped the politico-economic future of Western Europe is nonsense also. [A. S. Milward, *The Reconstruction of Western Europe, 1945–51*, 1984]

There was no evidence of a deliberate design to strangle British socialism at birth – liberal America would certainly have disowned any such aim – but the outward palpable expression of the inner compulsions of American society had its own menacing logic. [Michael Foot, *Aneurin Bevan*, 1975]

Remedies are also sought in various departments of knowledge – in academic economics and in a fashionable and Americanised sociology. [...]. Professionalism and bureaucracy grow together [...]. A new psychology appears [...]. Political 'managerialism' began to fuse with other manifestations of a similar kind elsewhere in the institutional structure. [...] With this went a growing faith in neat technical solutions within an existing institutional framework, and a rather pathetic faith in quantifiable social data [...] and in specific 'mysteries' of specialised knowledge [...]. [Donald G. MacRae, 'The ideological situation in the labour movement', *Political Quarterly*, XXIV, 1953]

This review of the different phases of the Marshall programme in action brings us back to the question raised in the Introduction: what was its long-term effect on the European labour movement, and was it a factor in the alleged deradicalisation of the political left? These are big issues. They tempt one to ask 'What would have happended if ——?', a question which simply cannot be answered. Nevertheless it is important to draw together some of the threads that have been running through this account and to make some general observations.

Industrial capitalism, which had looked so sickly in Europe in 1945, was enjoying by the 1960s a marvellous boom period and embarking on a new phase of prosperity based on multinational enterprise. Organised labour, which in 1945 seemed poised for bigger things as it looked forward to a social transformation in Europe, was experiencing in the 1960s a condition of unprecedented material affluence as part of this long boom. It had also carved out for itself, or was in the process of doing so, a stable niche in a settlement that permitted an ongoing collective bargaining relationship with employers and a role in government for parties pursuing moderate social democratic policies. It is in this sense that the Marshall Plan, America's big post-war economic offensive in Europe, is said to have played a major role in 'drawing the teeth' of European socialism. Of course, America's hegemonic influence operated not only in the world of economics but also in the broad field of foreign and military policy, and acceptance of United States leadership in these areas by large sections of the European labour and socialist movement was a major factor in their political moderation. But in economic terms the basis of the Atlanticism which characterised the non-communist left in Europe in the '50s and '60s had been laid by the Marshall Plan.

Communist – socialist divisions

Among the important developments of that period was the fact that the socialists and communists, who were part of a common front in most countries in 1945, had by 1948 pulled apart. It occurred in different ways in different countries but it is clear that an important element in this division was disagreement over whether to accept Marshall Aid. Whatever their misgivings about the long-term consequence most socialists felt they had no option but to accept, whereas communists were under clear instructions from Moscow to reject the programme, whatever misgivings the French and Italians had about forgoing necessary assistance. If unity of the communist and non-communist left is viewed as the essence of radical working-class politics or a precondition for it then clearly the Marshall Plan was substantially responsible for blunting the cutting edge of post-war European socialism. However, it is also clear that holes in this common front were beginning to appear in the earliest post-war months, well before the full weight of American policy began to have an impact on domestic European politics.

In France and Italy socialists who *were* very interested in developing a mass party of the left turned their backs on the idea of unity with the communists. And in Germany scope for socialist-communist collaboration was destroyed by the forced merger of the two parties in the Soviet-controlled sector. The cooling of ardour between the two was not at all explicable in terms of the greater radicalism of the communist parties over the socialists. Indeed, the policies embarked upon by Popular Front coalitions were quite restrained, and this was largely attributable to the moderation of the communists, whose reading of the world situation seemed to dictate the need for a period of quiet consolidation of the position of the working class in society while economic reconstruction took place. They were playing for time. Many socialists had a perspective that was far more radical than this. In rejecting the request for affiliation by the British Communist Party the Labour Party was not closing the door on a group likely to inject revolutionary politics into the British scene: after all, the CPGB had wanted a post-war continuation of the coalition with the Conservatives. And in France, among the followers of Léon Blum, the 1945–46 debate over the relative merits of Marxism and humanitarianism in socialism did not necessarily indicate their predisposition to jettison radical politics but reflected their search for something more ideologically penetrating than the PCF's obsession with production and its disregard of democratic procedure.[1]

Similarly the divisions in the trade union movement which led eventually to the fateful splits in France and Italy and internationally in the WFTU were already appearing before the question of American aid to Europe became the major issue of contention. True, the dispute over the role of the international trade secretariats in the WFTU was not what really caused the schism within that organisation, but nor was it an artificial issue invented by the TUC and the International Transport Workers' Federation. The conflict over this really did raise important questions of trade union practice for people who, before the war, had had first-hand experience of the disruptive tactics of communists in the labour movement. The factional alliance of Christian and communist trade unionists inside the unified Italian CGIL was fragile from the outset as communists practised partisan politics under the cover of a supposedly non-partisan organisation. And the dissidents in the French CGT who began to organise against the communists as early as 1945, and who two years later were to break away to form Force Ouvrière, included militant anarcho-syndicalists and Trotskyists who acted as they did for reasons of democracy and in the interests of preserving a militant trade union front. It would be wrong to read back from the moderate, white-collar, collaborationist organisation that FO became in the 1950s to identify its origins in 1945–46, just as it would be wrong to judge the Italian Social Democrats in terms of what they subsequently became in the years of the Cold War. The Saragat breakaway from the Italian Socialist Party over its continuing ties with the communists was not *simply* a *démarche* by right-wing Tammany politicians: the move was also supported by Matteo Matteotti's 'Socialist Initiative' group, whose politics were akin to those of the ILP and who acted for perfectly honourable democratic reasons.[2] With hindsight the labour movement may now lament those divisions and judge that the splits were tactically ill advised, that the dissidents should have remained to fight their corner. Such a judgement assumes the possibility of genuine trust and co-operation between democratic socialists and people schooled in the techniques of Leninism. Yet in 1946–47 there can be no doubting the genuine sense of grievance of those who broke away and their feeling that a lack of democratic practice in the movement made it impossible for their views to prevail.

This raises the issue of external financing of factions in the labour movement and leads to the question: would they have split without it? The first point to note is that there was outside financing on both sides. Without question the communist-led labour groups had at their disposal financial resources far in excess of their income from membership dues. In the early post-war months communist labour activities in the Western zones of Germany appear to have been much better financed than anything the Social Democrats could afford to mount – largely because of their access to resources provided by the Soviet occupation. In France and Italy, as Communist Party domination of the central labour organisations grew, they were able to dispense considerable patronage to their supporters in the form of resources and full-time staff positions, often financed indirectly by the state. And there was certainly an injection of financial aid to the French and Italian communists from the Soviet Bloc. In Italy communist-controlled import – export firms received 1 – 2 per cent commission on their annual trade with the Soviet Bloc – some $50 million worth, on average, meaning a subsidy to the party of $500,000 to $1 million. And during the 1948 mining strike in France the CGT received up to $1 million channelled through the Banque Commerical pour l'Europe du Nord, which was owned by two Soviet state banks.[3]

None of which is to deny the substantial nature of American financial assistance to non-communist labour groups in Europe, merely to place it in context. Such aid was given in cash and kind by the US labour movement as well as by government and business. It began to flow in small amounts as the war ended and so enabled dissident groups in France and Italy to maintain cohesion and develop an organisational structure. Until the late 1940s the amounts involved appear to have been much smaller than is often believed. The FTUC loudly proclaimed its own aim of building an international fund of $1 million in 1944, but never seems to have come close to raising that amount. On the other hand, it was not necessarily the size of the funding that counted but also its timing and targeting. Publicity about a large injection of cash from outside sources might be politically embarrassing and thus even counter-productive for the recipient, whereas a few hundred dollars here or there for a struggling journal or to facilitate travel to a meeting of rank-and-file activists could prove to be money well spent. For example, the CARE parcels sent to German labour officials every month or so cost the AFL some $500,000, but the foodstuffs and clothing they contained had a resale value on the black market equal to several months' wages for a worker. As such they were an important means of maintaining morale and also helped the recipients financially.[4]

While anti-communists were already receiving financial assistance in 1945 and 1946 it is arguable that genuine resentment over communist domination of the labour and socialist movements was, alone, probably sufficient to provoke the Saragat split from the Italian Socialist Party in 1947 and the FO break-away from the CGT a year later. The continued American funding of the two organisations thereafter was, of course, crucial in sustaining them, and it was not at all clear that FO had the capacity to survive on its own resources. Yet it is reasonable to suppose that, had FO collapsed for lack of finances, the CGT would not necessarily have benefited in terms of increased membership and that the tendency, already evident in France, for disillusioned workers to drop out of the labour movement altogether would have been accentuated. Without the CGT abandoning its instrumental tactics in its capacity as transmission belt for the PCF, it is hard to see how the radical aspirations of French labour would have been properly served.

In Italy the initial impetus for Pastore's Christian Democratic break-away from CGIL also seems to have stemmed from a genuine and widespread sense of outrage at the treatment of their followers by the majority communist faction. And in this case an autonomous base for oppositional organisation had long existed through Catholic Action. However, by 1948–49 the amount of American money received by Italian labour was substantially higher than in 1946–47 and it is quite apparent that US pressure was intense in securing social democratic trade union support for the LCGIL break-away. Here it is no exaggeration to talk in terms of the 'purchasing' of a labour movement. And the fact that Italian trade unionism split three ways rather than two was a direct result of this crude, and in some ways unsuccessful, application of financial pressure to buy loyalty. In subsequent years both the CISL and UIL were to become dangerously dependent on financial support from the United States and Italian employers. Yet although this had the effect of shifting the emphasis of trade union practice away from political protest and towards collective bargaining of the Anglo-American type, it would be hard to argue that the work of the CISL's American-financed training school at Florence, for example, inevitably produced a less radical form of trade unionism than the 'cyclone unionism'[5] of constant mass mobilisation for sectarian goals characteristic of the CGIL until the mid-1950s.

The socialist Third Force

Awareness of direct external funding of European labour groups in the Marshall Plan years is important for an understanding of international alignments and domestic developments in the countries concerned, but alone this factor does not explain the course of labour and socialist politics. Aside and apart from the splits induced by Cold War pressures there was a lack of common purpose and organisational cohesion on the part of European labour – reflected in the decision to delay the re-establishment of the Socialist International. This condition was certainly exacerbated by the Marshall Plan, but even before that Europeans were having considerable difficulty in agreeing on the nature of a socialist international policy in the context of super-power confrontation, let alone putting such a policy into operation. A cohesive international socialist organisation was a prerequisite of the development of the much discussed 'Third Force' – the idea that between the twin imperialisms of American capitalism and Stalinist communism a middle way might be opened up, based on democratic socialist values. Labour's failure to challenge American hegemony in western Europe was bound up with the failure of the Third Force.

Criticism of Ernest Bevin's pro-American leanings in foreign policy had been mouting throughout 1946 in the British Labour movement. In autumn that year the *New Statesman* published a series of articles on foreign policy arguing the case for Britain to reassert its independence of America in international affairs.[6] This viewpoint was echoed in Parliament when in November 1946 a substantial number of Labour MPs failed to support the government in a foreign policy debate – Bevin's famous 'stab in the back'. Dissatisfied back-bench Labour MPs now began to meet and discuss a range of domestic and foreign policy alternatives that were to be propounded in their pamphlet *Keep Left*, published in May 1947.[7] The Third Forcism in *Keep Left* was a modest proposal for Britain to distance herself from the United States. It was accepted that there could be no sudden break with the Americans, but the authors called for the creation of a Third Force through which a balance of power between the USA and USSR could be effected. How much of an alternative to American and Soviet policies this really was is open to doubt. There was no talk of establishing industrial or economic democracy, and the vague middle course proposed might well have resulted in little more than a blend of Stalinist economics and parliamentary democracy. Among the critics of government in Labour's ranks there were different emphases on this issue. More moderate than the *New Statesman*, *Tribune* held that the American presence in Europe was a necessary basis for the achievement of the social democratic middle way – though it soon had to admit the danger that socialists might be reduced to being the progressive wing of the US camp rather than an independent third group.[8]

Popular discussion of the Third Force tended to revolve round the perspectives of the *New Statesman* and *Tribune*, but a more determined effort to translate the Third Force idea into reality was already being made outside the Labour Party by the Independent Labour Party (ILP). They had adopted a policy in favour of a United Socialist Europe during the war, and in February 1947, in the context of growing discussion of the need for European unity, the ILP launched a campaign for a United Socialist States of Europe (USSE) at a conference in London in February 1947 attended by French, German, Dutch, Greek and Spanish socialists where an international co-ordinating committee was appointed.[9] The USSE concept was a more full-blooded approach to a democratic socialist alternative than the restrained balancing act envisaged by *Keep Left*. The ILP made no secret of its hostility not only to the imperialism of the two big powers but also to the mild reformism of Labour's domestic programme. As distinct from *Keep Left*, the USSE concept of the Third Force embraced the need for socialisation from below at the point of production.[10]

If the Third Force was to have any chance it would have to be based, in the first instance, on the joint efforts of British and French socialists. French pronouncements favoured such a development but the Labour Party leadership did little to foster closer links with France. In January 1947, with the socialist Leon Blum fleetingly at the head of a coalition government, Bevin did sign a Treaty of Alliance with France, recognising that in the interests of social democracy Britain should do anything possible to strengthen Blum's position. He was even open to suggestions of a customs union with France, though Stafford Cripps was wary of the prospect of Franco-British economic integration.[11] But the international climate was already changing for the worse, the winter of 1946–47 saw a sharp deterioration in the European economy, with Bevin leaning more than ever in the direction of America. At the Labour Party conference in May 1947 Bevin routed the critics of his foreign policy and reaffirmed the basic principles that guided him.

His position was that Britain was an island dependent on

trade, and to maintain this position and its standard of living it could not forsake power politics. This perspective influenced all Labour's foreign and domestic policies. There was no socialist ideology or notion of solidarity behind the thinking, merely a recognition of traditional national interest. Bevin did not believe that post-war Europe was on the verge of a socialist revolution, and so traditional power politics was the only practical game.[12] His instinctive approach was one for which Denis Healey was later to provide a theoretical justification: there was no room for a socialist foreign policy in a world characterised by anarchic international relations. The Third Force was therefore mere self-indulgence. Indeed, the Labour Party document on foreign policy, *Cards on the Table*, prepared by Healey in April 1947, argued that the United States had to be positively encouraged to abandon her desire for isolation, and asserted that between capitalist America and the communist USSR democratic socialism would survive as an alternative only if the Labour government survived as a world power.[13]

The difficulties facing the proponents of a Third Force became intense two months later when Secretary of State Marshall made his offer of aid. Critics of the Third Force could point to the inconsistency in British and French socialists, by their own admission desperately in need of aid, planning to launch a movement that would ensure independence from their benefactor. Moreover it was clear that, although the USA and the USSR were at loggerheads, they would both act to prevent the emergence of anything as radical as a Third Force that challenged their respective orthodoxies, as the USSE was certainly intended to do. From the outset supporters of the idea were clutching at straws. A common formulation prior to the communist coup in Prague in February 1948 was that socialist parties were in the business of creating a Third Force to *bridge* the gap between communism and capitalism. Socialists could not afford to concede that the world was split into hostile camps, but must fight for international co-operation and peace.[14] Up to the *coup* advocates of the middle way still talked in terms of a movement that would embrace socialists from eastern as well as western Europe.[15] The ILP urged the need to seek out supporters of a USSE among radical forces in the USA and (more speculatively) with 'the probably still underground oppositional forces in Russia to whom the present Stalinist police state is merely a temporary and reactionary interlude in Russian political evolution'. 'Across the frontiers we call upon the American and Russian workers to help with this crusade for reasons of peace.'[16]

With the Labour Party firmly in the grip of Bevinite foreign policy much seemed to depend on the French socialists for the success of the USSE project. Their formal commitment to Third Forcism was strong and within the SFIO the left wing appeared to be gaining the initiative in autumn 1947. However, it had long been Bevin's view that, despite their talk of a middle way, the French government were really as keen as any to secure American help. He had no faith in their ability to offer leadership in Europe or, indeed, to master their own domestic difficulties, faced as they were with growing opposition from Gaullists and communists. It was this weakness that attracted the French to European unity. That same weakness led Bevin to shun European unity and to seek salvation in an Atlantic milieu.[17] Bevin's assessment of French socialist weakness proved accurate. Compromised by its identification with ineffectual domestic and imperialist foreign policies, the SFIO and its partners in coalition began to lose support to the communists and the Gaullists towards the end of 1947. In the National Assembly Blum failed to win a majority for the idea of a Third Force against the Bonapartism of De Gaulle and the Stalinism of the PCF. Only six months after expressing great hopes for the SFIO the ILP had, therefore, to admit that the future of the Third Force really lay in the hands of the Labour Party, the only organisation with sufficient international influence to give a lead.[18] But there were few illusions as to the likelihood of Labour acting in this way, and, at least as far as the ILP was concerned, the cause of European socialist unity was pretty well lost by the end of 1947.

By 1948 the Third Force proposal had merged with other currents working in the direction of some form of European unity. The new factor was the projected conference on European unity at the Hague in May 1948, which would be dominated by Winston Churchill's idea of western Europe as an anticommunist bloc. It was the prospect of this event, coupled with the need to galvanise European labour support for Marshall Aid, that lent focus to Bevin's new idea of Western union. Bevin first floated the concept to Marshall and Bidault at the end of the

Foreign Ministers' Conference in London in December 1947, when all hope of agreement with the USSR over Europe had vanished.[19] The idea was to create a 'spiritual union' of Western nations sharing similar cultural values as part of a defence against Soviet expansionism.[20] It was a vehicle that would allow Britain to have a foot in Europe while simultaneously drawing the United States into an arrangement for common Western defence against the USSR. The strategy, which was announced to the House of Commons on 22 January 1948 and rapidly consummated in the Brussels Pact of March 1948, was explained in greater detail later that year in *Feet on the Ground*, a Labour Party document written by Denis Healey. In it he borrowed some of the phraseology from the USSE campaign, talking in terms of forming a third world power that would allow Europeans economic independence of America and political security from Russia.[21] As a third bloc it would, of course, be only a holding operation until such time as western Europe and the United States were linked in a comprehensive alliance.

The civil side of this joint military-civil initiative now included the objective of strengthening European socialist parties under the leadership of the Labour Party.[22] The Labour government had been under American pressure to generate more enthusiastic support for the Marshall Plan among its European neighbours. So far it had held back, but now Bevin gave the all-clear for the convening in March 1948 of a conference of European socialist parties at Selsdon Park on the question of the Marshall Plan. It paralleled the ERP–TUAC conference of trade unionists held the same month. The meeting was jointly convened by the Labour Party and the SFIO rather than COMISCO so as to avoid taxing that body's frail unity.[23] Bevin told the American ambassador that he attached great importance to this conference as part of his anti-communist strategy.[24] For its part the ILP was fearful of the outcome of the conference, warning darkly on the eve, 'European Socialism had now come to the parting of the ways. If it accepts either Russian Communism [...] or American Imperialism, as Western Social Democracy is obviously willing to do, it is a spent force.'[25]

Inevitably the Selsdon conference had to discuss the issue of European unity as part of the scenario for Marshall Aid, with papers presented by the British and French. Labour's contribution, prepared by Denis Healey with Foreign Office and Treasury guidance, set forth the pragmatic case for accepting American aid and, with little elaboration, observed that since the allocation of Marshall dollars would have to be planned it would strengthen the hand of the socialists, the natural planners in Europe.[26] The SFIO statement to the conference was couched in much bolder terms, arguing the case for a radical socialist strategy. It talked of the need for a real transformation of economic life in Europe, of the need for Europe-wide planning and the continental integration of the many industries that had already been socialised. There was a need for a European Economic Commission to plan, to supervise the dismantling of purely national military arms, the internationalisation of basic industries and the introduction of a common currency. A political structure was needed to support these measures and so steps would have to be taken to create a European Parliament. To concert the socialist position on a united Europe the SFIO wanted a further conference in Paris in April which would enable the supporters of a United Socialist Europe to go on to the Hague conference as a unified group. They raised still further ahead the prospect of the next USSE conference in June bringing together all progressive labour, republican and democratic groups who did not wish to be forced into a choice between the USA and the USSR, and addressing itself to potential supporters in Asia and Africa.[27] For the SFIO, Guy Mollet spoke strongly in favour of the USSE. If they were to counter American capitalism they had to be ready to give up a certain amount of national sovereignty. And in criticising the Labour Party's cautious pragmatism Ferrat, another French delegate, spoke of the United States of Europe as a 'revolutionary task'. But if the French were excited by the 'astounding possibilities' of the situation opening up before them the Labour spokesmen, Hugh Dalton and Morgan Phillips, warned against the creation of supranational structures, condemned the projected USSE conference as likely to impair Labour's European strategy, and announced their firm opposition to participation in the Hague conference.[28]

Along with a public declaration of support for Marshall Aid, the Selsdon conference closed with the parties agreeing to meet again in Paris in April to discuss the issue of European unity further. But as most delegations had indicated that they would take their lead from the Labour Party, SFIO ambitions for a concerted, radical strategy over the unity question were frustrated from the outset.

Labour's opposition to the Hague conference was, as much as anything, due to the fact that Churchill was likely to dominate the proceedings. But the truth was that the party's interest in European unity was minimal. In May 1948 its annual conference passed a resolution moved by Fenner Brockway in support of a United States of Europe. Dalton accepted the motion on behalf of the National Executive but damned it with faint praise in the process.

The march of events in 1948 made the prospects of a Third Force ever more doubtful while edging the western European countries nearer the American camp. The Prague *coup*, the Berlin blockade and the fact that Marshall Aid was already being received by May meant that the process of extricating Europe from the United States' fold would be that much harder. These events caused disillusionment among the Third Force supporters. Fissures appeared within the Keep Left group, but the moment of truth for the movement came at the USSE Paris conference in June, the most determined effort so far to forge the links of a Third Force.

The conference was sponsored by the SFIO, the ILP and the Indian Socialist Party. With 300 delegates present from thirty-eight countries, it was the first attempt to draw African and Asian groups into the movement. The report to the conference called for a Third Force to embrace Europe and countries of Asia and Africa. Though supported by the Asian delegations and some African socialist groups, it was rejected by African nationalist delegates on the grounds that their first priority was independence from colonial rule. They were therefore not prepared to become embroiled in European power politics. Moreover they identified the Third Force idea with coalition government in France and its imperialist policies. As elder statesman of the host party Leon Blum delivered an eloquent speech on the need for socialist fraternity, but his message was rendered hollow by his recent leadership of a government determined to preserve French colonial rule. The division between European socialists and African nationalists almost wrecked the conference. Unity was preserved only by diluting the proposed statement of policy.[29]

For all practical purposes Third Forcism, in the sense that it might embrace underdeveloped countries, was stillborn.

By 1949 the tide had well and truly turned for the Third Force. Socialists were losing political influence throughout Europe as the centre of gravity shifted rightwards. Labour governments suffered reverses in Australia and New Zealand, two outposts of British empire frequently talked of as potential supporters of a Third Force. When the next Labour Party conference met in May 1949, with Western union about to become the Atlantic alliance, it was clear that Bevinism had triumphed and that the Third Force was now a pipe dream. In France the SFIO policy was still to build an international force between the USA and USSR, but somehow the Atlantic Pact was now seen as a step in that direction.[30] In 1950 *Keeping Left*, the Parliamentary Labour left's successor to *Keep Left*, dropped the idea of a Third Force and tacitly accepted the fact of the American alliance. Almost every social democratic party followed suit at COMISCO's Copenhagen conference that year. True, popular support for neutralism began to grow in Europe in the first half of 1950 as fears of war increased and with the early successes of the Soviet-inspired Stockholm Peace Campaign.[31] But neutralism and the instinct to escape from military entanglements was not the same as positive politics in favour of a democratic socialist bloc with a viable economic base. The opportunity for creating such, if it ever existed, had passed.

The concept of a socialist Third Force was a bold, imaginative one, but in the circumstances of the day it is doubtful whether it could ever have been implemented. American and Soviet opposition to such a development would have been fierce, while variations on the theme conceived in terms of amicable relations with either of the blocs were Third Force in name only. The necessary basis in Franco-British economic and political collaboration was never really present. French socialists warmed to the proposal but could not deliver, the Labour leadership was not interested, while the other parties concerned carried insufficient weight. Vague popular support for such a high-minded scheme among the organised workers of Europe was no doubt substantial, but the leaders of the trade unions, and particularly the British, were almost to a man deeply caught up in Cold War politics and made no contribution to this radical movement. Walter Padley, who won the presidency of USDAW against communist opposition in this period, and Bob Edwards, General Secretary of the small Chemical Workers' Union, were unique among national trade union figures in their support for the Third Force.

There was always considerable doubt as to how much leverage socialists in an economically exhausted Europe could bring to bear against the United States in the proposal to bargain over Marshall Aid. Supplicants were, in any event, unlikely leaders of a movement to establish independence from their source of aid. As it happened, the failure of the CEEC countries in August 1948 to develop a genuine, cohesive programme for European recovery, going beyond the aggregation of their individual aid requirements, suggests that the hopes of European socialist planning would have been difficult to achieve. Beyond this there was some doubt about the viability of a European Third Force shorn of the Eastern Bloc countries. The division of Europe created an imbalance in the continent's economy and, given Soviet hostility to the project, the inclusion of the Eastern Bloc countries in some versions of the scheme reflected the triumph of optimism over common sense. The general drift of European Cold War politics from 1948 made the Third Force more and more necessary but at the same time ever less likely to materialise. And finally, the rejection of the USSE strategy by important nationalist groups in European colonies and the subsequent dilution of the policy undermined its credibility. The prospect of a Third Force had passed, neutralism would reappear and gain support at times in the 1950s, but a politico-economic bloc in Europe wholly independent of the Soviet or American spheres was not now on the cards.

The Socialist International was finally re-established at Frankfurt in 1951, where it adopted a definition of socialism so vague as to be almost meaningless. Affiliates were now hastening to shed their Marxist heritage and to present themselves as broad-based 'peoples' parties'. As had been the case at the founding of the ICFTU two years before, the emphasis was on developing an orientation acceptable to the non-socialist American labour movement.[32] In this spirit Denis Healey, one of the architects of this new socialist movement, argued that socialism, unlike communism, was not a uniform movement but rather a response by human beings to their economic and political environment, and therefore differed from place to place and time to time:

Internationally it is a community, but not an organisation and still less a machine. As an intellectual system it is an art, not a science. Its only rigid principles are moral imperatives, not political programmes.[33]

The absence of a sharp international socialist focus in circumstances where the labour movement was, in some instances, beset by organisational splits and with its political representatives almost everywhere in opposition or powerless prisoners of conservative-led coalitions constitutes the necessary background for understanding the politics of the non-communist European left in the 1950s. In danger of being marginalised, socialists and social democrats found it necessary to seek political realignments that would begin to afford them some purchase on political developments. In France the SFIO invited FO to combine forces with it so as to allow each to escape from the backwater into which they had drifted. Encouraged by the CIO, elements in FO and the often more militant Christian CFTC also began to collaborate closely.[34] And in 1955 there was even a dissident movement within the CGT that had enabled Lebrun to organise a substantial minority against Frachon's leadership, pointing to the possibility of their co-operating with non-communists outside the constraints of Communist Party discipline.[35] In Italy the Social Democrats called for a 'turn to the left' by which they hoped to woo Nenni and the PSI from the embrace of the Communist Party and back into a centre-left coalition so as to increase the leftward pressure on the Christian Democrat government. The idea was first floated in 1953 and though initially rejected it became a recurrent theme of political debate in Italian politics until it was put into effect in 1962–63. In Germany, with the trade union movement and the SPD in the early 1950s lacking strong leadership and frustrated by their exclusion from power and their inability to check the conservative tide in politics, there was an inclination to toy with the idea of a grand coalition which would facilitate a more effective marshalling of Social Democrat and progressive Christian Democrat forces.[36]

In some instances these developments assumed a radical gloss – as when in the mid-1950s the DGB's bid to become the political embodiment of a grand coalition blended with the CIO-backed militant wage bargaining strategy devised by Victor Agartz and Otto Brenner's Group of Ten;[37] or when in Italy the

CIO threw its weight behind a quasi-syndicalist strategy to make the UIL rather than the CISL or the Social Democrats the focal point of an effort to recruit the great mass of unorganised Italian workers who were oriented to a vague, ill defined socialism.[38] For the most part, however, these attempts at realignment reflected a coming to terms with the existing political and economic power structure in society. But the most important point is that little if any progress was made on any of these fronts in the 1950s. Political realignments had to await the 1960s. Meanwhile organised labour continued to be very much on the outside looking in. And the effect of years of frustration in opposition, lacking a strategic focus that seemed likely to pay political dividends, was to render labour and socialist movements prey to the 'revisionist' values that seemed particularly apposite in the context of the Marshall programme's great bequest – the consumer affluence that was beginning to appear in the late 1950s. Between 1949 and 1959, for example, the SPD in Germany had abandoned its strong Marxist legacy and adopted a programme so moderate that most liberals and many progressive conservatives could subscribe to it.

Revisionism: the Marshall Plan and managerial values

Revisionism – the tendency to abandon traditional Marxist and other class-based precepts in socialist analysis – did not originate in the Marshall Plan years (the elements were already there) but it was greatly encouraged by the vast programme of social engineering launched under Marshall Aid. In Britain the roots of Labour's post-war accommodation with capitalism were visible in the thinking of such people as Evan Durbin, Hugh Gaitskell and Douglas Jay as early as the late 1930s as they began to develop an economic theory of social democracy. By the 1940s they had already absorbed the ideas of Joseph Schumpeter on economic growth and James Burnham's concept of a managerial society. In the next decade they would assimilate the views of writers such as Peter Drucker and J.K. Galbraith on pluralist industrial society. Keen to discover ways of managing a capitalist economy and particularly concerned to improve economic efficiency while relying as much as possible on market forces, they took a great interest in the latest managerial practices in such areas as cost accounting and incentive schemes.[39]

Their emphasis on managerial notions of efficiency brought them into conflict with more traditional socialists such as G.D.H. Cole who were still concerned more with promoting non-market conditions for production than with gross output, with structures for administering socialised industry rather than with growth. However, in the late 1940s, as members of the Attlee government, Durbin and Gaitskell became very influential in preaching acceptance of the mixed economy and Keynesian values, the centrality of economic growth and a strategy for Labour that emphasised technical solutions to the problems of production for the creation of more wealth rather than class conflict over the distribution of existing wealth. The discovery of the key to sustained economic growth and commitment to it by national governments was an intrinsic part of the post-war value system of capitalism. It inspired and in turn fed on managerialist thinking, a growing productivity consciousness and the powerful notion of the 'end of ideology'. In what Raymond Aron termed the 'growth society', animated by the spirit of quantity and progress, economic growth was consonant with 'the true order of being'.[40] With a revolution in the mentality of business accompanying this, it was now fair to talk about an emerging ideology of growth.

The notion of the 'managerial revolution' that Burnham had identified had a profound effect on Labour Party thinking, and although it would gradually come to be criticised there is no doubt that in the late 1940s and into the 1950s it was widely regarded as a positive development. Typical was Stafford Cripps's comment at the founding conference of the British Institute of Management in April 1948 that industry had moved away from the authoritarian concept of management.[41] There was always a beguiling tendency for managerialism to be presented as neutral and universal in its application. Britain's first post-war gesture in the direction of managerial training, the establishment of the Administrative Staff College at Henley in 1946, was intended to provide common studies on the principles of organisation and administration in civil life for young executives in private enterprise, the public services and trade union officials alike. In this way the notion was fostered that management was, in the jargon of the day, a 'third force', standing between the polarities of labour and capital, and able, by dint of its technical competence, to bridge their differences. As Deputy Director of the BIM in 1948 Austen Albu, soon to become an influential member of the Parliamentary Labour Party, believed in the importance of management as a neutral activity. He and the Labour MP Ian Mikardo were prominently involved in launching the short-lived Society of Socialist Managers and Technicians in the late 1940s, an attempt to integrate this new group of 'knowledge workers' into the Labour Party. As an American observer of the Labour Party and Labour government wrote in 1950:

> The thesis of Burnham's Managerial Revolution seems to have been taken over by Labour spokesmen and Labour theoreticians, lock, stock and barrel. [...] One would gather from these references that businessmen in Britain are being led, as though by the unseen hand of technological logos, to encompass broad social ends which are not only no part of, but are actually contrary to, narrow objectives of their entrepreneurial intentions.[42]

With Stafford Cripps as Chancellor of the Exchequer from 1947 these managerialist values reinforced his preoccupation with output and productivity, matters which had concerned him since his wartime days as the Minister responsible for aircraft production. Economic planning in this environment became a technical exercise with a logic that transcended political considerations. The planning priorities of enhanced production and reduced inflation – part of Labour's adaptation to the requirements of the Marshall programme – inevitably displaced socialist objectives on the government's agenda. Productivity took precedence over equality. High production and the turn away from egalitarianism as a priority went hand-in-hand with the acceptance of the need for reasonable levels of profitability in industry, which in turn relied on the motivation of self-interest. In these ways Labour's economic strategy after 1947 marked the abandonment of any claim to be constructing a new economic order.[43] Thereafter the government's economic policy was marked by retrenchment and defensiveness. Psychologically and practically Labour had lost the initiative.[44] The Marshall Plan elevated 'productivity' to the level of a deity, but while Cripps was an instinctive worshipper at this shrine it was very much the circumstances of the American recovery plan for Europe that allowed his interest to flourish so.

The immediate effect of these new ideas was not to encourage wholesale revisionism in Labour's thinking, rather it resulted in 'consolidationism', that growing climate of opinion from 1948 that Labour had gone far enough, or as far as it was prudent to go, and that the need now was to iron out the kinks in the newly constructed mixed-economy welfare state. There would be no new major programme of socialisation, and a special effort would be made to retain the support of the middle class. Of course, the real political issue was not whether Britain should settle for a mixed economy, rather what the balance should be between socialised and private interests and the speed at which Labour should move to ensure that the essential instruments of planning and control were democratically controlled.[45]

Bit by bit the sentiment in favour of consolidation was taking hold. Labour's 1950 election manifesto listed only four candidates for nationalisation, a concocted programme of 'odds and ends', as Morrison was later to deride it. Even the parliamentary left was now in retreat on this issue: *Keeping Left* was concerned less about the ownership of industry than about who managed it, and therefore concluded that the next steps were not so obvious or so simple.[46] Consolidationism was generally accepted by the party, though only grudgingly by the left and the revisionists. The struggle between them would not be resolved until the second half of the 1950s, when the Gaitskellites took control of the party machine and infused its policy with revisionist values.

The transition from consolidation to revision in the early 1950s was reflected in the thinking of Labour intellectuals who contributed to *New Fabian Essays, Socialist Commentary* and were identified with the Socialist Union. When people like Richard Crossman argued that managerial society constituted a threat to human freedom he was countered by people who contended that such a society was capable of being civilised by socialism. This was a recurring theme in *New Fabian Essays*, one of the first post-war attempts at revising basic Labour thinking and establishing new values for socialism. In an exploratory essay that constituted a dry run for his famous treatise of four years later, *The Future of Socialism*, Anthony Crosland observed that managerialism had helped bring about a metamorphosis of British capitalism such that it no longer deserved the name. Austen Albu gave the line a further twist in arguing that, just as scientists were essentially team players and therefore adaptable to the egalitarian norms of a democratic socialist society, so also the application of the social sciences to business management would generate a co-operative and more socially responsible mentality among managers.[47] Thus although, at first blush, the managerial revolution seemed to substitute a new authoritarian hierarchy for the old class structure, such need not necessarily be the case. Business companies were rational in form and not in themselves anti-social. They needed to be tailored and refined to meet modern needs. How was this to be done? All supporters of this soft version of managerialism agreed it required a change in the relationship between management and labour, but equally most of them fought shy of concrete formulations that could reasonably be described as industrial democracy. On this point Cripps had set the tone in a famous speech in Bristol in October 1946 when he remarked that it would be almost impossible to have worker-controlled industry in Britain, 'even if it were on the whole desirable', without workers having more experience of the managerial side of industry.[48] In rejecting the authoritarian view of the managerial revolution the new Fabian essayists stood accused of opening a side door to a more beguiling form of managerialism, still resistant to democratisation. Their approach undervalued mass activity in industry while elevating to a lofty plane technicism and the logic of management science.[49]

In an organisational sense the revisionists were grouped around the magazine *Socialist Commentary* and the Socialist Union. *Socialist Commentary* was originally the journal of the Socialist Vanguard Group (SVG), the British section of the Internationalen Sozialistischen Kampfbundes (ISK), which had been expelled from the German SPD in 1928 for opposition to its Marxist materialist perspective. Though tiny, in Britain the SVG was an influential group, especially when after 1950, led by Allan Flanders and Rita Hinden, it ceased to operate as a sect and settled for being the driving force at the centre of the Socialist Union, which it launched in 1951 as both a focus for political activism and a think-tank – in its own eyes a more serious version of the Fabian Society. *Socialist Commentary* and the Socialist Union were plugged in direct to the Marshall Plan operation in Britain by virtue of the fact that William Gausmann, Labour Information

Officer in the London mission, was a member of the journal's editorial board.[50] In *Socialist Commentary* and the more considered publications of the Socialist Union an attempt was made to point Labour in a new direction, away from the Bevanite left and the pragmatic consolidators among the existing party and trade union leadership. The emphasis was on socialism as an ethical and moral movement; their concerns were with equality, freedom and, more nebulously, 'fellowship'. While there were expressions of disapproval over the contemporary obsession with productivity and materialism, they regarded this as necessary for freedom, simply needing to be tempered by a greater spirit of fellowship. And if they had some doubts about managerialism all they could suggest as a counterweight was 'responsible participation' by workers.[51]

While the Bevanites were still defending the old barricades against challenges to Labour's 1945 programme and concentrating especially on foreign-policy matters, the revisionists were quietly extending their influence and preparing the ground for the main attempt to reorient Labour orthodoxy which came with Anthony Crosland's *The Future of Socialism*. Heavily influenced by American liberal thought and written following an extended visit to the United States, *The Future of Socialism* was the quintessential expression of Marshall Plan values as applied to British social democracy. Emphasising economic growth, equality (social rather than economic) and the end of ideology, Crosland put forward the most comprehensive case for revisionism in the context of managerial society. Viewing the managerial revolution without alarm, he maintained that a shift in industry's moral consensus had already caused private industry to be humanised, and the trend needed to be extended. These were years when, as Coates observes, the capitalist element in British industry was gradually played down, it being referred to in increasingly bland terms as 'private enterprise', 'business' or simply 'industry'.[52]

The crucial problem now identified was that of the psychology of industrial relations. For Crosland this meant taking a further lead from United States industrial relations practice, where top executives were much more professional and enlightened than their British counterparts and, with their obsession with labour and personnel problems, were constantly searching for more progressive ideas: 'the talk is all about participation, co-operation, human relations, etc. Autocratic management is taboo; teamwork is in and Elton Mayo replaces Henry Ford as the symbol of management's attitude to labour.'[53] Again more consultation was called for, but this was not to come about through joint management or anything like that, rather as a consequence of enlightenment.[54] Attitudes were all-important. Crosland's increasingly harmonious view of industrial society was blind to any consideration of the purposes for which management was now keen to proffer a softer image. Had industrial management really moved so far away from authoritarian practices? Had Mayo and the proponents of motivation theory really superseded Ford and Taylor? Or was it simply, as Mant suggests, a case of British business, with its 'long and unlovely history of employee exploitation', falling with enthusiasm on American approaches to motivation.[55] The softening of management's image was a means of retaining managerial control in the changed environment of a welfare state. Control in the interests of managerial efficiency was still the prime objective, and when it was threatened, whether by labour or by government, industrial management was likely to mount a fierce resistance.[56] Whatever neutral, technical values applied to the concept of management in the United States, when American managerialism was imported into Britain it reinforced traditional class-based hierarchies.

Four years earlier in *New Fabian Essays* Richard Crossman had urged that citizens should be granted the right to participate in the control of industry – *even at the cost of some efficiency*.[57] In the United States Daniel Bell also speculated that the managerial revolution might be challenged by the substitution of some real thought about the labour process for the fashionable human relations values of the age – in effect reopening the study of the technology of work and challenging the accepted notion of 'efficiency'. But, of course, in an age of Marshall Plan productivity campaigning there was never any question of efficiency yielding to wider social values: efficiency was exactly what the proponents of managerialism were preoccupied with. Indeed, the whole thrust of Bell's writing was to show how an unquestioned acceptance of the ideal of efficiency underlay the technical and social organisation of industry.[58]

The managerial revolution in its 'civilised' form was an integral element in the much discussed 'end of ideology' which emerged as a powerful idea in the 1950s and on which Bell was an eloquent commentator. As he saw it, 'in a silently emerging "managerial revolution", technical decision-making by the economic expert now shapes the politician's pronouncements'. The consequence in Europe, he claimed, was the 'exhaustion of socialist thought'.[59] The end of ideology reflected the ascendancy of pragmatism in political systems and the eclipse of absolute principles and political dogmatism. The British labour movement was a case in point, with the Gaitskellite wing of the Labour Party formally in control after 1955 and, as Clark Kerr noted, its Croslandite thinking pragmatically oriented towards goals instead of ideologically towards method. 'England certainly is helped,' Kerr confidently assured his readers, 'by the fact that we are at the end of what might be called the "Socialist Century", the century when the socialist challenge and socialist thought were so important. By now it has been discovered [...] the eternal conflict of manager and managed may be subject to other and better solutions [...].'[60]

The notion of an 'end of ideology' drew heavily on American experience or, more specifically, American experience as filtered through the eyes of a school of intellectuals, often disillusioned radicals of the political left, whose prolific output of writing was a major factor in the spread of the idea. Among the most influential of the American ideologues of the 'end of ideology' school were the academics involved in the Inter-university Labour Project financed by the Ford Foundation, the revelance of whose work in the context of Marshall Plan productivity was discussed in chapter 11. The Inter-university Project was important in establishing an intellectual basis for American claims to world leadership in industrial practices, and the end of ideology which they detected in various parts of the world served to increase the legitimacy of the management-led American system. Industrialism was the common characteristic of all advanced countries and managerialism was its motor force, the guarantor of the inevitability of progress. In *Industrialism and Industrial Man*, the best known product of the Inter-university Project, the focus of attention in modern industrial society was no longer on the response of labour to capitalist development, but on how to

structure and manage the labour force. The need, then, was to
fashion a suitably harmonious labour relations system. As the
participants in this project recognised, there was a world-wide
contest going on over industrial relations systems no less than
over economic systems, the importance of industrial relations
systems being that they defined and established power and
authority relationships in industry. The labour issue that pressed
most heavily on modern industrial society was related to productivity: how could labour's pace of working be raised and then
maintained? The most lasting solutions were held to be found in
American experience, where a middle-class managerial elite
presided over a society in which ideologies had ceased to be
relevant. Here, as Crosland had pointed out, managers were
becoming increasingly benevolent and increasingly skilled, there
were no clear-cut divisions between workers and managers in
what was essentially an open society. And in this environment
the role of unions was simply to regulate management at the
workplace and to offer no greater challenge. American society
provided a model for other countries, for in industrial societies
the range of practical options was necessarily limited. The old
working-class utopias were no longer relevant and people seldom
had a real choice between ideological alternatives. There was, in
short, an inevitable tendency for ideology to wither as industrialism survived.[61]

It was indeed the American model that Anthony Crosland
embraced so enthusiastically and with such effect as he set about
providing an intellectual rationale for Labour revisionism in the
1950s. The greater class harmony in the United States was said
to be a function of the quality of management. Workers who rose
to management posts were not condemned as class traitors; trade
union leaders were not thought to be in danger of contamination
if they showed an interest in conspicuous consumption; the
unions were not deemed guilty of treachery if they co-operated
with management to boost sales or raise productivity, nor were
they regarded with suspicion, he argued with an eye on the EPA's
exchange visit scheme, if they sent their officials to Harvard for
training.[62] On the other hand, organised labour in Britain was
placed in the dock for its insufficient interest in managerial
efficiency and productivity drives. Sounding a note that was to
echo strongly throughout the rest of the 1950s and into the 1960s,

he argued that there would have to be a professionalisation of unions' staff to equip them for the managerial economy.[63]

As a well orchestrated press campaign built up in the mid-1950s attacking unions for their restrictive practices, and as prominent employers such as BMC, Ford and Standard Motors were encouraged to go on the offensive for the first time since the war in demanding that unions formally accede to managerial prerogative in a variety of ways, revisionist literature supplied the other cutting edge in this two-way attack, arguing for a complete rethink of union philosophy. The unions were accused of being 'robber barons', irresponsible and guilty of abusing their power,[64] and failing to see any virtues in capitalism.[65] They needed to adopt a more 'positive and constructive role'.[66] The argument was often presented in terms of the unions' technical failings but the underlying politics of the debate were never far from the surface. As a PEP study of trade unions pointed out, 'What is needed is [...] to rally behind the reformers the large body of trade unionists who are moderate and sensible but are at present defensive, sensitive to criticism and uncertain what to do.'[67]

In most revisionist literature there were positive appeals for some vague form of workers' participation – but never such as would leave them with any real influence. Industrial democracy was always presented as an attitude of mind, a form of managerial thinking rather than a concrete institutional arrangement in which workers had collective rights. In Shanks's gnomic formulation – industrial democracy was simply an aspect of good management.[68]

Thus Marshall Plan values, promoted through the extensive programme of social engineering, provided a congenial environment in which deradicalising pressures could operate on the labour movement in the 1950s. Marshall Aid cannot take total responsibility for revisionism, but it contributed mightily to the successes that it enjoyed. By the end of the 1950s organised labour in Britain and elsewhere in Europe had been steered away from some of the more radical objectives it had briefly and vaguely harboured in 1945. There was of course a dialectical process at work here, and the issue of workers' control and industrial democracy that had been forced off the agenda in the 1950s was to return in one form or another in the 1960s and 1970s. But the success of management's Taylorian values in undermining workers' scope for controlling the labour process was much more complete. Despite so-called 'labour process theory' being a fashionable subject of academic debate in the 1980s, there has been no significant counter-thrust from organised labour in this area. And for that result the Marshall Plan productivity programmes directed at labour must take much credit.

NOTES

Chapter 1

[1] Marshall later said his offer was something between a 'hint' and a 'suggestion' rather than a plan. William C. Crowell, 'The Marshall Non-plan, Congress and the Soviet Union,' *Western Political Quarterly*, Vol. 32, No. 4, December 1979, p. 429.

[2] The US loan negotiated in 1946 was running out fast, to a large extent as a result of uncontrolled American inflation, which had reduced its value by 25 per cent. In fact half Europe's balance of payments deficit in 1947 was due to price increases in the US, price controls having been terminated there in June 1946. J. J. Joseph, 'European recovery and United States aid,' *Science and Society*, summer 1948, p. 296.

[3] Military expenditure was responsible for more than half Britain's total balance of payments deficit for 1946–47. *Ibid.*, p. 340.

[4] Scott Newton, 'How successful was the Marshall Plan?' *History Today*, Vol. 33, November 1983, p. 12.

[5] McGeorge Bundy, *The Pattern of Responsibility*, Houghton Mifflin, 1952, p. 49.

[6] Harry Price, *The Marshall Plan and its meaning*, Cornell University Press, 1955, p. 12.

[7] Paul Hoffman, *Peace can be Won*, Michael Joseph, 1951, pp. 16–18, 76.

[8] George Kennan, *Memoirs, 1925–50*, Little Brown, 1967, p. 336.

[9] Scott Jackson, 'Prologue to the Marshall Plan: the origins of the American commitment for a European Recovery Programme,' *Journal of American History*, Vol. 65, No. 4, March 1979, p. 1046.

[10] For example, *Newsweek*, 12 May 1948, p. 74; *Time*, 26 May 1947, p. 85.

[11] Council of Economic Advisers, *The Impact of Foreign Aid on the Domestic Economy: A Report to the President*, 1947, pp. 30–1.

[12] Joyce and Gabriel Kolko, *The Limits of Power*, Harper & Row, 1972, p. 367.

[13] The 'Krug Committee', one of the three committees set up by President Truman to advise on Marshall Aid, emphasised that the US was dependent on expanding trade if only to secure such raw materials and strategic commodities. *National Resources and Foreign Aid*, 19 November 1947.

[14] *Department of State Bulletin*, 25 January 1948.

[15] Karl Schriftgiesser, *Business Comes of Age*, Harper Bros., 1960, p. 117.

[16] Thomas G. Smith, 'From the Heart of the American Desert to the Court of St. James's: the Public Career of Lewis W. Douglas of Arizona, 1894–1974,' unpublished PhD thesis, University of Connecticut, 1977, p. 396.

[17] *Department of State Bulletin*, 11 July 1948, p. 36.

[18] Senate Foreign Relations Committee, *Executive Session 1947*, pp. 153–4.

[19] President's Committee on Foreign Aid, *European Recovery and American Aid*, Washington, DC, November 1947.

[20] *New York Times*, 14 May 1948.

[21] *Business Week*, 9 October 1948, p. 124.

[22] Hadley Arkes, *Bureaucracy, the Marshall Plan and the National Interest*, Princeton University Press, 1972, p. 300.

[23] Senate Foreign Relations Committee, *Hearings on Extension of ERP*, 1949, p. 61.

[24] See, for example, Lewis Douglas's evidence to the Senate Foreign Relations Committee, *ERP Hearings in Executive Session*, 1948, pp. 247–51.

25 Immanuel Wexler, *The Marshall Plan Revisited*, Greenwood Press, 1983, pp. 100–7.

26 John G. Gurley, 'Excess liquidity and European monetary reforms 1944–52,' *American Economic Review*, Vol. 43, No. 1, March 1953, p. 76.

27 Senate Foreign Relations Committee, *Hearings on Extension of ERP*, 1949, p. 160–1.

28 Robert Oshins, interview, 1952, *Harry Price Oral History Project*, Truman Library.

29 Bissell to Golden and Jewell, 23 January 1950, ECA Admin. 5.

30 Minutes of Meeting of National Advisory Committee, 26 December 1950, cited in Wexler, p. 113.

31 Hoffman, *Peace can be Won*, pp. 79–80.

32 Thomas Finletter, *Oral History*, p. 7, Truman Library.

33 Bissell to Hoffman and Foster, 'Counterpart and Investment Policy,' 20 January 1950, ECA Policy Series.

34 Milton Katz, Harriman's deputy as Special Representative in Europe for the Marshall Plan, believed that this was a tactical blunder. Milton Katz, *Oral History*, Truman Library.

35 *American Federationist*, February 1948, p. 17.

36 Carey statement to the Committee for the Marshall Plan, 2 April 1948, CIO Sec. Treas. 39. Just a few months earlier, in stating the CIO's position on Marshall Aid, Carey had told the WFTU Executive Board: 'I am here to talk to you not about ideologies, because we have no American ideologies to export, but about food and coal and fertilisers and agricultural machinery, and power plants, and transportation, and cotton, and steel [...].' Statement to WFTU EB, November 1947.

Chapter 2

1 George Ross, *Workers and Communists in France*, University of California Press, 1982, pp. 22–3; Richard F. Kuisel, *Capitalism and the State in Modern France*, Cambridge University Press, 1981, pp. 202–4.

2 Val Lorwin, *The French Labour Movement*, Harvard University Press, 1954, pp. 106–7; Walter Kendall, *The Labour Movement in Europe*, Allen Lane, 1975, p. 55.

3 S. J. Woolf, 'The rebirth of Italy, 1943–50,' in S. J. Woolf (ed.), *The Rebirth of Italy, 1943–50*, Longmans, 1972, pp. 216, 231.

4 F. Catalano, 'The rebirth of the party system, 1944–48,' in Woolf, p. 60.

5 Danield L. Horowitz, *The Italian Labour Movement*, Harvard University Press, 1963, pp. 253–5.

6 Leo Panitch, *Social Democracy and Industrial Militancy*, Cambridge University Press, 1976, p. 10.

7 Lorwin, pp. 109–10.

8 E. Drexel Godfrey, *The Fate of the French Non-communist Left*, Doubleday, 1955, pp. 39–44.

9 Henry W. Ehrmann, 'The decline of the Socialist Party,' Edward Mead Earle, *Modern France*, Russell & Russell, 1964, p. 183; Alexander Werth, *France, 1940–55*, Robert Hale, 1956, p. 267.

10 Catalano, p. 66.

11 Muriel Grindrod, *The Rebuilding of Italy*, RIAA, 1955, p. 48.

12 For the views of two of the key protagonists in the US Manpower Division see George S. Wheeler, *Who Split Germany?*, Confederation of Free German Trade Unions, Berlin, 1962, and Paul Porter, 'Conflict within American

Military Government concerning the Revival of German Trade Unions,' 15 November 1983, Porter Papers, Truman Library. For accounts by academics see Michael Fichter, 'Non-state organisations and the problems of redemocratisation,' in John H. Hertz (ed.), *From Dictatorship to Democracy*, Greenwood Press, 1982, and Carolyn Eisenberg, 'Working class politics and the Cold War: American intervention in the German labour movement, 1945–49,' *Diplomatic History*, Vol. VII, No. 4, fall 1983.

13 Val Lorwin, 'The struggle for control of the French trade union movement, 1945–49,' in Earle, pp. 202–3.

14 Ross, pp. 28–9.

15 Lorwin, *The French Labour Movement*, p. 285.

16 Maurice Neufeld, *Italy: School of Awakening Countries*, Greenwood Press, 1974, pp. 459, 462, 466.

17 B. Salvati, 'The rebirth of Italian trade unionism, 1943–54,' in Woolf, p. 197.

18 *Ibid.*, p. 194.

19 Horowitz, pp. 208–9.

20 Joseph La Palombara, *The Italian Labour Movement*, Cornell University Press, 1957, p. 17; Neufeld, p. 473.

21 Horowitz, pp. 258, 206.

22 *Ibid.*, pp. 338–9.

23 Ross, p. 43; Lorwin, 'The struggle', pp. 203–6.

24 Henry Pelling, *The Labour Governments, 1945–51*, Macmillan, 1984, pp. 59–60.

25 Ben Pimlott, *Hugh Dalton*, Cape, 1985, pp. 434–5.

26 Sir Richard Clarke, *Anglo-American Economic Collaboration in War and Peace, 1942–49*, Clarendon, 1982, pp. 52–4, 145, 152.

27 Kuisel, p. 232.

28 Werth, pp. 295, 313–14, 316.

29 Vernon Van Dyke, 'The communists and foreign relations in France,' in Earle, p. 241.

30 Lorwin, *The French Labour Movement*, p. 216; Ross, p. 42; Werth, p. 349.

31 Lorwin, *The French Labour Movement*, pp. 116–17.

32 Werth, pp. 355–8.

33 *Ibid.*, p. 357.

34 *Ibid.*, p. 360.

35 Lorwin, *The French Labour Movement*, p. 118.

36 *Ibid.*, p. 119; Werth, p. 366.

37 Ross, pp. 53–4.

38 Werth, p. 389.

39 Charles A. Micaud, 'The Third Force today,' in Earle, p. 139.

40 Grindrod, p. 47; Neufeld, p. 470.

41 G. Warner, 'Italy and the powers, 1943–49,' in Woolf, p. 52.

42 Following the break Nenni's section of the PSIUP had become the PSI.

43 Neufeld, p. 473.

44 La Palombara, p. 18.

45 Horowitz, p. 212.

46 Neufeld, p. 474.

47 C. S. Maier, 'Two post-war eras and the conditions for stability in twentieth century western Europe,' *American History Review*, 1981, pp. 338–9.

48 US Embassy, London, to State Department 21 January 1948, State 800.00S.

49 US Consul, Antwerp, to State Department, 8 December 1947, State 800.00S.

Chapter 3

[1] Thomas G. Paterson, 'The Economic Cold War: American Business and Economic Foreign Policy, 1945–50,' unpublished PhD thesis, University of California (Berkeley), 1969, pp. 73, 100.

[2] William Appleman Williams, 'The large corporation and American foreign policy,' in David Horowitz (ed.), *Corporations and the Cold War*, Monthly Review Press, 1969, p. 94.

[3] Walter Lippmann, *The Method of Freedom*, Macmillan, 1934, p. 105.

[4] Williams, p. 95.

[5] Robert A. Pollard, *Economic Security and the Origins of the Cold War, 1945–50*, Columbia University Press, 1985. p. 2.

[6] Paterson, pp. 9, 20, 22.

[7] G. William Domhoff, 'Who made American foreign policy, 1945–63,' in Horowitz, *op. cit.*, p. 27.

[8] Karl Schriftgiesser, *Business Comes of Age*, Harper Bros., 1960, pp. 162–3.

[9] Paterson, pp. 21–7, 36. Many other prominent businessmen served in the Truman administration, including Robert Lovett of Brown Bros. Harriman & Co., who became Under-Secretary of State; William Clayton, the cotton millionaire, who served as Under-Secretary for Economic Affairs; and Willard Thorp, director of numerous utilities, who became Assistant Secretary for Economic Affairs. James Forrestal, who served as Secretary for Defence, was the main recruiter of businessmen for the administration, pressing for appointment as ambassadors business leaders who would push vigorously the interests of American business.

[10] Schriftgiesser, pp. 46–50.

[11] 'The Marshall Plan: a way to peace,' speech delivered to the Engineering Society of Detroit, 18 February 1948, Batt Collection, 3, Truman Library.

[12] Schriftgiesser, pp. 136–7.

[13] Charles S. Maier, 'The politics of productivity: foundations of American international economic policy after World War II,' *International Organisation*, Vol. XXXI, fall 1977, p. 615.

[14] Porter letter to Norman Thomas, 30 June 1947, *Porter Collection*, 1, Truman Library.

[15] *Newsweek*, 3 October 1938.

[16] Paul Hoffman, *Peace can be won*, Michael Joseph, 1951, p. 124.

[17] Maier, p. 609.

[18] Pollard, p. 248.

[19] Maier, pp. 616–18, 627.

[20] Lovett to Caffrey, 25 October 1947, State, 851.00.

[21] Maier, p. 631.

[22] Charles Maier, 'Two postwar eras and the conditions for stability in twentieth century western Europe,' *American History Review*, 1981, p. 347.

[23] Paterson, p. 202.

[24] Howell John Harris, *The Right to Manage*, University of Wisconsin Press, 1982, pp. 39, 99, 131 and 195.

Chapter 4

[1] David Brody, *Workers in Industrial America: Essays on the Twentieth Century Struggle*, Oxford University Press, 1980, p. 176.

[2] Steve Fraser, 'Dress rehearsal for the New Deal: shop floor insurgents, political elites, and industrial democracy in the Amalgamated Clothing Workers,' in

Michael H. Frisch and Daniel J. Walkowitz, *Working Class America: Essays on Labour, Community and American Society*, University of Illinois Press, 1983, p. 214.

[3] *Ibid.*, p. 223.

[4] Sumner Slichter, *Union Politics and Industrial Management*, Brookings Institute, 1941, p. 378.

[5] Clark Kerr, *Labour and Management in Industrial Society*, Anchor, 1964, p. 261.

[6] Philip Murray and Morris Cooke, *Organised Labour and Production*, Harper Bros., 1940.

[7] Clinton Golden and Harold Ruttenberg, *The Dynamics of Industrial Democracy*, Harper Bros., 1942; Harold Ruttenberg, 'Strategy of industrial peace,' *Harvard Business Review*, Vol. 17, 1939.

[8] Thomas R. Brooks, *Clint: a Biography of a Labour Intellectual*, Atheneum, 1978. In the mid-1950s Golden became part of the secretive and highly influential international Bildergerg group, comprising businessmen, politicians and selected labour leaders from various 'Western' countries.

[9] Clinton Golden, 'A tribute to Joseph N. Scanlon,' in Frederick G. Lesieur (ed.), *The Scanlon Plan: a Frontier in Labour–Management Co-operation*, MIT Press, 1958.

[10] Nelson Lichtenstein, *Labour's War at Home*, Cambridge University Press, 1982, p. 41.

[11] *Ibid.*, .81.

[12] Victor G. Reuther, *The Brothers Reuther*, Houghton Mifflin, 1976, pp. 247–8.

[13] Lichtenstein, p. 81.

[14] *Ibid.*, p. 217.

[15] Irving Richter, 'The Decline of Organised Labour from 1945,' *Papers in the Social Sciences* (Washington, DC), Vol. 4, 1984, p. 40.

[16] *Ibid.*

[17] Brody, pp. 176–7.

[18] Lichtenstein, p. 221.

[19] *Ibid.*, p. 229.

[20] Jack Stieber, *US Industrial Relations, 1950–80*, IRRA, 1981, p. 175.

[21] Brody, p. 188.

[22] Nelson Lichtenstein, 'Conflict over workers' control: the automobile industry in World War II,' in Frisch and Walkowitz, *op. cit.*, p. 303.

[23] R. Herding, *Job Control and Union Structure*, Rotterdam University Press, 1972, p. 30.

[24] Lichtenstein, 'Conflict over workers' control,' p. 301.

[25] Harris, pp. 143–53.

[26] Brody, p. 185.

[27] 'GM's five-year plan,' *New Leader*, 3 June 1950.

[28] Clinton Golden and Virginia Parker, *Causes of Industrial Peace under Collective Bargaining*, Harper Bros, 1955, p. x.

[29] See below, chapter 11.

[30] Golden and Parker, p. 9.

[31] *Ibid.*, p. 10.

[32] *Ibid.*, p. 47.

[33] *Ibid.*, p. 332.

[34] *Ibid.*, p. 51.

[35] Herbert R. Northrup and Harvey A. Young, 'The causes of industrial peace revisited,' *Industrial and Labour Relations Review*, Vol. 22, No. 1, October 1968, p. 47.

[36] Report of Special CIO Committee to Europe to CIO Committee on International Affairs, March 1951, CIO Washington Office, 64 (16).

[37] Harris to Mullin (undated, 1950?), Golden 4 (9).

[38] Jay Lovestone, Labour's Stake in Democracy: American Labour Looks Ahead, October, 1940, Dubinsky 262, (A).

[39] *Washington Post*, 10 January 1941.

[40] Representation in International Relations, Report of Post-war Planning Committee of AFL, Dubinsky 176 (3A)

[41] ALCIA records are in Dubinsky Papers 173.

[42] Varian Fry, 'How to Help the Free and Democratic Labour Movements in Liberated Europe', April 1945, Dubinsky 173, (3B).

[43] Abramovitch to Woll, 3 December 1945, Dubinsky 173 (3A).

[44] Bluestein to Woll, 'Free Trade Union Fund,' 16 July 1945, Thorne 16.

[45] Lie to Woll, 14 June 1944, Dubinsky 78 (3A).

[46] Brown to Woll, 28 December 1945, Thorne 16.

[47] Brown to Woll, December 1945, Zimmerman 21 (1).

[48] Brown to Bluestein, 27 November 1945; Brown to Woll, 5 December 1945 and 10 December 1945, Thorne 16.

[49] Brown to Woll, 14 December 1945, Zimmerman 11 (16).

[50] Brown to Woll, 1 January 1946, Thorne 16; 17 February 1946, Zimmerman 21 (1).

[51] Brown to Woll, 22 February 1946, Zimmerman 21 (1).

[52] Brown to Zimmerman, 14 March 1946, Dubinsky 11 (16).

[53] Zimmerman to Dubinsky, 12 April 1946, Dubinsky 7, (3).

[54] Brown to Woll, 22 March 1946, Zimmerman 21 (1).

[55] Brown to Woll, 24 May 1946, Zimmerman 21 (1).

[56] AFL Committee on International Labour Affairs, 19 July 1946, Thorne 16.

[57] *Ibid.*, 26 April 1950, Thorne 17.

[58] American-Italian Labour Conference – Financial Statements, Dubinsky 256 (2A/B).

[59] Brown, Report on Greece, France and England, 7 July 1947, Thorne 17; 'Confidential' from Brown, 10 November 1947, Zimmerman 13 (4).

[60] Germer, Diary, 15 November 1946, Germer 15.

[61] Brown to Woll, 1 January 1946, Thorne 16; Editor of Frankfurter Runschau Appeal, 6 January 1946, Zimmerman 21 (1).

[62] AFL Committee on International Labour Affairs, 3 November 1946, Thorne 16; Rutz to Woll, November 1947, Thorne 11.

[63] Rutz to Woll, 5 November 1947, Thorne 17.

[64] Minutes of 2nd Quarterly Meeting of ILGWU, GEB 20 January 1948.

[65] Brown Report to CILR, 10 November 1947, Thorne 17.

[66] AFL, Committee of International Labour Affairs, 5 January 1948, Thorne 17.

[67] In January 1949 Lovestone told the ECA Office of Labour Advisers (no doubt with tongue in cheek) that a consignment of FTUC pamphlets intended for France was bundled up and ready to go, but that the FTUC could not afford to send them air mail. 'Our Committee is too poor to do that. We live strictly and solely on trade union funds.' Lovestone to Pratt, 5 January 1949, ECA Lab. Div. 145.

[68] Krane to Cope, 5 December 1948, Krane 1 (3); Brown to Dubinsky 16 December 1947 and 19 May 1948; Dubinsky to Brown 5 January 1948; Verdier to Dubinsky, October 1948; Berger to Dubinsky 2 September 1949; Dubinsky to Josephson 22 November 1950; Dubinsky to Robert Blum 27 February 1953, Dubinsky 249 (6).

[69] In mid 1951 FTUC expenditure appears to have been at the rate of $8,000 per

month. However, Dubinsky did not seem to be strictly limited to regular union sources of finance for his international work. For example, Lovestone's name was not on the official ILGWU payroll and it was claimed by some that his salary came from expenses for which Dubinsky did not have to account. The source was never disclosed. Martin Arundel, 'Jay Lovestone: mystery man', May 1956, North American Newpaper Alliance Syndicate. Loosely attached to the Garment Workers' Union as he was, and deeply involved in clandestine international activities, it was said of Lovestone that he was 'part cloak and suit, part cloak and dagger'.

70 The *Detroit Free Press* claimed (21 August 1951) that Lovestone was spending in excess of $250,000 per year. The following year *Time* stated that Brown had doled out a total of $500,000 since coming to Europe and was operating on a budget of $2,000 per month. *Time*, 17 March 1952, p. 15. The *Chicago Daily News* said in 1950 that Brown was spending $250,000 annually and, adding in special union gifts, as much as $5 million. On the other hand, Brown told Sidney Lens in 1965 that over twenty years he had spent $100,000. Sidney Lens, 'Lovestone diplomacy,' *Nation*, 5 July 1965, p. 15.

71 The allegation by Tom Braden, former head of the CIA's Psychological, Political and Paramilitary Division, that the CIA was financing Irving Brown as early as 1947 is not supported by the available evidence. Braden himself only came on the scene some years later. Braden, 'I'm glad the CIA is immoral', *Saturday Evening Post*, 20 May 1967. See also Ronald Radosh, *American Labour and United States Foreign Policy*, Random House, 1969, p. 439.

72 Final Report of the Senate Select Committee to Study Governmental Operations with Respect to Intelligence Activities, Washington, 1976 (Supplementary Detailed Staff Reports on Foreign and Military Intelligence, Box IV) pp. 28–9, 35.

Chapter 5

1 Joseph C. Goulden, *Meany*, Atheneum, 1972, p. 126.

2 John Windmuller, *American Labour and the International Labour Movement, 1940–53*, New York State School of Industrial and Labour Relations, 1954, pp. 50–1.

3 *Ibid.*, p. 20.

4 US Embassy, Prague, to State Department, 6 June 1947, State 800.5043.

5 V. L. Allen, *Trade Union Leadership*, Longmans, 1957, pp. 292–9; Elmer Cope to Corrinne Cope, 29 June 1947, Cope Papers 17 (2), State Historical Society of Ohio.

6 Germer, Diary, 16 November 1946, 27 January 1947, 9 April 1947, 12 May 1947, Germer Papers 15, State Historical Society of Wisconsin.

7 Deakin to Germer, 21 March 1947, Germer 28; Elmer Cope to Corrinne Cope, 5 July 1947, Cope 17 (2).

8 Windmuller, p. 120.

9 The basis of this interpretation was an article in *Bolshevik*, 15 November 1947, reported in British ambassador, Moscow, to Hankey, 17 December 1947, FO 371/71648, PRO, London.

10 Allen, p. 298.

11 Ross to Cope, 30 October 1947, Cope 17 (5).

12 US Embassy, Paris, to State Department, 21 November 1947, State 800.5043.

13 Bevin to British ambassador, Washington, 24 December 1947, Bevin Papers, FO 800/493.

14 US ambassador, London, to State Department, 30 December 1947, State 800.5043.

15 Memorandum of conversation, Marshall, Murray, Carey and Ross, 20 January 1948, State 840.5043.
16 US Embassy, London, to State Department, 30 December 1947, State 800.5043; Tomlinson to Deakin and Tewson, 27 January 1948; Kolarz to Tewson, 3 February 1948; Bell to Tewson and Deakin, 4 February 1948, TUC 564.19.
17 Allen, p. 289.
18 Tewson to Saillant, 28 January 1948, TUC 564.19; Kuznetsov to Deakin, 29 January 1948, TUC 564.19.
19 US Embassy, Stockholm, to State Department, 30 January 1948, State 840.50 Recov.
20 US ambassador, London, to Lovett, 21 February 1948, State 840.50 Recov.
21 See Anthony Carew, 'The schism within the World Federation of Trade Unions: government and trade union diplomacy,' *International Review of Social History*, Vol. XXIX, 1984, part 3.

Chapter 6

1 Report of a Conference of ECA Mission Heads, 23 July 1948, ECA Admin. 1.
2 *ECA Labor Who's Who*, 1950.
3 Functions and Requirements for Labour Personnel outside the United States for the Operation of the ERP, undated, ECA Lab. Div. 143.
4 Harry Price, *The Marshall Plan and its Meaning*, Cornell University Press, 1955, p. 104.
5 *Ibid.*, p. 248; 'Role of Information Service', undated, 1949, ECA/OSR Cent. Sec. 15.
6 Friendly to Harriman, 19 January 1949, ECA/OSR Cent. Sec. 15; Functions and Requirements, *op. cit.*
7 Paul Porter, quoted in Price, *op. cit.*, p. 246.
8 Martin to H. J. Heinz II, 13 December 1950, ECA LI 130.
9 Director of European Affairs to Secretary of State, 23 March 1948; Memorandum of conversation, Green, Fenton and Under-Secretary Lovett, 6 April 1948, State 840.50.
10 Silvey to Murray, 15 April 1950, Silvey Papers.
11 Cope to Ross, 13 March 1949, CIO Sec. Treas. 115.
12 Rutz to Meany, 9 May 1951, Meany Series 7, 1 (13).
13 Silvey to Murray, *op. cit.*; Golden to Martin, 16 July 1950, Golden 4 (17).
14 *Ibid.*; in summer 1950 Golden demanded more staff for the office or suggested that the function be liquidated.
15 Report of a Conference of ECA Mission Heads, *op. cit.*
16 Golden to Harris, 1 January 1949, Golden 5 (6).
17 The very same day as Carey's leter to Hoffman, Golden noted in is diary, 'Developed proposal for an information specialist to go to Paris.' Diary, 11 June 1948, Golden 1.
18 Martin to Foster, 14 November 1948, ECA Lab. Div. 164.
19 Gausmann to Martin, 3 January 1950, ECA LI 130.
20 Golden to Harris, 1 January 1949, Golden 5 (5).
21 Shishkin to Katz, 16 May 1950, ECA Cent. Sec. 15.
22 Krane to Cope, 7 November 1948 and 15 December 1948, Krane 1 (3).
23 Shishkin to Green, 18 April 1949, Thorne 16.
24 Silvey to Golden and Jewell, 24 August 1948, Silvey Papers.
25 Silvey to Murray, *op. cit.*
26 Gausmann to Thomas, 18 April 1951, ECA LI 130.

[27] Golden to Heaps, 4 June 1953, and to Hutchison, 27 April 1950, Golden 5 (5) and 3 (27).

[28] Golden to Harris, 30 December 1950, Golden 5 (5).

[29] Silvey to Murray, *op. cit.*

Chapter 7

[1] Vandenberg to Carl M. Saunders, 2 January 1948, cited in Thomas G. Paterson, 'The Economic Cold War: American Business and Economic Foreign Policy, 1945–50,' unpublished PhD thesis, University of California (Berkeley), 1969, p. 26.

[2] This was how he was described on the dust jacket of his book, *Peace can be Won*, Michael Joseph, 1951.

[3] Hadley Arkes, *Bureaucracy, the Marshall Plan and the National Interest*, Princeton University Press, 1972, p. 311.

[4] Senate Foreign Relations Committee, *Hearings on the Extension of ERP*, 1949, pp. 85–6.

[5] Karl Schriftgiesser, *Business Comes of Age*, Harper Bros., 1960, pp. 136–7.

[6] For more detail on the corporate connections of ECA personnel see Paterson, *op. cit.*, pp. 26–9.

[7] Italy, like France, had received substantial 'interim aid' while the Marshall programme was being negotiated, so critical was her politico-economic situation. See Hoffman, *op. cit.*, pp. 82–83.

[8] Immanuel Wexler, *The Marshall Plan Revisited*, Greenwood Press, 1983, p. 47.

[9] Philip M. Williams (ed.), *The Diary of Hugh Gaitskell, 1945–56*, Cape, 1983, pp. 160, 184; *Fortune*, April 1950, p. 25.

[10] *New York Times*, 14 May 1948.

[11] Indeed, it was at this point that the importance of Marshall Aid to the domestic American economy became obvious. As Bissell conceded, the revival of the US economy in the latter part of 1949 might not have occurred without the ERP, and the continuation of the programme into 1950 was 'important from the view of maintaining domestic employment'. Bissell to Arrow, 2 December 1949, ECA Admin. 33.

[12] Text of speech 24 November 1948, Finletter Papers, Truman Library.

[13] Muriel Grindrod, *The Rebuilding of Italy*, RIIA, 1955, p. 209.

[14] Finger to Golden, 28 June 1949, ECA Lab. Div. 150.

[15] Martin to Harriman, 20 March 1950, ECA/OSR Cent. Sec. 15.

[16] Alexander Werth, *France, 1940–1955*, Robert Hale, 1956, p. 422.

[17] Paris Mission Paper for European Labour Staff Conference, 22–24 May 1950, ECA Lab. Div. 144.

[18] *Ibid.*; Delaney to Harriman, 6 November 1949, Lab. Div. 149.

[19] Shishkin to Harriman, 9 January 1950, ECA Lab. Div. 144.

[20] Douty to Parkman, September 1950, ECA Lab. Div. 149; Report of Special CIO Committee to Europe to CIO Committee on International Affairs, 1 March 1951, CIO Washington Office 64 (16).

[21] Henry Pelling, *The Labour Governments, 1945–51*, Macmillan, 1984, p. 189.

[22] Philip M. Williams, *op. cit.*, p. 139.

[23] *Ibid.*, p. 125; William C. Mallalieu, *British Reconstruction and American Policy, 1954–55*, Scarecrow Press, 1956, pp. 187, 191.

[24] Alan Bullock, *Ernest Bevin: Foreign Secretary*, Heinemann, 1983, p. 707.

[25] Douglas to Acheson, 15 August 1949, Acheson Papers, 64, Truman Library.

[26] Roger Eatwell, *The 1945–1951 Labour Governments*, Batsford, 1979, p. 104;

Michael Foot, *Aneurin Bevan, 1945–60*, Paladin, 1975, p.274; Ozer to Shishkin, 25 October 1949, ECA Lab. Div. 152.

[27] Unsigned memorandum, 'The Lesson of British Foreign Exchange Crisis of 1949,' 26 January 1950 ECA/OSR Cent. Sec. 11.

[28] Germany, File 943, TUC Archives.

[29] Joyce and Gabriel Kolko, *The Limits of Power*, Harper & Row, 1972, p.434.

[30] Transcript of radio broadcast by Victor Reuther, 1 September 1948, State 840.50 Recov.

[31] Shishkin to Daspit, 25 July 1950, ECA Lab. Div. 149.

[32] Harvey Brown Report, Transcript of Proceedings, European Labour Staff Conference, 22–24 May 1950, ECA Lab. Div. 144.

[33] Beckner memorandum, 'Labour Employment Situation,' July 1950; Beckner to Lovell, 7 January 1950 and 19 January 1950, ECA Lab. Div. 149.

[34] Council on Foreign Relations, Records of Groups, 24 April 1950, cited in Wexler, *op. cit.*, p.100.

[35] AFL Committee on International Labour Affairs, 19 October 1948, Thorne 17 (4); Ambassador Dunn to Secretary of State, 12 March 1948, cited in R. Faenza and M. Fini, *Gli Americani in Italia*, Feltrinelli, 1976, p.304. FO also obtained from the Minister of Labour two-thirds of the funds confiscated from the Vichy labour front – some $75,000 in all. E. Drexel Godfry, *The Fate of the French Non-communist Left*, Doubleday, 1955, pp.55–6.

[36] Golden to Harris, 6 December 1948; Golden to Strachan, 5 December 1948; Golden to Harris, 1 January 1949, Golden 4 (17); Diary 15–16 December 1948.

[37] Krane to Cope, 14 September 1949, 29 October 1949 and 8 November 1949, Krane 1 (7) and 1 (8).

[38] Lane was a mystery man. A lawyer formerly attached to the Bricklayers' Union, he held the army rank of colonel and had previously served as a labour officer in the American mission in Trieste. In the course of lobbying for the ECA Labour Adviser's job in Rome he claimed that he had travelled to Rome 'at his own expense' to help the anti-communist forces during the April 1948 election campaign. He appears to have been well connected and knew Harriman and Zellerbach personally before being appointed in Rome. Silvey to Golden and Jewell, 24 August 1948, Silvey Papers. He worked very closely with Irving Brown for a number of years, though it would seem that he had his own direct source of supply of CIA funds for Italian labour.

[39] The audience was in February 1949, also attended by Toughill and ECA Labour Consultants William Gausmann, Neal Miller and Pete Swimm. Toughill to author, 7 July 1984.

[40] Dunn to Acting Secretary of State, 21 September 1948, State 865.5043.

[41] Rome Embassy to State Department, 15 January 1949, State 840.50 Recov.

[42] W. E. Knight, Memorandum of conversation, 1 October 1948, State 840.50 Recov.

[43] Martin to Golden and Jewell, 26 April 1949, ECA Policy and Planning 164; Acheson to Dunn, 12 April 1949, State 865.504.

[44] Joseph La Palombara, *The Italian Labour Movement*, Cornell University Press, 1957, p.57.

[45] File: Information Function, ECA/OSR Cent. Sec. 15.

[46] Toughill to author, 7 July 1984.

[47] Jewell to Crouch, 11 August 1949, Silvey Papers.

[48] Dubinsky to Harriman, July 1949, Dubinsky 255 (3B). These views were expressed in a draft letter. There is no evidence as to whether or not it was sent. Dubinsky's line on this issue is interesting. The records suggest that he assumed a highly ethical position. Yet it seems unlikely that he would have

been unaware of any arrangements for securing external funding – whether from the ECA or from the intelligence services. It is just possible that in this draft letter (left for the record) and the minutes of the AFL International Committee, Dubinsky was seeking to cover himself against future allegations of irregular practice. See Dubinsky's own autobiographical account of how he kept the CIA at arm's length. David Dubinsky and A. H. Raskin, *David Dubinsky: a Life with Labour*, Simon & Schuster, 1977, pp. 259–61.

49 AFL International Labour Relations Committee, 27 October 1949, Thorne 17 (5).

50 Brown to Lovestone, 4 September 1949, Dubinsky 255 (3B).

51 Norman Thomas, 'Memorandum on the Unity of Non-communist Labour Groups in Italy,' undated 1949, Dubinsky 255 (3B).

52 Golden and Jewell to Hoffman, 27 August 1948, ECA Admin. 2.

53 Krane, Diary, 16 March 1949, Krane 1 (5).

54 Philip M. Williams (ed.), *The Diary of Hugh Gaitskell, 1945–46, op. cit.*, p. 90; Val Lorwin, *The Labour Movement in France*, Harvard University Press, 1954, p. 130.

55 Harris to Golden, 11 March 1949, Golden 4 (17); Krane, Diary, 18 May 1949 and 4–6 June 1949, Krane 1 (7).

56 Krane to Cope, 6 September 1949, 9 September 1949 and Diary, 23 September 1949, Krane 1 (7).

57 Krane, Diary, 23 September 1949, Krane 1 (7).

58 Tasca to Katz, 9 November 1950, ECA/OSR Cent. Sec. 15; Hoffman speech to Washington Conference of Labour Leaders, 5 May 1950, ECA Admin. 4.

59 Lovestone Report on Second ERP Trade Union Conference, 29–30 July 1948, Dubinsky 276 (4B).

60 Clay to Woll, 5 January 1949, Thorne 17 (5).

61 Harvey Brown Report, Transcript of Proceedings of European Labour Staff Conference, *op. cit.*

62 Woll to Clay, 14 February 1949, Thorne 17 (5).

63 HICOG Labour Staff job description, Trade Union Policy and Relations Branch, 1949 ECA Lab. Div. 149.

64 Lovestone Report, *op. cit.*

65 *Ibid.*

66 Beckner, 'Labour Employment Situation', *op. cit.*; Harvey Brown Report, *op. cit.*

Chapter 8

1 *ADA World*, December 1949.

2 Krane to Cope, 4 December 1948, Krane 1 (3).

3 Krane to Cope, 14 December 1948, Krane 1 (3).

4 Krane to Cope, 11 January 1949, Krane 1 (3).

5 Shishkin to Katz, 31 August 1949, ECA/OSR Cent. Sec. 15.

6 Ozer memorandum, 'A Suggestion for an Ad Hoc Committee to Evaluate,' 8 September 1949, ECA Lab. Div. 143.

7 Martin to Harriman, 15 December 1949, ECA/OSR Cent. Sec. 15.

8 Turtledove to Martin, 31 January 1950, ECA LI 130.

9 Douty to Bingham, 7 February 1950, ECA LI 5.

10 Douty to Golden, 15 February 1950, ECA Lab. Div. 149.

11 See pp. 12–13.

12 Special Assistant to the Under Secretary of State to Hoffman, 31 December 1948, ECA Admin. 5.

[13] On this se Arkes, *op. cit.*, pp. 314–15.

[14] Turtledove to Martin, 1 April 1950, ECA LI 130.

[15] Shishkin to Katz, 16 May 1950, ECA/OSR Cent. Sec. 15.

[16] *Ibid.*

[17] Martin to Douty, 2 May 1950, ECA LI 130.

[18] Golden and Jewell to Wood and Stone, 4 April 1950, ECA Lab. Div. 149.

[19] Memorandum of meeting in the office of Donald Stone, 17 April 1950, ECA LI, 131. Two days later Stone, the Director of Administration, ECA Washington, told Hoffman: 'The use of confidential funds was viewed as very unsuitable for the above purposes, although there are certain ways, as Jewell realises, in which they might possibly be employed.' Stone to Hoffman and Foster, 19 April 1950, ECA Admin. 5. General counsel to OSR had previously advised that it was legally possible to finance special projects from this source even though they could not be justified as direct costs of mission administration. General Counsel OSR to Deputy Chief of Mission, Bizone, 2 October 1948, ECA LI 163.

[20] Bingham to Secretary of State, 27 April 1950, ECA Lab. Div. 144.

[21] *Labour News from the US*, 14 September 1950; Jewell to Smith, 3 October 1950, ECA Lab. Div. 146.

[22] Gausmann to Martin, 3 January 1950, ECA LI 130. Sheyer to Shishkin, 5 April 1950, ECA Lab. Div. 146.

[23] Jewell to Stone, 14 April 1950, ECA Admin. 5.

[24] Report on France by three American Trade Unionists, 1 October 1950, ECA Lab. Div. 149.

[25] Programme to Expand CIO Staff in Europe, 23 October 1950, CIO International 64 (16).

[26] 'International functions of the US Government', undated, UAW International, Reuther-Carliner 1956–62, 64.

[27] Report of CIO Committee to Europe to CIO Committee on International Affairs, March, 1951, CIO International 64 (16).

[28] *Ibid.*

[29] *Ibid.*

[30] Brown to Lovestone, 2 December 1951; AFL Paper on ICFTU, undated (February 1952?), Dubinsky 260 (6A).

[31] William J. Humphreys, 'Bevanism on the Continent', *New York Herald Tribune*, 23 April 1952.

[32] Martin to Katz, 21 March 1950, ECA Lab. Div. 143.

[33] Martin to Katz, 21 March 1950; Hutchison to Golden, 20 April 1950, Golden 3 (27); ERP–TUAC Conference, Rome, 18–20 April 1950, ECA Lab. Div. 143; Martin to Golden, 8 July 1950, Golden 4 (17).

[34] Transcript of Proceedings, European Labour Staff Conference, *op. cit.*

[35] Memorandum: Some Comments on Future ECA Programming, ECA/OSR Cent. Sec. 15.

[36] Bissell to Golden and Jewell, 27 March 1950, ECA Lab. Div. 149.

[37] Hoffman to Harriman, 12 January 1950, ECA/OSR Cent. Sec. 15.

[38] Harriman to Katz, 18 June 1950, ECA/OSR Cent. Sec. 15.

[39] Oliver to Foster, 20 October 1950, ECA Lab. Div. 131.

[40] Shishkin to Katz, Programme Objectives of Labour Division 1950–51, 7 July 1950 ECA/OSR Cent. Sec. 15.

[41] Transcript of Proceedings, European Labour Staff Conference, *op. cit.*

[42] *Ibid.*

[43] Functions of Mission Labour Division in Relation to the Defence Programme, February 1951, ECA LI 130.

44 Gausmann, Monthly Reports of Major Activities, February 1950–September 1951, ECA LI 130 and 137.

45 Gausmann to Evans, 2 April 1951, ECA LI 130; Lyn Smith, 'Covert British propaganda: the Information Research Department, 1947–77', *Journal of International Studies*, Vol. 9, No. 1, pp. 75–8. A Foreign Office file on the circumstances surrounding the publication of *The Curtain Falls* which should now be open under the thirty-year rule is closed indefinitely.

46 Gausmann to Martin, 3 February 1950, ECA LI 130.

47 Socialist Union papers are in the Socialist Vanguard Group Collection, Modern Record Centre, Warwick University.

48 Philip Williams (ed.), *The Diary of Hugh Gaitskell, 1945–56*, Cape, 1983, p. 384. Information on the dispute between Gausmann and Godson comes from Murray Weisz, who served as acting chief of the FOA Labour Division in Europe in 1953–54. Interview, 28 August 1986.

49 Gaitskell to Dubinsky, 20 June 1956, Dubinsky 248 (8A).

Chapter 9

1 Wexler, *op. cit.*, p. 144.

2 Kolko, *op. cit.*, pp. 443–4.

3 Price, *op. cit.*, p. 113.

4 Wexler, p. 206.

5 Acheson to Truman, 16 February 1950, Acheson Papers, Truman Library.

6 *Business Week*, 1 April 1950.

7 William Y. Elliott (ed.), *The Political Economy of American Foreign Policy: its Concepts, Strategy and Limits*, Henry Holt, 1955, p. 55.

8 NPACI 23 July 1948; TUC GC Min., 28 July 1948; Hansard, 28 July 1948.

9 Memorandum of conversation, Golden, Swayzee and Tobin, 24 August 1948, State 840.5043 Recov.; Golden had attended the ERP–TUAC conference.

10 Manchester and Salford Trades Council to Tewson, 20 August 1948; Taunton Trades Council to Tewson, 3 September 1948; Croydon Trades Council to Tewson, 4 September 1948, TUC 552.3 R.

11 Edwin Fletcher, then head of the TUC's Research Department, claims that he was notified by a Marshall Plan productivity expert before any steps were taken to launch the AACP, that the Americans were thinking in terms of sponsoring a series of visits by Britons to the United States. Interview, 24 February 1984.

12 *Draft History of the Council's Activities*, undated (1952?), TUC, 552.32 III; Hoffman, *op. cit.*, p. 91.

13 *Ibid.*

14 Report of AACP Full Council, 26–29 October 1948, TUC 552.31, and Transcript TUC 659.

15 *Ibid.*

16 *Foreign Report*, Economist Intelligence Unit, 3 February 1949.

17 Douglas to Marshall, 12 August 1948, ECA Admin. 6.

18 AACP, Report of Second Session, 7 April 1949; informal meeting, 17 October 1949, TUC 552.31.

19 *Daily Telegraph*, 19 August 1949.

20 *Draft History of the Council's Activities*; 'Organised Labour and Productivity in Western Europe,' Labour Productivity Branch PTAD/SRE, 28 August 1952, Gomberg Papers.

21 Graham Hutton, *We too can Prosper*, Allen & Unwin, 1953, pp. 233–4.

22 Tewson to Sir Thomas Hutton, 20 January 1950, TUC 552.3.

[23] NPACI – General Council Side, 30 March 1950.

[24] Tewson to Sir Thomas Hutton, *op. cit.*

[25] The practice adopted was for the British section of the AACP to submit to the Special Branch of the CID the names of nominees with a view to obtaining a speedy indication of whether the people in question were acceptable. If the Special Branch had a file on them there was little chance of their passing the American vetting process.

[26] *Building Report*, p. 55.

[27] *Letterpress Report.* Other reports that referred to unemployment as a spur to greater effort by workers were the *Drop Forge Report* and *Internal Combustion Report*.

[28] *Grey Ironfounding Report*, p. 20.

[29] Leo Goldstone, *A Critical Analysis of the Anglo-American Productivity Reports*, undated (1951?), mimeographed, p. 22. Goldstone has many useful insights into the contradictions in these reports.

[30] *Letterpress Report*, p. 4.

[31] *Trade Union Comments on the Letterpress and Lithographic Printing Productivity Reports*, undated, TUC 552.372 II.

[32] *Steel Founding Report*, p. 33.

[33] John Cates, 'The politics of free enterprise,' *New Statesman*, 29 December 1951.

[34] Howell John Harris, *The Right to Manage*, University of Wisconsin Press, 1982, p. 186.

[35] *Grey Ironfounding Report*, p. 17.

[36] *Ibid.*, p. 20.

[37] Holmes to OSR, 26 September 1949, ECA Lab. Div. 152.

[38] For example, *Cotton Yarn Doubling, Zinc, Aluminum Die Casting Reports.* See also Goldstone, *op. cit.*

[39] *Building Report*, p. 55.

[40] This was still the line being pushed in 1953 with the fall in profits and the rise in unemployment. *Cf.* Hutton, *We too can Prosper*, pp. 224–5.

[41] *Some Conclusions drawn from the Reports of the Anglo-American Productivity Teams*, Ministry of Labour, March 1952, TUC 552.372 II.

[42] Kimble, *Report of Trip to Europe*, 19 October 1949, TUC 552.3.

[43] AACP – British Section Interim Report, 31 January 1950, TUC 552.32 III.

[44] *Final AACP Report*, TUC 552.3.

[45] AACP – British Section Interim Report, *op. cit.*

[46] *Foundations of High Productivity*, 10 October 1950, TUC 552.31.

[47] Tewson to Fletcher, 4 January 1952, TUC 552.372 II.

[48] Hutton to Tewson, 13 November 1951, TUC 552.372 II.

[49] Hutton to Tewson, 22 November 1950, TUC 552.372 II.

[50] Fletcher, *The Anglo-American Council on Productivity*, 21 April 1952, TUC 552.32 III.

[51] Fletcher to Horne, 22 August 1952, TUC 557.374.

[52] Fletcher to Tewson, 30 January 1953, TUC 557.374.

[53] Paradise, Transcript of European Labour Staff Conference, *op. cit.*; Killen to Golden and Jewell, 3 June 1949, ECA Lab. Div. 152.

[54] US Embassy, London, to OSR, 5 October 1949 and 21 September 1949, ECA Lab. Div. 152.

[55] Killen to Forbes, 31 May 1949, ECA Lab. Div. 152.

[56] Paradise to Kenny, 28 December 1949, ECA Lab. Div. 152.

[57] Transcript of 3rd Round Table ECA Discussion with Members of the UK Trade Union Production Engineering Team, New York, 28 November 1949, TUC HD 21

58 NPACI – General Council Side, 1 August 1950.

59 *Trade Unions and Productivity*, TUC, 1950, pp. 60–1.

60 *Ibid.*, pp. 59–60.

61 *Ibid.*, p. 66.

62 Gomberg Report on Special Mission to United Kingdom, Netherlands and Germany, ECA Lab. Div. 146.

63 *Trade Unions and Productivity, op. cit.*, pp. 51–2.

64 *Ibid.*, p. 59.

65 Moving adoption of the General Council's report on production matters at the 1951 annual conference, Jack Tanner spoke of the movement's general appreciation of the importance of increasing productivity, 'which is just a simple commonsense attitude', and then went on to remark, 'How it is to be shared, of course, is another matter and we are not discussing that at the present moment.' *TUC Annual Report*, 1951, p. 482. This reflected the General Council's unwillingness to grapple with a fundamental question that had been raised on the floor of Conference the previous year when H. G. Knight (ASSET) pointed out, '[...] my organisation is very distressed to learn that, while the General Council is making these continual pleas for greater productivity, they have not really got down to thinking in concrete terms of what is going to happen to the results of that productivity. So far all we have seen is inflated profits.' *TUC Annual Report*, 1950, p. 506.

66 Interview, 16 November 1984.

67 Paradise to Kenny, 18 December 1949, *op. cit.*

68 This is confirmed by Fletcher, interview, 24 February 1984, and Paradise, interview, 29 March 1984. Harle himself plays down Paradise's role. Telephone interview, 12 April 1984.

69 Gausmann to Toughill, 18 May 1950; Gausmann to Evans and Martin, 16 August 1950, ECA LI 137; Paradise, statement to European Labour Staff Conference, *op. cit.* The proposal to reprint the report in popular format was killed off by Fletcher, who evidently had misgivings about the logic behind its findings. Interview, 24 February 1984.

70 Gausmann to Beck, 18 May 1950, ECA LI 137.

71 *Labour Developments – United Kingdom*, 18 August 1950, ECA Lab. Div. 152.

72 *Report of European Labour Staff Conference*, 23 May 1950, *op. cit.*

73 *TUC Annual Report*, 1950, pp. 507–12. See note 65 above.

74 *Labour Developments – United Kingdom*, 20 January 1950, ECA Lab. Div. 152.

75 Paradise to Cassels, 5 January 1951, ECA LI 130.

76 AACP – British Section Interim Report, *op. cit.* Tewson corroborated this view, telling the Americans some months later that in recent years there had been 'a revolution of thought in these [productivity] matters in the Trade Unions', AACP Joint Session, aide-mémoire, 18 October 1950, TUC 552.32 III.

77 NPACI – General Council Side, 27 July 1950.

78 Tewson, 'In defence of the unions,' *Spectator*, 10 December 1954, p. 738.

79 *Report of Footwear Industry Productivity Conference*, 9–11 November 1953, TUC HD 21. Four years later the link between politics and productivity appears to have become clearer to Crawford, by now perhaps *the* foremost British trade union evangelist of the productivity religion and soon to take his missionary zeal with him to the National Coal Board when he became a director. Speaking at a 1957 conference on productivity, he said, 'The hydrogen bomb may prove an effective deterrent to armed action, but unless we keep raising productivity, no bomb on earth can satisfactorily protect us from the potential domination of a national group which raises the productivity per man by 44 per cent between 1950 and 1955, as Russia did.' *British Productivity Council Bulletin*, 21 June 1957.

80 *Brassfounding Productivity Conference*, 21 December 1951, TUC HD 21.
81 *Consumer Capitalism*, United States Information Service, 1952.
82 AACP Full Council, 6 April 1949, TUC 557.32.
83 Minutes of 5th and Final Session of AACP, May 1952, TUC 552.3.

Chapter 10

1 James Stern memorandum, 1951, Mark Starr Papers 6 (1).
2 Herbert C. Mayer, *German Recovery and the Marshall Plan, 1948–52*, Edition Atlantic Forum, 1969, pp. 47, 74.
3 P. Armstrong, *et al.*, *Capitalism since World War II*, Fontana, 1984, pp. 126–7.
4 Milton Katz, *Oral History*, 25 July 1975, 262, Truman Library.
5 Krane Diary, 4 January 1950, Krane 1 (8).
6 Richard F. Kuisel, *Capitalism and the State in Modern France*, Cambridge University Press, 1981, p. 263; 'Organised Labour and Productivity in Western Europe,' Labour Productivity Branch, PTAD/SRE, 28 August 1952, Gomberg (4); Pier Paolo D'Attorre, *ERP Aid and the Politics of Producitivty in Italy during the 1950s*, European University Institute Working Paper 85/159, 1985, p. 12.
7 'Organised Labour and Productivity,' *op. cit.*
8 Cited in Hutchison to Harriman, 11 May 1950, ECA LI 149.
9 Paradise and Gausmann to Cruikshank and Martin, 22 December 1950, ECA Lab. Div. 144.
10 Bissell to Hoffman, 12 September 1949, ECA Admin. 5.
11 Shishkin to Harriman, 29 April 1950, ECA Lab. Div. 146.
12 File 'France–Productivity General', ECA LI 149.
13 'Organised Labour and Productivity,' *op. cit.*
14 D'Attorre, p. 12.
15 Kelly, Report of Productivity Trip to Italy, 11–16 June 1950, ECA LI 150.
16 OSR to Secretary of State, 2 August 1950, ECA Lab. Div. 145.
17 Kern to Harvey Brown, 24 January 1950, ECA LI 149.
18 Gomberg, speech to 5th International Conference on Social Problems of the Organisation of Labour, 1–3 June 1951, Abbaye de Royaumont, Gomberg 1.
19 Golden to Foster, 'European Trip, January 3–February 5, 1951', Golden 4 (9).
20 Harvey Brown to Golden, 23 March 1951, Golden 4 (9).
21 US Consulate, Frankfurt, to OSR, 24 November 1950; Bernstein to Shishkin, 17 November 1950, ECA LI 149; Golden to Foster, *op. cit.*
22 Mayer, *op. cit.*, p. 90.
23 Harris to Golden, 25 January 1952 and 15 December 1952, Golden 5 (6).
24 Bissell to OSR, 5 June 1951, Gomberg 1.
25 *Ibid.*; Scherbak to Gomberg, 22 January 1952, Gomberg 5.
26 Gausmann to Martin, 5 September 1950, ECA LI 130.
27 Dos and Be Wary Ofs in Productivity Case Histories, 8 September 1950, ECA LI 130. The instructions read: 'Utilise case histories where productivity rises have directly affected and increased wages or earnings. [...] Be wary of case histories entailing the installation of new machines where one man can now do the job of 100.'
28 Bissell to OSR.
29 Gomberg, Report on Third Trip to Europe, 22 June–31 July 1952, Gomberg 1.
30 Gomberg paper on inadequacy of US engineers in foreign aid programmes, undated (1953?), Gomberg 1.

[31] 'Organised Labour and Productivity.'

[32] The Benton amendment became Section 516 of the Mutual Security Act of 1951. The Moody amendment became Section 115 of the Economic Co-operation Act of 1948.

[33] Fletcher to Tewson, 3 March 1953, TUC 564.8.

[34] Arrangements for the Expenditure of Counterpart Funds, 25 February 1953, Cmd 776; BPC EC, 18 June 1953; TUC Production Committee 27 May 1954, TUC 557.1 II: BPC Bulletin, October 1955. Policy and Progress, BPC, October 1955, November 1957.

[35] Preliminary Proposals for Work to be Undertaken within the 'Conditional Aid' Programme, BIM, 12 March 1953, TUC 564.8.

[36] Martin to Gausmann, 9 September 1950, ECA LI 130; Cruikshank to Tyler Wood, 13 June 1951, Dubinsky 260 (3A); Productivity Section OSR to Mission Productivity Officers, undated 1950, ECA Lab. Div. 131.

[37] Porter was a former prominent member of the Socialist Party and editor of Kenosha Labour.

[38] Cruikshank to Dubinsky, 28 September 1951; Porter to McGowan, September 1951, Dubinsky 260 (3A); Shishkin to Wood, 4 November 1950, ECA-OSR Cent. Sec. 15.

[39] Oliver, 'The Production Assistance Programme in France,' 18 March 1952, CIO International 80 (11).

[40] 'Organised Labour and Productivity.'

[41] Harriş to Golden, 9 January 1953, Golden 5 (6).

[42] Harris to Weinberg, 17 February 1953, CIO Washington Office 6 (19).

[43] Jockel to Reuther, 10 September 1953, CIO Washington Office 73 (20).

[44] Golden to Foster, op. cit.

[45] 'A Recommended Programme for France,' undated ECA-OSR Cent. Sec. 15.

[46] Gomberg to Irving Brown, 3 November 1952; Brown to Gomberg, 24 January 1953, Gomberg 2 and 5.

[47] Memorandum for OSR Conference on Pilot Projects (undated 1951), Gomberg 3.

[48] Scherbak to Gomberg, 22 January 1952, Gomberg 5.

[49] 'Organised Labour and Productivity.'

[50] Levinson to Reuther, 8 November 1952, CIO Washington Office 64 (18).

[51] 'Organised Labour and Productivity.'

[52] Gomberg, Report on Third Mission to Europe, op. cit. Gomberg 2.

[53] Memorandum for OSR Conference, op. cit.; Scherbak to Gomberg, op. cit.

[54] Gomberg to Irving Brown, op. cit.

[55] Douty to Timmons, 10 September 1952, Gomberg 3. Interestingly Golden's principal disciple in France was an old friend of his, Hyacinthe Dubreuil, whose support for productivity values and especially the Scanlon Plan endeared him to the Gaullists while causing FO to regard him as a pariah. Martin to Hedges, 20 July 1950, Martin to Golden, 20 September 1950, Golden 5 (17).

[56] Levinson to Reuther, 6 November 1952, CIO International 64 (18).

[57] Le Figaro, 23 September 1952; Gomberg to Brown, op. cit.

[58] OSR to Washington, 27 December 1952 and 1 January 1953, Gomberg 2 and 5.

[59] Ibid.; Douty to Labouisse, 18 December 1952, Gomberg 4.

[60] Gomberg reply to CIERP memo, December 1952, Gomberg 2.

[61] OSR to Washington, 1 January 1953, op.cit.

[62] D'Attorre, pp. 17–18.

[63] 'Organised Labour and Productivity'; Gomberg Report on Third Trip to Europe, op. cit.

[64] Croce to Taylor, 24 October 1955, Gomberg 1; Time Magazine, 19 April 1954;

Shapiro to Cabot, undated, CIO International 67 (7); Adriano Oivetti, 'How US aid boomeranged in Italy', *World*, November 1953, p. 62.

[65] 'Higher Productivity through European Co-operation', EPA, 1956; UIL Paper for ICFTU Productivity Conference, 1953. TUC 557.291.

[66] Peter Lange *et al.*, *Unions, Change and Crisis: French and Italian Union Strategy and Political Economy, 1945–80*, Allen & Unwin, 1982, p. 115.

[67] Report on 5th National Congress of ACLI, 1955, CIO Washington Office 67 (7).

[68] Joseph La Palombara, *The Italian Labour Movement*, Cornell University Press, 1957, p. 148; 'Trade union education as an anti-communist weapon in Italy,' *Southwestern Social Science Quarterly*, Vol. 37, June 1956.

[69] D'Attorre, p. 21.

[70] La Palombara, pp. 148–9.

[71] *Ibid.*, pp. 87, 136, 163, 168.

[72] *Attitude of the Trade Unions towards the Present Productivity Campaign in Europe*, 3rd Session of the European Regional Council, ICFTU-ERO, 9–10 June 1953, TUC 557.291.

[73] Fletcher to Geddes, 4 June 1953, TUC 557.291.

[74] Crawford, Report on ILO Conference on Productivity, February 1953, TUC Production Committee 557.1 II; Gomberg to Michel Verhulst, July 1951, Gomberg 1.

[75] ICFTU-ERO Productivity Conference Report, October 1953, TUC 557.291.

[76] ERP-TUAC Circular, 9 March 1955, TUC 546-8.

[77] Levinson to Reuther, 6 November 1952.

[78] Jockel to Reuther, 10 September 1953, CIO Washington Office 73 (20).

[79] Levinson to Reuther, 22 November 1952, CIO Washington Office 64 (18).

[80] *Le Figaro*, 23 September 1952.

[81] In its early days the ICFTU was very much an appendage of the Marshall Plan. ECA Labour staff had observer status at a top-level ICFTU emergency committee when American aid for rearmament and anti-communist activities were being discussed; the Confederation accepted material help from the US embassy in Paris in printing literature for distribution in the Middle East – the cost being borne by embassy funds – and at an early meeting of the ICFTU Executive Board the presence of ECA officials was so marked that OSR Labour chiefs were warned that they risked embarrassing their European union friends. Stauffer contribution to ECA Labour Staff Conference, *op. cit.*; Labour Adviser Reports OSR, 13 February 1950, ECA Lab. Div. 144; Gausmann observed graphically that such people 'don't like to have their fig leaves torn off them in the public streets'.

[82] The Ferguson tractor company of Coventry was thought of as a possible benefactor, since it had an obvious interest in the underdeveloped world and was seen as typical of those firms which valued free trade unions as the strongest defence against communism. W. Kemsley, Suggestions for the Paper on the International Free T.U. Education Foundation Inc., 31 August 1953, CIO Washington Office 74 (1).

[83] Brown to Dubinsky, 29 October 1951, Dubinsky 260 (6A).

[84] Assistant Director of Supply (MSA) to Golden, 24 March 1952; Casserini to Reuther, 5 May 1952; Guaranty Trust Co. to Golden, 27 May 1952; Oldenbroek to Reuther, 12 June 1952, Golden 5 (21).

[85] Victor Reuther, *The Brothers Reuther*, Houghton Mifflin, 1976, pp. 424–5.

[86] William Kemsley to author, 9 August 1986.

[87] Status of USRO Labour Projects, 15 March 1954; Ross to Reuther, 31 May 1954, CIO Washington Office 52 (2).

[88] Woll to Thorne 7 April 1952; Thorne to Woll 9 April 1952, Thorne 8; AFL International Labour Relations Committee, 15 April 1952, Thorne 17.

[89] ICFTU Executive Board Sub-committee on Education, 24–29 May 1954, CIO Washington Office 69 (25).

[90] Levinson to Reuther, 6 November 1952.

[91] 'Section 115k Briefing Paper', 4 October 1954, FOA Lab. Div.

Chapter 11

[1] Holme to Joint AACP Secretaries, 23 October 1951, TUC 552.3.

[2] The Advisory Board's best known trade union figure was Jack Tanner, President of the Amalgamated Engineering Union.

[3] Memorandum, 'European Productivity Agency', NPACI Minutes, 18 May 1953, TUC 557.126.

[4] Harten speech, ICFTU Productivity Conference, October 1953, TUC 557.291.

[5] *The European Productivity Agency*, OEEC, Paris, 1958.

[6] EPA Advisory Board Minutes, 14 April 1959.

[7] *European Productivity Agency, op. cit.*

[8] NPACI Minutes, 20 November 1953, TUC 557.1 II; 20 February 1954, TUC 557.126.

[9] Clement Watson, Report on EPA, 25 February 1954, FOA 32.

[10] ICFTU-ERO Productivity Conference, October 1953, TUC 557.291.

[11] The MSA/FOA had in fact covered a substantial part of the cost of the ICFTU conference.

[12] V. Reuther, 'Proposed Transfer of MSA Productivity Programme to OEEC', undated 1953, Gausmann 4 (12); Mintzes to Meskimen, 'EPA and ICA Labour Programme Activities in Europe,' 29 July 1955, FOA 32.

[13] European Productivity Agency, Minstry of Labour Files, Lab. 13/713.

[14] Stewart to Hancox, 26 April 1954, Lab. 13/713.

[15] *European Productivity Agency, op. cit.*

[16] Fletcher to Tewson, 21 December 1951, TUC 557.378.

[17] Fletcher to Morgan, 8 April 1954; Stewart to Hancox, *op. cit.*, Lab 13/713.

[18] Mintzes to Meskimen, 29 July 1955; ISPR to FOA, 8 April 1955, FOA 32; OEEC PRA Committee Minutes, 4–5 April 1955, Lab 13/713; Charles Ford, *The Role of the Trade Unions in the Social Development of Europe*, ICFTU, 1966, p. 24.

[19] Ford, *op. cit.*, p. 21.

[20] Taylor to Meskimen, 10 January 1956, FOA 32.

[21] Gausmann to Reuther, 26 August 1955, CIO International 66 (19), Meskimen to Taylor, 28 September 1956, FOA 32.

[22] Haskel to Mintzes, 9 November 1955, FOA 32.

[23] Reuther, Report to Joint Meeting of International Affairs Committee and Latin American Affairs Sub-committee, 6 October 1954, CIO Washington Office 56 (12); Meany to W. Reuther, 12 July 1956; Peer to Reuther, 1 June 1956, UAW International, Reuther-Carliner 1956–62, 52 (16).

[24] TUC Production Committee Minutes, 24 February 1955, TUC 557.1 vi; *The European Productivity Agency*.

[25] R. Cottave, address to TUC Conference on Britain and European Productivity, 13 January 1959, TUC HD 21.

[26] EPA Circular, 7 November 1957; R. Cottave, address; *Report of Activities of EPA for Financial Year 1959–60; Programme of Action of EPA and Part 1 Budget for 1959–60.* TUC HD 21.

[27] Brooks, *op. cit.*, p. 323.

[28] Programme of Action.

[29] Joe Mintzes, 'FOA Position in Regard to European Productivity Agency', 5 May 1954, FOA 32.

[30] Labour Productivity Projects, December 1953, CIO Washington Office 74 (1).

[31] Brooks, pp. 204, 330.

[32] Report, 7 January 1959, Columbia University Trade Union Technicians Course, TUC 810.736.

[33] 'America revisited', *New Dawn*, 14 November 1959, p. 719.

[34] Chairman's address, G&MWU Conference Report, 1959, p. 36.

[35] The Trade Union Programme of EPA, 1957, TUC HD 21 (emphasis added).

[36] BPC Council Minutes, 6 March 1956, TUC 552.41 I.

[37] *The European Productivity Agency.*

[38] President of the Board of Trade, Report to NPACI, 26 April 1953, TUC 557.126.

[39] BPC Council Minutes, March 1956; Argyris address to Joint DSIR/MRC Committee, 23 March 1955, TUC 571.772.

[40] The Human Sciences and their application in Industry: Programme of Action, EPA, 29 September 1957, TUC HD 21.

[41] Education for Management, 26 May 1954, FOA 32.

[42] Conway to Meskimen, 28 October 1955, FOA files 32.

[43] Haskel to van Dyke, 18 November 1955, FOA files 32.

[44] Ford to Gaither, 22 November 1948, Mark Starr Collection, 4 (5), Tamiment Institute, New York.

[45] Memoranda of conversation, Acheson, Hoffman and Ford, 13 April 1951 and 16 July 1951, Acheson Collection, 66–67.

[46] Starr to Wood, 18 February 1949, Wood to Starr, 24 February 1949, Starr 4 (5).

[47] Hoffman Statement to Board of Adult Education Fund, 1951, Golden 4 (29).

[48] Golden Papers, 2 (4).

[49] Richard Bissell interview, September–October 1952, Harry Price Papers, Truman Library.

[50] John Goldthorpe, 'Theories of industrial society: reflections on the recrudescence of historicism and the future of futurology', *Archives Européennes de Sociologie*, vol. 12, part 2, 1971, p. 266.

[51] J. T. Dunlop *et al.*, *Industrialism and Industrial Man Reconsidered*, Interuniversity Study of Human Resources in National Development, 1975.

[52] Sir George Schuster, 'Human Relations in Industry', Paper to BMA, Cambridge, 1 July 1948, TUC 571–1.

[53] Schuster to Tizzard, 10 January 1950, TUC 571.71.

[54] Boyfield to Winterbottom, 8 October 1953, NJAC Human Relations Subcommittee, TUC 571.771.

[55] Schuster to Tizzard, *op. cit.*

[56] TUC Production Committee Minutes, 23 July 1953, TUC 557.1 I; Human Relations – DSIR/MRC Joint Committee, TUC 571.772.

[57] 'EPA Project for the Setting up of a European Trade Union College', ERO, 7 November 1959, UAW International, Reuther-Carliner, 98 (34).

[58] *Opinion of the Council of European Industrial Federations on the Future of the EPA*, 13 April 1959, TUC HD 21.

[59] Minutes of EPA Advisory Board, 14 April 1959, TUC HD 21.

Chapter 12

[1] Ian Mikardo, 'Trade unions in a full employment economy', in R. H. S. Crossman (ed.), *New Fabian Essays*, Turnstile Press, 1953, p. 157.

[2] *T & GWU Record*, September 1950.

[3] H. D. Roberts, 'Training of shop stewards', *Socialist Commentary*, November

1952, pp. 262–4. The practice of training by management consultants was opposed by William Gomberg, the US productivity consultant. He felt there was a risk that training would be given without any critical examination of fundamental assumptions, the result being that the union did not get a trained time study technician, but management did secure a hostage in the union ranks. Gomberg to Professor Thomas Mathews (Birmingham University), 6 June 1949, Gomberg 2.

4 G&MWU Conference Report, 1954, p. 33; 1955, pp. 336–7.
5 Williamson to Tewson, 18 November 1954, TUC 564.8.
6 Bowers to Tewson, 3 December 1954, TUC 564.8.
7 'Wages and efficiency – our responsibility,' *T&GWU Record*, June 1953; 'Living standards depend upon production', September 1954.
8 G&MWU Conference Report, 1953, p. 34.
9 USDAW, Annual Delegate Meeting, 1958, p. 50.
10 *Operative Builder*, September–October, 1956, p. 290.
11 USDAW Annual Delegate Meeting, 5 April 1953, p. 56.
12 G&MWU Conference Report, 1953, pp. 35–6.
13 G&MWU Conference Report, 1954, p. 255.
14 *T&GWU Record*, August 1950.
15 T&GWU, GEC Minutes, 28 February 1949.
16 *T&GWU Record*, January 1954.
17 *Ibid.*, July 1953; ASW Conference Report 1954.
18 Crawford speech, ICFTU Productivity Conference, October 1953, TUC 557.291.
19 J. E. Mortimer, *Trade Unions and Technological Change*, Oxford University Press, 1971, p. 47.
20 *Man and Metal*, November 1952.
21 'The only way to raise real wages,' *Sunday Times*, 26 August 1951.
22 G&MWU Conference Report, 1950, pp. 25–6.
23 *Ibid.*, 1959, p. 36.
24 TUC Production Committee Minutes, 19 May 1955, TUC 557.1 VI.
25 *EPA Information Bulletin*, Nos. 6–7, December 1954–January 1955; No. 10, May 1955.
26 TUC Production Committee Minutes, 19 May 1955.
27 Fletcher to BPC, 11 March 1957; BPC to Fletcher, 3 April 1957, TUC 552.4 III.
28 TUC Production Committee Minutes, 14 October 1954; 19 May 1955, TUC 557.1 VI.
29 Fletcher, 'Trade Unions and Industrial Productivity', paper read to first European International Summer School, ICFTU, 21–28 April 1951, Gomberg 3; Fletcher draft for Tewson's speech to ICFTU Productivity Conference, October 1953, TUC 557.291.
30 Les Cannon, 'The productivity drive,' *Marxist Quarterly*, April 1955, Vol. 2, No. 2, pp. 91–2, 95.
31 Sidney Sober, 'US Government Organisation for the Conduct of International Labour Affairs,' paper to Economics Department, Northwestern University, June 1953, Kaiser Collection, 1, Truman Library. The programme brought student workers over to the US for a year, placed them in unionised jobs and gave them training in industrial management techniques. The plan was to bring 2,000 workers over from Europe, and 500 came in the first year.
32 J. R. Campbell, 'Rearmament's bitter fruits,' *Labour Monthly*, September 1951, p. 426.
33 *New Dawn*, 29 December 1956, p. 805.
34 J. R. Horth, 'Work study alone not enough,' *Scientific Worker*, May 1954, p. 12.

[35] USDAW, Annual Delegate Meeting, 1956, p. 69.
[36] G&MWU Conference Report, 1953, p. 269.
[37] *Ibid*. Lucas were also one of the first firms to sponsor academic work in production engineering at Birmingham University.
[38] USDAW, Annual Delegate Meeting, 1959, p. 44.
[39] Cannon, 'The productivity drive,' p. 94.
[40] Graham Hutton, 'Productivity and the £,' *BPC Bulletin* (Supplement), October 1955, p. 8.
[41] C. A. R. Crosland, *The Future of Socialism*, Schocken, 1963, pp. 286–7.
[42] Report by UILM on the Situation of the Democratic Trade Union Movement in Italy, 26 January 1954, CIO Washington Office 67 (4). Levinson to Reuther, 8 September 1953, CIO Washington Office 74 (12); D'Attorre, *op. cit.*, pp. 34–5.
[43] D'Attorre, pp. 29–30.
[44] Hilary Partridge, 'Italy's Fiat in Turin in the 1950s,' in T. Nichols (ed.), *Capital and Labour*, Fontana, 1980, pp. 416–17.
[45] D'Attorre, pp. 34–5.
[46] *Ibid.*, pp. 32, 34.
[47] Joseph La Palombara, *The Italian Labour Movement*, Cornell University Press, 1957, p. 162.
[48] Viglianesi to Walter Reuther, 17 September 1953, CIO Washington Office 67 (7).
[49] D'Attore, p. 25.
[50] Peter Lange *et al.*, *Unions, Change and Crisis: French and Italian Union Strategy and Political Economy, 1945–80*, Allen & Unwin, 1982, p. 115.
[51] Murray Edelman and R. W. Fleming, *The Politics of Wage–Price Decisions: a Four Country Analysis*, University of Illinois Press, 1965, pp. 50–1; Daniel L. Horowitz, *The Italian Labour Movement*, Harvard University Press, 1963, p. 295.
[52] D'Attorre, p. 25.
[53] Benedict Report on European Trip, July 1955, *op. cit.*
[54] Croce to Taylor, 24 October 1955, Gomberg I.
[55] *Wall Street Journal*, 4 February 1963.
[56] *Ibid.*; Mintzes to Meskimen, 'Proposed EPA Project for Middle Trade Union Leadership,' 26 October 1955, FOA 32.
[57] D'Attorre, p. 16.
[58] *Ibid.*, p. 27. In 1956, in the absence of university courses in business administration or personnel management, the IRI instiued its own training programme for industrial relations specialists.
[59] *Ibid.*, p. 38.
[60] Richard F. Kuisel, *Capitalism and the State in Modern France*, Cambridge University Press, 1981, pp. 227–44.
[61] *Ibid.*, p. 271.
[62] Victor Reuther, 'Between Moscow and Main Street,' *Look Magazine*, March 1952.
[63] 'Works agreements of the Renault type,' *International Labour Review*, Vol. LXXXI, No. 3, March 1960, pp. 205–32.
[64] Kuisel , pp. 263, 273.
[65] A. S. Milward, *The Reconstruction of Western Europe, 1945–51*, Methuen, 1984, p. 101.
[66] Volker Berghahn, *The Americanisation of West German Industry, 1945–1973*, Berg, 1986, p. 79.
[67] H. C. Hillmann, 'American aid and the recovery of Germany,' *American Review*, Vol. II, No. 4, March 1963, pp. 125, 128.

68 K. Van der Pijl, *The Making of an Atlantic Ruling Class*, Verso, 1986, provides a good example of this approach.

69 Werner Link, *The Contribution of Trade Unions and Businessmen to German-American Relations, 1945–75*, Bloomington, Institute of German Studies, 1978, pp. 124, 141.

70 Mayer, *op. cit.*, p. 95.

71 Cited in Berghahn, p. 176.

72 *Ibid.*, pp. 174–81.

73 *Ibid.*, pp. 204–5.

74 *Ibid.*, pp. 229–30.

75 Link, pp. 83–4.

76 *Ibid.*, p. 35.

77 Berghahn, p. 249.

78 *Ibid.*, pp. 242, 245.

79 *Ibid.*, p. 251; Heinz Hartmann, *Authority and Organisation in German Management*, Greenwood Press, 1970, pp. 89–91.

80 Berghahn, p. 257.

81 *BPC Bulletin*, 31 January 1957; 25 October 1957.

82 *Ibid.*

83 Arthur Ross, 'Prosperity and labour relations in Europe: the case of West Germany', *Quarterly Journal of Economics*, August 1962, Vol. LXXVI, No. 3, p. 332.

Chapter 13

1 E. Drexel Godfrey, *The Fate of the French Non-communist Left*, Doubleday, 1955, p. 39.

2 Healey, Report on 2nd Annual Conference of PSLI, 23–26 January 1949, Labour Party International Files.

3 Edmund Stevens, 'Behind the Italian crisis,' *New Leader*, 18 January 1954, p. 9; Lorwin, *The French Labour Movement*, p. 241. Lorwin actually gives a higher figure for Soviet aid to France. For what it is worth, the CIA estimate of Soviet spending on front organisations was $250 million per annum. *New York Times*, 8 May 1967.

4 Germer, Diary, 15 November 1946, Germer 15.

5 Daniel Horowitz, *The Italian Labour Movement*, Harvard University Press, 1963, pp. 229–30, 227, 239.

6 *New Statesman*, August–September 1946.

7 Mark Jenkins, *Bevanism*, Spokesman, 1979, p. 44.

8 *Tribune*, 3 January 1947; 10 October 1947.

9 *Socialist Leader*, 15 March 1947.

10 Draft Document by the International Committee for Study and Action for the USSE Conference, 21–22 June 1947, Labour Party International Files.

11 Alan Bullock, *Ernest Bevin: Foreign Secretary*, Heinemann, 1983, pp. 357–8.

12 *Ibid.*, p. 164.

13 Bruce Reed and Geoffrey Williams, *Denis Healey and the Policies of Power*, Sidgewick & Jackson, 1971, pp. 60–1.

14 Views of Haakon Lie, Secretary of Norwegian Labour Party, US Embassy, Oslo, to State, 29 January 1948, State 840.50 Recov.

15 M. Merker, 'The Marshall Plan and western Europe,' *Socialist Commentary*, March 1948, pp. 138–9.

16 *Socialist Leader*, 15 July 1947; 6 December 1947.

17 Bullock, pp. 541, 591, 640–1.

[18] *Socialist Leader*, 29 May 1948.

[19] Kenneth O. Morgan, *Labour in Power, 1945–51*, Oxford University Press, 1984, p. 274.

[20] F. K. Roberts, minute, 5 March 1948, FO 800/460; Working Party on Spiritual Aspects of the Western Union, FO 953/144. The 'spiritual aspects' that were highlighted for propagandistic purposes and where 'Western values' were said to differ from Russian ones were areas such as women's equality, trade union philosophy, the role of the arts, the role of law and the constitution, and religious freedom. On the latter point the Foreign Office used influence to encourage the Archbishop of Canterbury and the Cardinal of Westminster to stage a World Congress of Churches in 1948 as an anti-communist rallying point.

[21] *Feet on the Ground*, Labour Party, October 1948.

[22] Roberts, minute, *op. cit.*

[23] Selsdon Park Conference, 21–22 March 1948, Verbatim Proceedings, Labour Party International Files.

[24] Record of Conversation, Bevin and Douglas, 26 February 1948, FO 800/460.

[25] *Socialist Leader*, 20 March 1948.

[26] *European Co-operation within the Framework of the Recovery Programme: Memorandum submitted by the British Labour Party to the Socialist Conference on the European Recovery Programme*, 21–22 March 1948; senior civil servants Otto Clarke of the Treasury and Roger Makins of the Foreign Office went with Healey over his draft paper, after which he duly amended it. As Clarke wrote, 'Our two hours with Mr. Healey [...] was well spent.' Clarke to Makins, FO 371-72855.

[27] *The Point of View of the French Delegation at the Conference of the Socialist Parties from the Countries having accepted the Principle of American Aid*, London, 21–22 March 1948, Labour Party International Files.

[28] Verbatim Proceedings, Selsdon Park Conference, *op. cit.*

[29] *Socialist Leader*, 3 July 1948.

[30] Krane to Cope, 23 May 1949, Krane Papers 1 (6), reporting a conversation with Robert Pontillon of SFIO's International Department.

[31] Bullock, p. 766.

[32] Haakon Lie, 'Democratic socialism for our time,' *Socialist Commentary*, July 1951, pp. 160–3.

[33] Denis Healey, 'European socialism today,' *New Leader*, 16 September 1957, p. 15.

[34] Developments in European Labour, week ending 27 August 1952, OSR, Gomberg 2.

[35] Benedict, Report of European Trip, *op. cit.*

[36] Saposs, 'Recent Elections: Italy and Germany,' undated, ECA Lab. Div., Box 150; V. Reuther to W. Reuther and Potofsky, 'Recent Critical Developments in Germany and Possible CIO Action,' undated 1953, CIO International 64 (19); Link, *op. cit.*, p. 59.

[37] William D. Graf, *The German Left since 1945*, Oleander Press, 1976, p. 127.

[38] Programme for UIL (undated), UAW International, Reuther-Carliner 1956–62, 96 (5).

[39] Elizabeth Durbin, *New Jerusalems*, Routledge, 1985, pp. 263–76.

[40] Raymond Aron, *The Industrial Society*, Weidenfeld & Nicolson, 1967, pp. 14, 60, 99.

[41] A. A. Rogow, *The Labour Government and British Industry, 1945–51*, Greenwood, 1974, p. 103.

[42] R. A. Brady, *Crisis in Britain*, Cambridge University Press, 1950, p. 563.

[43] David Howell, *British Social Democracy*, Croom Helm, 1976, p. 159.

[44] Morgan, pp. 357–8.

[45] Michael Foot, *Aneurin Bevin*, Vol. II, Paladin, 1975, p. 256.

[46] Ralph Miliband, *Parliamentary Socialism*, Merlin, 1973, p. 306.

[47] C. A. R. Crosland, 'The transition from capitalism,' and Austen Albu, 'The organisation of industry,' in R. H. S. Crossman (ed.), *New Fabian Essays*, Turnstile Press, 1953, pp. 33–5, 38–9, 131, 135, 142.

[48] *Times*, 28 October 1946.

[49] Andrew Filson, *Socialist Commentary*, June 1952, p. 141.

[50] On the internal affairs of the Socialist Union see Socialist Vanguard Group Papers, Modern Record Centre, Warwick University. Gausmann was a founding member of the Socialist Union and in the mid-1950s chaired its working party on Labour Party democracy.

[51] Socialist Union, *Twentieth Century Socialism*, Penguin, 1956, pp. 7, 16, 58; *Socialism: a New Statement of Principles*, Lincolns-Prager, 1952, p. 51.

[52] David Coates, *The Labour Party and the Struggle for Socialism*, Cambridge University Press, 1975, p. 90.

[53] C. A. R. Crosland, *The Future of Socialism*, Schocken, 1963, p. 157.

[54] *Ibid.*, p. 263.

[55] A. Mant, *The Rise and Fall of the British Manager*, Pan, 1977, p. 76.

[56] A. A. Rogow, pp. 178–9.

[57] R. H. S. Crossman, 'Towards a philosophy of socialism,' in Crossman, *op. cit.*, p. 29.

[58] Daniel Bell, *The End of Ideology*, Free Press, 1965, pp. 15, 251, 262.

[59] *Ibid.*, p. 295.

[60] Clark Kerr, 'Productivity and labour relations,' in *Labour and Management in Industrial Society*, Doubleday, 1964, pp. 279–80.

[61] Clark Kerr et al., *Industrialism and Industrial Man*, Heinemann, 1962, p. 283.

[62] Crosland, *The Future of Socialism*, pp. 180, 253.

[63] *Ibid.*, pp. 263–4.

[64] Eric Wigham, *What's wrong with the Unions*, Penguin, 1961, p. 14.

[65] Michael Shanks, *The Stagnant Society*, Penguin, 1961, pp. 45 and 64.

[66] PEP, *Trade Unions in a Changing Society*, Vol. XXIX, No. 472, 10 June 1963, p. 207.

[67] *Ibid.*, p. 218.

[68] Shanks, pp. 161–2.

Collections cited are located as follows: British Foreign Office and Ministry of Labour papers at the Public Record Office, Kew; US State Department papers in Record Group 59 at the National Archives, Washington DC; ECA and FOA papers in Record Group 286 at the Federal Record Centre, Suitland, Maryland; AFL, Thorne and Germer papers at the State Historical Society of Wisconsin, Madison; CIO, UAW, Krane and Gausmann papers at the Walter Reuther Library, Detroit; Dubinsky, Antonini and Zimmerman papers at the International Ladies Garment Workers Union Archives, New York; Acheson, Finletter and Kaiser papers at the Truman Library, Independence; Starr and Cope papers at the Tamiment Institute, New York; Golden papers at Pennsylvania State University, State College; Gomberg papers at the London School of Economics; TUC papers at the Trades Union Congress, London; Labour Party papers at the Labour Party, London; Meany papers at the AFL-CIO Archives, Washington DC; Socialist Vanguard Group papers at the Modern Record Centre, Warwick University, Coventry; Silvey papers in the personal possession of Mr Ted Silvey.

BIBLIOGRAPHY

Unless otherwise indicated the place of publication is London

Books

Abruzzi, Adam, *Work, Workers and Work Measurement*, New York, Columbia University Press, 1956.

Agee, Philip, and Wolf, Louis, *Dirty Work: the CIA in Western Europe*, Zed Press, 1978.

Allen, V. L., *Trade Union Leadership*, Longmans, 1957.

Anderson, Terry H., *The United States, Great Britain and the Cold War, 1944–1947*, Columbia, University of Missouri Press, 1981.

Arkes, Hadley, *Bureaucracy, the Marshall Plan and the National Interest*, Princeton University Press, 1972.

Armstrong P., Glyn, A., Harrison, J., *Capitalism since World War II*, Fontana, 1984.

Aron, Raymond, *The Industrial Society*, Weidenfeld & Nicolson, 1967.

Bailey, Thomas A., *The Marshall Plan Summer*, Stanford University Press, 1977.

Ball, M. Margaret, *NATO and the European Union Movement*, Stephens, 1959.

Barker, Elisabeth, *The British between the Superpowers, 1945–50*, University of Toronto Press, 1984.

Barnet, R. J., *The Roots of War*, New York, Atheneum, 1972.

—, *Allies: America, Europe and Japan since the War*, Cape, 1984.

Bell, Daniel, *The End of Ideology*, New York, Free Press, 1965.

Berghahn, Volker R., *The Americanisation of West German Industry, 1945–73*, New York, Berg, 1986.

Berner, Wolfgang, 'The Italian left, 1944–1978; patterns of co-operation, conflict and compromise', in William E. Griffith (ed.), *The European Left: Italy, France and Spain*, Lexington, Lexington Books, 1979.

Blackwell, T., and Seabrook J., *A World still to Win*, Faber, 1985.

Brock, Clifton, *Americans for Democratic Action: its Role in National Politics*, Washington, DC, Public Affairs Press, 1962.

Brown, Geoff, *Sabotage*, Nottingham, Spokesman, 1977.

Bullock, Alan, *Ernest Bevin: Foreign Secretary*, Heinemann, 1983.

Busch, Gary, K., *The Political Role of International Trade Unions*, Macmillan, 1983.

Caute, David, *The Fellow Travellers*, Weidenfeld & Nicolson, 1973.

Carew, Anthony, *Democracy and Government in European Trade Unions*, Allen & Unwin, 1976.

Citrine, Lord, *Two Careers*, Hutchinson, 1967.

Clarke, Sir Richard, *Anglo-American Collaboration in War and Peace 1942–49*, ed. Sir Alec Cairncross, Clarendon, 1982.

Coates, David, *The Labour Party and the Struggle for Socialism*, Cambridge University Press, 1975.

Cochran, Bert, *Labour and Communism*, Princeton, Princeton University Press, 1977.

Copeland, Miles, *The Real Spy World*, Weidenfeld & Nicolson, 1974.

Crosland, C.A.R., *The Future of Socialism*, New York, Schocken, 1963.

Crosland, Susan, *Tony Crosland*, Cape, 1982.

Crossman, R.H.S. (ed.), *New Fabian Essays*, Turnstile Press, 1953.

D'Attorre, Pier Paolo, *ERP Aid and the Politics of Productivity in Italy during the 1950s*, Florence, European University Institue Working Paper 85/159, 1985.

Davies, Andrew, *Where did the Forties go?*, Pluto, 1984.

Dubsinky, David and Raskin, A.H., *David Dubinsky: a Life With Labour*, New York, Simon & Schuster, 1977.

Dunlop, J.T., *et al.*, *Industrialism and Industrial Man Reconsidered*, Princeton, Inter-university Study of Human Resources in National Development, 1975.

Earle, Edward Mead, *Modern France*, New York, Russell, 1964.

Edelman, Murray, and Fleming, R.W., *The Politics of Wage–Price Decisions: a Four Country Analysis*, Urbana, University of Illinois Press, 1965.

Elliott, William Y., *The Political Economy of American Foreign Policy: its Concepts, Strategy and Limits*, New York, Holt, 1955.

Epstein, Leon D., *Britain: Uneasy Ally*, University of Chicago Press, 1954.

Faenza, R., and Fini, M., *Gli Americani in Italia*, Milan, Feltrinelli, 1976.

Fichter, Michael, *Besatzungsmacht und Gewerkschaften*, Berlin, Westdeutscher Verlag, 1982.

Fitzsimons, M.A., *The Foreign Policy of the British Labour Government, 1945–51*, Notre Dame, University of Notre Dame Press, 1953.

Fleming, R.D., *The Cold War and its Origins*, Vol. I, Allen & Unwin, 1961.

Fletcher, Richard, 'How CIA money took the teeth out of British socialism', in Philip Agee and Louis Wolf (eds.), *Dirty Work: the CIA in Western Europe*, Zed Press, 1981.

Foot, Michael, *Aneurin Bevan, 1945–60*, Paladin, 1975.

Foote, Geoffrey, *The Labour Party's Political Thought: a history*, Croom Helm, 1985.

Fraser, Steve, 'Dress rehearsal for the New Deal: shop-floor insurgents, political elites, and industrial democracy in the Amalgamated Clothing Workers', in Michael A. Frisch and Dabiel J. Walkowitz (eds.), *Working Class America: Essays on Labour, Community and American Society*, Urbana, University of Illinois Press, 1983.

Gannon, Francis X., *Joseph D. Keenan: Labour's Ambassador in War and Peace*, New York, University Press of America, 1984.

Gautiere, Lewis, *et al.*, *America and the Mind of Europe*, Hamish Hamilton, 1951.

Gimbel, John, *The Origins of the Marshall Plan*, Stanford University Press, 1976

Glyn, A., and Harrison, J., *The British Economic Disaster*, Pluto, 1980.

Godfrey, E. Drexel, *The Fate of the French Non-communist Left*, Garden City, Doubleday, 1955.

Godson, Roy, *American Labour and European Politics*, New York, Crane Russack, 1976.

Golden, Clinton and Parker, Virginia, *Causes of Industrial Peace under Collective Bargaining*, New York, Harper Bros., 1955.

Golden, Clinton and Ruttenberg, Harold, *The Dynamics of Industrial Democracy*, New York, 1942.

Gomberg, William, *A Trade Union Analysis of Time Study*, New York, Prentice Hall, 1955.

Goulden, Joseph C., *Meany*, New York, Atheneum, 1972.

Gourevitch, Peter, *et al.*, *Unions and Economic Crisis: Britain, West Germany and Sweden*, Allen & Unwin, 1984.

Graf, William, D., *The German Left since 1945*, Cambridge, Oleander Press, 1976.

Grant, Alan, *Against the Clock*, Pluto, 1983.

Griffith, Robert, and Theoharis, Athan, *The Spectre: Original Essays on the Cold War and the Origins of McCarthyism*, New York, Franklin Watts, 1974.

Grindrod, Muriel, *The Rebuilding of Italy*, RIAA, 1955.

Grove, J. W., *Government and Industry in Britain*, Longmans, 1962.

Hamilton, Richard F., *Affluence and the French Worker in the Fourth Republic*, Princeton University Press, 1967.

Harris, Howell John, *The Right to Manage*, Madison, University of Wisconsin Press, 1982.

Harrison, Martin, *Trade Unions and the Labour Party since 1945*, Allen & Unwin, 1960.

Haseler, Stephen, *The Gaitskellites*, Macmillan, 1969.

Hero, Alfred O., and Starr, Emil, *The Reuther–Meany Foreign Policy Dispute*, Dobbs Fery, Oceana, 1970.

Hildebrand, George H., *Growth and Structure in the Economy of Modern Italy*, Cambridge, Mass., Harvard University Press, 1965.

Hoffman, Paul, *Peace can be Won*, Michael Joseph, 1951.

Horowitz, Daniel L., *The Italian Labour Movement*, Cambridge, Mass., Harvard University Press, 1963.

Horowitz, David (ed.), *Corporations and the Cold War*, New York, Monthly Review Press, 1969.

Howell, David, *British Social Democracy*, Croom Helm, 1976.

Hutton, Graham, *We too can Prosper*, Allen & Unwin, 1953.

Hutton, Graham, (ed.), *Source Book on Restrictive Practices in Britain*, Institute of Economic Affairs, 1966.

Jenkins, Mark, *Bevanism: Labour's High Tide*, Nottingham, Spokesman, 1981.

Keeran, Roger, *The Communist Party and the Auto Workers' Union*, Bloomington, Indiana University Press, 1980.

Kendall, Walter, *The Labour Movement in Europe*, Allen Lane, 1975.

Kerr, Clark, 'Productivity and labour relations', in *Labour and Management in Industrial Society*, New York, Doubleday, 1964.

—, *Labour and Management in Industrial Society*, New York, Anchor, 1964.

Kerr, Clark, *et al.*, *Industrialism and Industrial Man*, Heinemann, 1962.

Kolko, Joyce and Gabriel, *The Limits of Power*, New York, Harper & Row, 1972.

Kuisel, Richard F., *Capitalism and the State in Modern France*, Cambridge University Press, 1981.

Lange, Peter, *et al.*, *Unions, Change and Crisis: French and Italian Union Strategy and the Post-war Political Economy, 1945–80*, Allen & Unwin, 1982.

La Palombara, Joseph, *The Italian Labour Movement*, Ithaca, Cornell University Press, 1957.

Lee, Jennie, *My Life with Nye*, Cape, 1980.

Lens, Sidney, 'Labour lieutenants and the Cold War', in Burton Hall (ed.), *Autocracy and Insurgency in Organised Labour*, New Brunswick, Transaction Books, 1972.

Lesieur, Frederick G., (ed.), *The Scanlon Plan. a Frontier in Labour–Management Co-operation*, Cambridge, Mass., MIT Press, 1958.

Levenstein, Harvey A., *Communism, Anticommunism and the CIO*, Westport, Greenwood Press, 1981.

Lichtenstein, Nelson, *Labour's War at Home*, Cambridge University Press, 1982.

—, 'Conflict over workers' control: the automobile industry in World War II,' in Michael F. Frisch and Daniel J. Walkowitz, *Working-class America: Essays on Labour, Community and American Society*, Urbana, University of Illinois Press, 1983.

Lincoln, John A., *The Restrictive Society: a report on Restrictive Practices*, London, 1967.

Link, Werner, *The Contribution of Trade Unions and Businessmen to German–American Relations, 1945–75*, Bloomington, Institute of German Studies, 1978.

Lipset, S. M., 'The End of Ideology and the Ideology of the Intellectuals,' in J. Ben-David and T. Clark, *Culture and its Creators*, Chicago, University of Chicago Press, 1977.

Lorwin, L., *The International Labour Movement*, New York, Harper & Row, 1953.

Lorwin, Val, *The French Labour Movement*, Cambridge, Mass., Harvard University Press, 1954.

Mallalieu, William C., *British Reconstruction and American Policy, 1945–1955*, New York, Scarecrow Press, 1956.

Mant, A., *The Rise and Fall of the British Manager*, Pan, 1977.

Mayer, Herbert C., *German Recovery and the Marshall Plan, 1948–52*, New York, Atlantic Forum, 1969.

McCreary, Edward A., *The Americanisation of Europe*, Garden City, Doubleday, 1964.

Meany, George, *The Last Five Years*, Washington, DC, American Federation of Labour, 1951.

Meyer, Cord, *Facing Reality: from World Federalism to the CIA*, New York, Harper Bros., 1980.

Middlemas, Keith, *Industry, Unions and Government*, Macmillan, 1983.

Miliband, Ralph, *Parliamentary Socialism*, Merlin, 1973.

Milward, A. S., *The Reconstruction of Western Europe, 1945–51*, Methuen, 1984.

Morgan, Kenneth O., *Labour in Power, 1945–51*, Oxford University Press, 1984.

Morgenthau, Hans J. (ed.), *Germany and the Future of Europe*, Chicago, University of Chicago Press, 1951.

Morris, George, *CIA and American Labour*, New York, International Publishers, 1967.

Mortimer, J. E., *Trade Unions and Technological Change*, Oxford University Press, 1971.

Murray, Philip, and Cooke, Morris, *Organised Labour and Production*, New York, Harper Bros., 1940.

Neufeld, Maurice, *Labour Unions and National Politics in Italian Industrial Plants*, Ithaca, Institute of International Industrial and Labour Relations, 1953.

—, *Italy: School for Awakening Countries*, Westport, Greenwood Press, 1974.

Niethammer, Lutz, 'Structural reform and a compact for growth: conditions for a united labour union movement in western Europe after the collapse of fascism,' in Charles Maier (ed.), *The Origins of the Cold War in Contemporary Europe*, New York, New Viewpoints, 1978.

Paige, D., and Bombach, Gottfried, *A Comparison of National Output and Productivity of the United Kingdom and the United States*, Paris, OEEC, 1959.

Pakenham, Lord, *Born to Believe*, Cape, 1953.

Panitch, Leo, *Social Democracy and Industrial Militancy*, Cambridge University Press, 1976.

Peck, Winslow, 'The AFL-CIA', in Howard Frazier (ed.), *Uncloaking the CIA*, New York, Free Press, 1978.

Pelling, Henry, *America and the British Left*, A. & C. Black, 1956.

—, *The Labour Governments, 1945–51* Macmillan, 1984.

Persico, Joseph E., *Piercing the Reich*, New York, Viking, 1979.

Pimlott, Ben, *Labour and the Left in the 1930s*, Cambridge University Press, 1977.

—, *Hugh Dalton*, Cape, 1985.

Pollard, Robert A., *Economic Security and the Origins of the Cold War, 1945–50*, New York, Columbia University Press, 1985.

Pomian, John (ed.), *Joseph Retinger: Memoirs of an Eminence Grise*, Sussex University Press, 1972.

Powers, Thomas, *The Man who kept the Secrets: Richard Helms and the CIA*, New York, Knopf, 1979.

Price, Harry, *The Marshall Plan and its Meaning*, Ithaca, Cornell University Press, 1955.

Radosh, Ronald, *American Labour and United States Foreign Policy*, New York, Random House, 1969.

Reed, Bruce, and Williams, Geoffrey, *Denis Healey and the Policies of Power*, Sidgwick & Jackson, 1971.

Reuther, Victor G., *The Brothers Reuther*, Boston, Houghton Mifflin, 1976.

Rogow, A. A., *The Labour Government and British Industry, 1945–51*, Westport, Greenwood Press, 1974.

Roll, Eric, *The World after Keynes*, Pall Mall Press, 1968.

—, *Crowded Hours*, Faber, 1985.

Romero, Federico, *Post-war Reconversion Strategies of American and Western European Labour*, Florence, European University Institute, Working Paper 85/193, 1985.

Ross, George, *Workers and Communists in France*, Los Angeles, University of California Press, 1982.

Rostas, L., *Comparative Productivity in British and American Industry*, Cambridge University Press, 1948.

Rothwell, Victor, *Britain and the Cold War, 1941–47*, Cape, 1982.

Sassoon, Donald, *The Strategy of the Italian Communist Party*, Pinter, 1981.

Schriftgiesser, Karl, *Business Comes of Age*, New York, Harper Bros, 1960.

Sissons, Michael and French, Philip (eds.), *Age of Austerity*, Hodder & Stoughton, 1963.

Slichter, Sumner, *Union Politics and Industrial Management*, Washington, DC, Brookings Institute, 1941.

Smith, A. D., *et al.*, *International Industrial Productivity*, Cambridge University Press, 1983.

Smith, R., Harris, *OSS: the Secret History of America's First Central Intelligence Agency*, Berkeley, University of California Press, 1972.

Smuts, Robert W., *European Impressions of the American Worker*, New York, King Crown Press, 1953.

Socialist Union, *Socialism: a New Statement of Principles*, Lincolns-Prager, 1952.

—, *Socialism and Foreign Policy*, Book House, 1953.

—, *Twentieth Century Socialism*, Penguin, 1956.

Spiro, Herbert, *The Politics of German Codetermination*, Cambridge, Mass., Harvard University Press, 1958.

Swanberg, W. A., *Norman Thomas: the Last Idealist*, New York, Scribner, 1976.

Taft, Philip, *Defending Freedom: American Labour and Foreign Affairs*, Los Angeles, Nash, 1973.

Terrill, Ross, *R. H. Tawney and his Times*, Deutsch, 1974.

Truman, Harry, *Years of Trial and Hope, 1946–53*, Hodder & Stoughton, 1956.

Van der Beugel, Ernst H., *From Marshall Aid to Atlantic Partnership*, Amsterdam, Elsevier, 1966.
Van der Pijl, K, *The Making of an Atlantic Ruling Class*, Verso, 1984.
Watt, D. C., *Personalities and Policies*, Longmans, 1965.
—, *Succeeding John Bull: America in Britain's Place, 1900–75*, Cambridge University Press, 1984.
Werth, Alexander, *France, 1940–1955*, Hale, 1956.
Wexler, Immanuel, *The Marshall Plan Revisited*, Westport, Greenwood Press, 1983.
Wheeler, George S., *Who Split Germany?* Berlin, Confederation of Free German Trade Unions, 1962.
Who were they Travelling with? London, Radical Research Services, 1975.
Williams, Philip M., (ed.), *The Diary of Hugh Gaitskell, 1945–56*, Cape, 1983.
Wilson, Theodore A., *The Marshall Plan, 1947–51*, New York, Foreign Policy Association, 1977.
Windmuller, John, *American Labour and the International Labour Movement, 1940–53*, Ithaca, New York State School of Industrial and Labour Relations, 1954.
Windrich, Elaine, *British Labour's Foreign Policy*, Stanford University Press, 1952.
Woolf, S. J. (ed.), *The Rebirth of Italy, 1945–50*, Longmans, 1972.
Yergin, Daniel, *The Shattered Peace*, Penguin, 1977.

Journals

Balfour, W. Campbell, 'Productivity and the worker,' *British Journal of Sociology*, Vol. 4, September 1953.
Barkin, Sol, 'The technical engineering service of an American trade union,' *International Labour Review*, Vol. LXI, No. 6, June 1950.
Boyle, Peter G., 'The British Foreign Office view of Soviet-American relations, 1945–46,' *Diplomatic History*, summer 1979.
Cannon, Les, 'The productivity drive,' *Marxist Quarterly*, Vol. 2, No. 2, April 1955.
Carew, Anthony, 'The schism within the World Federation of Trade Unions: government and trade union diplomacy,' *International Review of Social History*, Vol. XXIX, part 3, 1984.
Crick, Bernard, 'Socialist literature in the 1950s,' *Political Quarterly*, July–September 1960.
Davies, Lane, 'British socialism and the perils of success,' *Political Science Quarterly*, December 1954.
De Hanne, Hugo, 'Scientific management to productivity,' *Manager*, September 1952.
Dubofsky, Melvyn, 'American labour and foreign policy,' *Monthly Review*, June 1971.
Earle, Edward Mead, 'The American stake in Europe: retrospect and prospect,' *International Affairs*, October 1951.

Eisenberg, Carolyn, 'Working class politics and the Cold War: American intervention in the German labour movement, 1945–49,' *Diplomatic History*, Vol. VII, fall 1983.

Fourastie, Jean, 'Towards higher labour productivity in the countries of western Europe,' *International Labour Review*, April 1953.

Goldthorpe, J. H. 'Theories of industrial society,' *Archives Européennes de Sociologie*, Vol. 12, part 2, 1971.

Gomberg, William, 'Union participation in high productivity,' *Annals of the American Academy of Political and Social Science*, November 1946.

—, 'Labour's participation in the European Productivity Programme: a study in frustration,' *Political Science Quarterly*, Vol. LXXIV, No. 2, June 1959.

Hamilton, Richard, F., 'Affluence and the worker: the West German case,' *American Journal of Sociology*, Vol. LXXI, No. 2, September 1965

Harbison, F., and Burgess, E., 'Modern management in western Europe,' *American Journal of Sociology*, Vol. LX, No. 1, July 1954.

Heaps, David, 'Union participation in foreign aid programmes,' *Industrial and Labour Relations Review*, Vol. IX, October 1955.

Hillmann, H. C., 'American aid and the recovery of Germany,' *American Review*, Vol. II, No. 4, March 1963.

Hogan, Michael J., 'The search for a "creative peace": the United States, European unity and the origins of the Marshall Plan,' *Diplomatic History*, Vol. 6, part 3, 1982.

Jackson, Scott, 'Prologue to the Marshall Plan: the origins of the American commitment for a European recovery programme,' *Journal of American History*, Vol. 65, No. 4, March 1979.

Joseph, J. J., 'European recovery and United States aid,' *Science and Society*, summer 1948.

Kassalow, Everett, M., 'European union research and engineering services,' *Monthly Labour Review*, July 1959.

Kerr, Clark, 'Collective bargaining in Germany,' *Industrial and Labour Relations Review*, April 1952.

—, 'The trade union movement and the redistribution of power in post-war Germany,' *Quarterly Journal of Economics*, 1954.

La Palombara, J., 'Trade union education as an anti-communist weapon in Italy,' *Southwestern Social Science Quarterly*, Vol. 37, June 1956.

Lewis, Gordon, K., 'Twentieth century capitalism and socialism: the present state of the Anglo-American debate,' *Western Political Quarterly*, Vol. XII, No. 1, part 1, March 1959.

Maier, Charles, S., 'The politics of productivity: foundations of American international economic policy after World War II,' *International Organisation*, Vol. XXXI, fall 1977.

—, 'The two postwar eras and the conditions for stability in twentieth-century western Europe,' *American History Review*, 1981.

Neufeld, Maurice, F., 'The Italian labour movement in 1956: the structure of crisis', *Annals of the American Academy of Political and Social Sciences*, Vol. CCX, March 1957.

Newton, C. C. S., 'The sterling crisis of 1947 and the British response to the Marshall Plan,' *Economic History Review*, Vol. XXXVII, No. 3, August 1984.

Newton, Scott, 'How successful was the Marshall Plan?' *History Today*, Vol. 33, November 1983.

Northrup, Herbert R., and Young, Harvey A., 'The causes of industrial peace revisited,' *Industrial and Labour Relations Review*, Vol 22, No. 1, October 1968.

Phillips, Paul, 'The German trade union movement under American occupation,' *Science and Society*, fall 1950.

Richard René, 'Productivity and the trade unions in France,' *International Labour Review*, Vol. LXVIII, 1953.

Richter, Irving, 'The decline of organised labour from 1945,' *Papers in the Social Sciences*, Vol. 4, 1984.

Ross, Arthur M., 'Prosperity and labour relations in Europe: the case of West Germany,' *Quarterly Journal of Economics*, Vol. LXXVI, No. 3, August 1962.

Rostas, L., 'Changes in the productivity of British industry, 1945–50,' *Economic Journal*, March 1952.

Saville, John, 'The politics of encounter,' in R. Miliband and J. Saville (eds.), *The Socialist Register*, Merlin Press, 1964.

Scammel, W. M., 'British economic recovery, 1945–51,' *American Review*, Vol. II, No. 4, March 1963.

Schneer, Jonathan, 'Hopes deferred or shattered: the British Labour left and the Third Force movement, 1945–49,' *Journal of Modern History*, Vol. 56, No. 2, June 1984.

Sedgewick, Peter, 'Varieties of socialist thought,' *Political Quarterly*, 1969.

Smith, Lyn, 'Covert British propaganda: the Information Research Department, 1947–77,' *Millenium: the Journal of International Studies*, Vol. 9, No. 1, 1980.

Weiler, Peter, 'The United States, international labour and the Cold War: the breakup of the World Federation of Trade Unions,' *Diplomatic History*, Vol. 5, Part 1, winter 1981.

'Works agreements of the Renault type,' *International Labour Review*, Vol. LXXXI, No. 3, March 1960.

Theses

Balfour, William Campbell, 'Productivity and the Worker', MA, University of Wales, 1958.

Bremner, Marjorie, 'An Analysis of British Parliamentary Thought Concerning the United States in the Post-war Period,' PhD, London University, 1950.

Childs, D. H., 'The Development of Socialist Thought within the SPD, 1945–58,' PhD, London University, 1962.

Manderson-Jones, R. B., 'American Attitudes towards Britain's Relations with Western Europe, 1947–56', PhD, London University, 1969.

Meehan, Eugene J., 'The British "Left" and Foreign Policy, 1945–51,' PhD, London University, 1954.

Paterson, Thomas, G., 'The Economic Cold War: American Business and Economic Foreign Policy, 1945–50,' PhD, University of California, Berkeley, 1969.

Smith, Thomas G., 'From the Heart of the American Desert to the Court of St. James's: the Public Career of Lewis W. Douglas of Arizona,' PhD, University of Connecticut, 1977.

Wood, Jonathan, 'The Labour Left in the Constituency Labour Parties, 1945–51,' MA, Warwick University, 1977.

INDEX